WORSHIP
A Symphony for the Senses

VOLUME 2
ANNOTATED ORDERS OF WORSHIP:
VARIATIONS ON A THEME

Soli Deo Gloria

For
Julia Mae Grabiel Gaddy, John Paul Gaddy, and James Welton Gaddy
Catherine Lowe Nixon and Jordan Burgess Nixon

WORSHIP
A Symphony for the Senses

**VOLUME 2
ANNOTATED ORDERS OF WORSHIP:
VARIATIONS ON A THEME**

C. Welton Gaddy & Donald W. Nixon

Smyth & Helwys Publishing, Inc.
6316 Peake Road
Macon, Georgia 31210-3960
1-800-747-3016
©2002 by Smyth & Helwys Publishing

Worship: A Symphony for the Senses
Volume 2: Annotated Orders of Worship
C. Welton Gaddy & Don W. Nixon

Library of Congress Cataloging-in-Publication Data

Gaddy, C. Welton & Don W. Nixon
   Worship: A Symphony for the Senses/
   C. Welton Gaddy and Don W. Nixon
   p. cm.
   ISBN 978-1-57312-199-6 (pbk)
   Contents: v. 2 Annotated Orders of Worship
   1. Worship programs. 2. Church year. 3. Baptists—Liturgy.
   4. Free churches—Liturgy.
   I. Nixon, Donald. II. Title.

BV198.G33   1995
264—dc   94-17454
                                                           CIP

CONTENTS

Introduction vii

General Worship

The Work of Worship 3
The Visions of Worship 17

Advent

First Sunday of Advent 25
Second Sunday of Advent 32
Third Sunday of Advent 36
Fourth Sunday of Advent 42
Contemporary Advent 47

Christmas

Christmas Eve 57
Christmas Day 61
First Sunday after Christmas 67

Epiphany

Epiphany Sunday 73
First Sunday after Epiphany 78
Third Sunday after Epiphany 83
Transfiguration Sunday 89

Lent

Ash Wednesday 95
First Sunday in Lent 100
A Sunday in Lent 102
Preparation for Holy Week 105

Holy Week

Palm Sunday 111
Maundy Thursday 117
Good Friday 121

Easter

Easter Sunday 129
First Sunday after Easter 133
A Sunday in Easter 138
Ascension Sunday 142

Pentecost

Pentecost Sunday	149
Trinity Sunday	154
A Sunday after Pentecost	158
A Sunday after Pentecost	161
A Sunday after Pentecost	164
A Sunday after Pentecost	168
A Sunday after Pentecost	171

Civil Holidays

New Year's Day	177
Martin Luther King Jr.'s Birthday/Black History	182
Memorial Day	187
Independence Day	191
Labor Day	196
Thanksgiving Day	200

Special Services

World Communion Sunday	205
World Hunger Sunday	210
Reformation Sunday	216
Minister Ordination	222
Holocaust Memorial	230
Arts Festival/Honoring an Artist	239
Christian Education	243
Renewal/Revival	249
Dedication of a Hymnal/Music	253
Family Sunday	257
Mother's Day	261
Father's Day	266
Heritage Sunday	271
Baptismal Service	278
Funeral Service	282
The Service of Christian Marriage	286
The Dedication of a Baby	294
Appendix	302

INTRODUCTION

How do you *do* worship? What have you planned for Advent this year? Do you observe the season of Lent and, if so, how? What can you do to bring freshness and vitality to worship in your church?

These questions and scores of other inquiries of a similar nature prodded work on this book. Few days pass without either Don Nixon or me receiving a phone call or a letter from someone requesting assistance in worship planning. Frankly, each of us finds pleasure in responding to a burgeoning interest in the public worship of God. Subsequently, with joy we share the thoughts, plans, and resources presented in this volume.

Believing that worship is the primary task of the people of God, Don and I are eager to do our part in contributing to experiences of worship that cause persons to arrive for worship with a sense of expectation, participate in worship with genuine enthusiasm, and think of worship with profound appreciation.

Contents

Contained in this book are annotated orders of worship for congregational experiences of the worship of God. These suggested approaches grow out of our efforts in worship planning across the years—mostly during our tenure of ministry together at Northminster Church in Monroe, Louisiana, but also from our occasions of worship leadership in numerous conferences and assemblies. Though we now serve different congregations (Don is Associate Pastor and Minister of the Arts at Willow Meadows Baptist Church in Houston, Texas, and I am Pastor for Preaching and Worship at Northminster Church in Monroe, Louisiana), we continue to talk about worship-related ideas regularly and to plan worship experiences cooperatively. A few of the service plans that appear in this book are the products of our long-distance conversations.

The orders of worship included in this volume profile services that have "worked" for us. We have had the good fortune of observing people lower their defenses, open their minds, express their emotions, and uninhibitedly give themselves to the adoration of God as cooperative members of a worshiping community. Simultaneously, in many instances, we have known the unmitigated wonder of sensing our work in worship leadership transformed into an overpowering joy that took us and those around us into realms we never could have envisioned much less intentionally led others to experience. We have looked on with awe as God honored careful worship planning and the Spirit of God brought liturgy to life.

On the pages that follow you will find orders of worship arranged according to the seasons of the Christian Year, Sundays given special significance because of a particular date on the civil calendar, and Sundays devoted to a special emphasis in the life of the church. Each service plan contains the full texts of calls to worship, litanies, various types of prayers, invitations, and commissions. In addition, you will find titles for selections of instrumental and choral music, scripture references, and a sermon title, if you include a sermon (complete texts of the sermons cited in this volume appear in volume 3 of this series). We introduce each service with a brief description of its nature and purpose, details of resources needed to execute the service described, and recommendations regarding floral arrangements, material designs, and other sensory components of the worship setting that will enhance the worship experience of those present. We also provide comments and instructions on how each part of a service relates to the whole of that service.

The manner in which worship leaders move members of a congregation from one act of worship to another in a given service significantly affects the total impact of that service. Thus, we offer specific suggestions about how to negotiate various transitions in worship. We encourage you to pay attention to the detailed annotation that accompanies each order of worship. After all, in worship as in the total lives of worshipers, grace is in the details.

Developed and structured from the perspective that worship is a symphony for the senses, these service plans aim at appealing to all of an individual's senses. We intend to draw the total personhood of every member of a congregation into an encounter with God. In addition to an organ, a piano, and voices of the worshipers, essential instruments of worship include fabrics, scents, flowers, drama, vegetables, fruits, silence, objects of art, and dance.

Worship Types

The plans for public worship presented in this book draw from the vast richness of many different worship traditions. We find great meaning and inestimable value in the rites and rituals as well as the liturgies of informality that characterize various "schools" or "styles" of worship. On the following pages you will discover classical music, gospel songs, and beloved spirituals contributing to the same worship service in which silence and hallelujahs, confessions of faith and displays of fabric, candles, and incense serve an important purpose. We are not convinced that to be meaningful worship must be slavishly committed to the dictates of a singular tradition of worship.

You will discover in our service suggestions of a few elements of worship that stand apart from any one tradition of worship. As a matter of fact, a few of our ideas for worship may strike you as so different from the norm as to seem suspect. Keep in mind, though, that the spiritual efficacy of the varied suggestions in these services has been measured by biblical and theological integrity as well as proven in the crucible of actual congregational experiences of worship.

The orders of worship in this volume differ from the orders of worship that we prepare for our congregations each week only in two respects. First, most of the litanies and prayers in these services are previously-unpublished expressions of worship. In our local congregations, in addition to the original materials we write, we often draw from the many fine collections of worship resource materials available from publishing houses, journals, and web sites (a list of many of these resources can be found in the Introduction to volume 1 in this series). Second, we prefer to include communion in every major experience of corporate worship. Such a plan assures that every service involves a call to confession, a congregational confession of sin offered in silence or spoken in unison, an assurance of forgiveness, a communion prayer, and an offering of elements that bring to mind the body and blood of Christ. Though we have not included communion in every service in this volume, no one of these services is of a nature that makes communion an inappropriate part of it.

Suggestions for Use

Please use this book in the way that best inspires, supports, and enhances your planning and leadership of worship in a local congregation. You are welcome to reproduce both the orders and the substantive materials of the services presented here or to draw from our work the parts that prove most beneficial to your work. Certainly the services that you plan in interaction with the materials in this book should take seriously the context, needs, interests, and gifts of the people who comprise the congregation in which those services will take place.

Though we have attempted to detail specific directions related to worship leadership in each service, we intentionally have not offered counsel regarding the following aspects of worship that we feel should reflect the distinctive character of each respective congregation and worship leader:

- *The Welcome.* Presence in worship is the first major gift that a worshiper makes to God. Congregational worship does not occur unless individuals choose to come together for worship. Thus, a welcome to worship serves an important theological function and also fulfills a very practical purpose. To be effective, however, the welcome to worship must convey the sincere thoughts and feelings of the one voicing it.

- *The Offering.* Worship does not take place without an offering—an offering of monetary gifts, individual talents, and personal commitments. Different congregations have various means of stressing the importance of offerings appropriate to worshiping God.

- *The Distribution of the Elements of Communion.* In the course of a year we serve communion in several different ways. Most of the time, however, we ask members of the congregation to come forward to receive communion. We offer bread (different kinds of bread in different services) in the form of one loaf broken, as was the body of Christ, and wine in a chalice from which all can drink or grape juice in individual cups for worshipers who prefer not to drink from a common cup.

Introduction

- *The Invitation.* God entrusts to worship leaders the call to discipleship and to the church the invitation for others to become a part of a local expression of the body of Christ. Each congregation and each worship leader should convey God's invitation in the manner that is most personal and persuasive.

- *The Pealing.* Through the centuries, bells have been used to call people to corporate worship and to send people out from corporate worship. Using handbells, carillons, or organ chimes, a free improvisation on a hymn tune or a melodic line of an anthem can capture and instill in worshipers the character of a particular service.

Pouring over these materials for a period of many months has given me an appreciation for another use of this book—a private and individual use of it. Many of the prayers, contemporary readings, and litanies in this volume can greatly enhance one's personal meditation, devotional reading, and prayers. Much like reading a hymnal, engaging liturgies prepared to enhance the lives of the gathered people of God can have a profound impact on the life of any one member of the people of God.

Liturgy: The Work of the People

The worship materials in this book have been drawn from the contributions of a variety of worship traditions and the spiritual leadership of scores of individuals. Various components of the liturgy for each service reflect the true meaning of the word liturgy—the work of the people. Indeed, this volume incorporates the fruits of the work of worship on the part of many people.

We have suggested hymns, songs, and choruses for congregational singing well aware of the variety of hymnals and musical preferences found in different congregations. Our recommendations for congregational singing have been drawn from the following hymnals:

- *A Singing Faith* by Jane Parker Huber (Philadelphia: Westminster Press, 1987)
- *For the Living of These Days,* edited by Michael Hawn (Macon GA: Smyth & Helwys Publishing, Inc., 1995)
- *Taize: Songs for Prayer* (Chicago: G.I.A. Publications, 1998)

- *The Baptist Hymnal* (Nashville: Convention Press, 1991)
- *The New Century Hymnal* (Cleveland: The Pilgrim Press, 1995)

Don and I could not have produced this resource for worship planning without the interest, cooperation, and generous sharing of materials on the part of numerous individuals. Along with the worship materials in this volume that we have written, you will find thoughtful contributions from the following worship-sensitive people:

- **John Ballenger** (JB)—minister and creative writer, Atlanta, Georgia
- **Jane Webb Childress** (JWC)—Freelance writer, Nacogdoches, Texas
- **D. H. Clark** (DHC)—physician, hymn writer, and Minister of Music of Northminster Church, Monroe, Louisiana
- **L. Katie Cooke** (LKC)—Editor of *Seeds* magazine, Waco, Texas
- **Ragan Courtney** (RC)—creative writer, dramatist, poet, and Co-Pastor of Terry Town Baptist Church, Austin, Texas
- **Philip Cunningham** (PC)—Theology Ministry Institute, Notre Dame College, Manchester, New Hampshire
- **Sue Enoch** (SE)—Pastor of Prescott Memorial Baptist Church, Memphis, Tennessee
- **Julia (Judy) Mae Gaddy** (JMG)—educator, Monroe, Louisiana
- **Kathy Manis Findley** (KMF)—Director of Victim Support and Prevention Programs, Family Service Agency, North Little Rock, Arkansas
- **Paul Richardson** (PR)—Professor of Music and Associate Dean for Graduate Studies, Samford University, Birmingham, Alabama
- **Sharlande Sledge** (SS)—Associate Pastor of Lake Shore Baptist Church, Waco, Texas
- **James R. Spence** (JRS)—deacon, Willow Meadows Baptist Church, Houston, Texas
- **Tommy Simons** (TS)—Minister to Youth, Willow Meadows Baptist Church, Houston, Texas
- **Elizabeth Turner** (ET)—Professor of History, Rice University, Houston, Texas
- **Dawn Darwin-Weeks** (DDW)—Pastor of First Christian Church, Rowett, Texas

Mary Ann Fore, Secretary for Northminster Church in Monroe, Louisiana, prepared more drafts of this manuscript than I can or want to remember. The depth of gratitude that Don and I owe to Mary Ann is directly proportionate to the inestimable help that she has provided for us at every step we took toward the completion of this project.

A Personal Word

When I first mentioned the idea for this project to Don Nixon and subsequently suggested it to David Cassady and Cecil Staton at Smyth & Helwys Publishing, Inc., I honestly had no idea of how much work would be involved in bringing such an endeavor to conclusion. I was excited about the possibility of the project from the first moment the idea of it dawned in my mind. Don never blinked at the challenge. Each time the two of us have discussed the project and spent long hours together working on innumerable details, the invigoration of worship planning and the excitement we share about the potential value of this volume have far outweighed concerns about deadlines and physical fatigue. Fortunately, the good people at Smyth & Helwys have demonstrated great patience as Don and I continued to nudge this project toward publication.

Across the years I have read many books on worship and utilized numerous volumes of resource materials for planning worship. Honestly, I do not know of another volume like this one. Here are insights into both the substance and the spirit of the corporate worship of God: texts and suggestions on how to speak them or to dramatize them, directions for creating floral arrangements that reflect the nature of a specific service, suggestions for processionals and congregational acts of commitment, recent personal works of devotional literature alongside ancient hymn texts and contemporary ideas for blending the two to fulfill a particular purpose in worship, materials for use as different components of worship, and suggestions on how best to move from one component of worship to another to achieve an offering that flows as a single piece of tapestry. Though I have helped assemble this resource volume, I have learned from it as much as I have contributed to it. I wish I had known the benefit of this kind of book early in my ministry. I am elated that it is available now.

—C. Welton Gaddy

General Worship

THE WORSHIP OF GOD
The Work of Worship

The holistic nature of public worship is apparent in the following service, which is intended as an exercise in preparation for worship that becomes an actual experience of worship. Each of the five senses serves as a medium for a revelation from God, an invitation to encounter God, and an instrument with which to praise God.

The Gathering
(By means of an announcement printed in the order of worship or by spoken words, instruct worshipers to gather outside the worship center—either remaining outside the building at the entrance to the sanctuary or congregating in an enclosed space adjacent to the room in which worship will occur.)

    Leader: Most of our worship occurs in a set-aside place, a designated sanctuary. Worship can emerge behind four walls or erupt under an open sky, unfold while kneeling at an altar, or form while propped up against the trunk of a tree. Usually our worship site is close to home, a familiar place. But holiness knows no bounds. Today we worship here.
                                                                                                (CWG)

(Invite all present to participate in the litany.)

The Prologue
    Leader: Through these doors have stumbled pilgrims, outcasts, unwashed saints, sin-wounded sisters and brothers, the rich and the impoverished, people with the learning of ages, and children with only the word of love at their command. Magdalenes and Simon Peters have stumbled through these doors, all crying out for shelter from a raging storm, each seeking a balm for wounds they could not even name. For mercy dwells where the flame of grace is kindled and is kept. And love doth make its nest among a people of steadfast compassion.

People: **We are a colony of heaven, a redeemed people, a royal priesthood, a ministering body of God's healing grace, a sacred isle of peace, and a beacon of hope in a broken and suffering world.**

Leader: Sing, angels of grace, and break forth you ministers of mercy. For God has chosen and formed a people. The Spirit has been bestowed and shall not be taken back.

People: **What God has given us, no power in heaven or earth can take away.**

Leader: We shall not die, but live to tell the story of God's unconquerable love, to sing and dance—that all generations of God's children shall see and know the salvation of our God. Heaven may pass away. Offerings of grain and of our bounty may cease. Kings and royal families may rise and fall.

People: **But Christ's church shall never be defeated. The church shall rise again and again and again, until the word of God's love runs deep in every heart of all that lives and breathes. And all creation will be holy, and the hosannas of our thanksgiving shall rise unto the heavens forever and ever. Amen.**

—Garth House[1]

Leader: Worship is a gift, a gift from God that allows us to achieve our full potential as persons, and a gift to God that acknowledges God as Creator and Redeemer. Without gifts at its center, worship does not occur. God's people gather for worship not so much to receive a blessing as to make an offering.

Worship is an experience, not a time for thinking about God but a time for encountering God; not a moment for contemplating praise, beauty, and holiness but for engaging and enjoying praise, beauty, and holiness. Worship requires the involvement of all we are as persons—our senses as well as our minds. Unless the whole person is involved in worship, we deprive God of one of our gifts, and we risk leaving important dimensions of our lives untouched by God's gift.

Today we will seek to include every aspect of our lives in the worship of God. Fidelity to that intention requires preparation; but, of course, all meaningful worship requires preparation. Many times we fail to experience the total potential of worship because of limited preparation that stops short of a full understanding of the encounter between God and us. Let us pray that in the next brief segment of time we can become aware of new possibilities in worship and for worship.

This entire service is a prologue to worship—a prelude to worship—that we pray will become an experience of worship. As we go inside, I want to introduce to you the different gifts to God that will be a part of our corporate worship today. Each gift represents a potential medium for engagement with God. We will try to understand each offering so we can experience the fullness of the worship experience.

A line from the Broadway musical *Phantom of the Opera* comes to mind. "Silently the senses abandon their defenses." That's what we are about in this experience—opening all of our senses to an encounter with God.

So let's get on with it.

(CWG)

(The worship leader motions for the worshipers to follow and all move into the sanctuary together.)

The Enlightenment

Refreshing Water

(All pause just inside the entrance to the sanctuary where a worship leader stands filling a vessel with water. [The vessel can be as common as a concrete birdbath, as elegant as a large shell, or as rustic as a household dishpan. Whatever the nature of the vessel, the container needs to be elevated on a stand for easy access.] Worshipers are requested to stand where they can see the water-filled vessel.)

Leader: What would it feel like to touch God? Perhaps like a burning coal taken from a cleansing fire as in Isaiah's experience. Or maybe like a wrestling match in which losing turned out to be winning as with Jacob. Touching God can feel as rough as the splintery wood of a manger, as prickly as the sharp point of a thorn, or as smooth as the fabric of a burial cloth.

What touch can we give to God in worship today? The tackiness of the dough we knead in making bread for hungry people, the burning singe of a broken blister on a hand roughed up by a hammer pounding nails while building a shelter for the homeless. What touch can we give to God?

Today the gift is water. Touching water is a cleansing, refreshing experience integrally related to repentance, a reception of forgiveness, a commitment dramatized in baptism, a touch filled with communion with God.

When you enter this room for worship today, I encourage you to stop here and touch water. Think about your baptism. Ponder the meaning of being immersed in faith, getting soaking wet for God.

Touch the water. Immerse your hands. Splash some of the water on your face if you will. Sprinkle it on a friend if that is meaningful. But, be sure and touch God in worship today.

(CWG)

Perfumes of Holiness

(Ask worshipers to move to another spot in the sanctuary where a worship leader is preparing incense. As worshipers approach this station, the leader begins to ignite coals and apply incense to the heated charcoal. Within seconds the aroma of incense fills the air.)

Leader: What is the scent of God? What does God smell like? I know that's a rather strange question. Perhaps we best get in touch with our sense of scent generally before focusing our scent in worship. Smell the heavy sweetness of crowded floral arrangements at a funeral. Inhale the odor of a newly mowed lawn or a hayfield just cut. Incorporate into your senses the scent of a spring rain falling on a hot pavement.

What does energy smell like? Black smoke belching from an industrial furnace, natural gas escaping from a leak in a line, dried sweat on a spent athlete or dancer? What does repentance smell like—a burning dove, a roasted lamb, a charred offering of grain?

Now, what is the scent of God?

What scent can we offer to God in worship today? Contrast the apostle Paul's praise for a "sweet smelling offering" to God with the prophet Jeremiah's disdain for the scents of frankincense and sweet Cain that accompanied sacrifices unacceptable to God. Obviously, God finds offense as well as takes pleasure in fragrances. What scent can we offer to God in our worship today that will please God?

Some traditions of the church use incense to help sanctify a place for worship. The odor conveys distinction, uniqueness—some would say holiness. As we worship God today, please don't just look at what is happening with the incensor. Smell what is happening. Offer God your sense of smell.

(CWG)

(Direct each worshiper to move past the smoldering incensor and inhale the scent of incense.)

Cry of the Soul

(Worshipers move to the midpoint of the worship center. Ask them to take seats in that area.)

Leader: What does God sound like? Ah, at last, a familiar sense—the sense of sound. Do we know what God sounds like? Amos said a roaring lion. Isaiah described an inquiring voice. Elijah thought of the whisper of a gentle wind.

What does God sound like? The whimper of a baby among pawing cattle and bleating sheep. A soft invitation to fellowship. A scream from a cross or some other lonely place of dying. Someone weeping. Someone laughing.

God sounds like Bach's "St. Matthew Passion" and like Handel's "Hallelujah Chorus."

What sound can we offer to God in worship today? Music is always a good gift of worship. Please do more than voice it or hear it, though. Experience the music.

From the Taize Community comes music to help us in our engagement with God. Let's hear and learn this music that we may sing it as an offering to the One who created music and sound.

(CWG)

(A musician conducts a short rehearsal to familiarize congregants with the simple melodies of Taize music. Musical scores should be provided in the order of worship. Choose three of the simple chants to be used in the meditative processional.[2])

Reflections of Majesty

(Worshipers stand, move to the front of the sanctuary, and take seats in close proximity to the communion table.)

Leader: What does God look like? How do you see God? That vision will make all the difference in the way you worship God. Do you see God as an angry judge, a restless tyrant, a loving parent, a smiling friend, a dim image in a smoky mirror, an indefinable spirit shrouded in mystery, a broken body, a luminous angel, a monarch with scepter in hand, a servant holding a towel? How do you see God?

Does your sight of God make you want to run and hide or to sit down and rest? Maybe the look of God inspires you to dance. Or does it evoke quiet reverence? Does God look like someone you enjoy or someone you don't want to meet when alone? Does God appear as Mother or Father, Lover or Friend? Or in some inexplicable manner, does God look like all of that?

What sight, what vision, can we give to God in worship today? Oh, we all know about candles that convey light, symbols that incite a vision of remembrance that takes us to the heart of the story of redemption, a cross, a pulpit.

But what about the sight of praise? What does praise look like? Look for it. Watch it. As I read words from the psalms of David and the lyrics of Saint Francis of Assisi, please see the truth rather than hear it. Experience praise.

Offer the sight of praise to God here at this table for the Eucharist, a table present in a place of worship to evoke praise for God.

(CWG)

(While one worship leader reads the following words selected from the psalms and the lyrics by Saint Francis of Assisi commonly known as the hymn "All Creatures of Our God and King," another stands behind the communion table and creates an arrangement that interprets the texts of the Psalm and the hymn. The visible sign of praise is constructed with flowers, fruits, vegetables, altar books, hymnals, and brass musical instruments while the spoken words of praise are being read.)

Leader: Praise the Lord! How good it is to sing praises to our God (Ps 147:1)!

All creatures of our God and King, Lift up your voice ... O praise God. Praise God in God's sanctuary. Praise God in God's mighty firmament. Praise God for God's mighty deeds. Praise God according to God's surpassing greatness. (Ps 150:1-2)

Thou burning sun with golden beam, Thou silver moon with softer gleam! O praise God. O praise God. Alleluia. Praise God with trumpet sound. Praise God with lute and harp. Praise God with tambourine and dance. Praise God with strings and pipe. Praise God with clanging cymbals . . . Let everything that breathes praise the Lord! Dear mother earth, who day by day unfoldest blessings on our way, O praise God. The flowers and fruits that in thee grow, let them God's glory also show! O praise God! Great is the Lord and greatly to be praised. God's greatness is unsearchable. (Ps 145:3)

Let all things their Creator bless and worship God in humbleness. O praise God. I will praise the Lord as long as I live. I will sing praises to my God all my life long.

(When the visible declaration of praise has been completed and worshipers have experienced the completed expression of praise, the worship leader can proceed to the next experience of preparation at the same location in the sanctuary.)

Sweetness of Promise

Leader: What does God taste like? The psalmist admonishes us to taste the goodness of God. What is that like—the sweetness of honey or the bitterness of parsley? Our predecessors in the faith tasted God. For some, God tasted like bitter herbs. For others, God tasted like fine wine. God tasted like manna and fresh meat after a period of hunger; cool water and soothing grape juice after a thirst symptomatic of dehydration. And now?

Surely if sin tastes like poison, God tastes like all the foods of a feast available in abundance.

What taste can we give to God in worship today? Not all tastes appeal to God. God finds repulsive the taste of wishy-washy mediocrity. God threatened to spit out the bad taste associated with the middle-of-the-road crowd in the church at Laodicea. Prejudice, envy, spitefulness, and the like strike in God an unpalatable taste akin to the vinegar rammed into the mouth of Jesus on the cross.

We want to give to God in worship a taste that pleases God. What is it?

Here are bread and honey—two staples in the scriptural history of redemption; tastes that convey love, generosity, grace, kept promises, new adventures, and a promised land. When we come here again in worship, taste the bread and honey well as you ponder the taste you will give to God.

(CWG)

(The worship leader who has been speaking directs the congregants' attention to a small table placed at the front of the worship center to the left of the communion table and easily accessible to all worshipers. On this table set a large loaf of bread and an oversized bowl into which the worship leader pours honey while speaking about taste. Preparations for this worship experience are complete.)

Leader: Now you are equipped to use and understand your senses in the worship of God. It's all here for you. Together we can experience God and relish with our entire beings the beauty of holiness.

You now have witnessed the full scope of "the symphony of the senses," which is worship. We are now ready to return to the beginning and, fully aware of the vehicles that can enrich the experience, worship God. During the silent moments of preparation after reentering the sanctuary, enjoy the ministry of each of the senses we bring to worship.

(CWG)

(Congregants are led to the entrance of the sanctuary. Once all are reassembled there, a worship leader begins the litany.)

The Litany
- Leader: The stage is now set, the actors have taken their places, and the grand drape begins its upward pull to reveal another offering of worship.
- **People: Our Creator God has promised to be present, to give ear to our offerings, to give grace to our confessions, and to be renewal for our celebrations of life.**
- Leader: So come, all who are corrupt and all faithful ones, all who know the text by heart and those who will hear the lines for the first time. Come, for in this place the Eternal One brings light to the dark shadows of our souls.
- **People: We will speak our hearts, we will learn of the way, and our souls shall be freed to share the story and to bear the light so that others may come.**
- Leader: The revelation of truth that God made known to those before us are meant also for us and for this day.
- **People: With the unnumbered multitudes we now gather to praise the God of our salvation.**
- Leader: Open your hearts to the presence of the Almighty and to the words of Christ. Children of God, come now for worship and celebration.
- **People: Alleluia.**
- Leader: Thanks be to God.

(DWN)

(At the conclusion of the litany, worship leaders open the doors of the entrance to the sanctuary and invite the worshipers to enter. A worship leader with a towel stands beside the vessel filled with water and extends the towel to worshipers as each touches the water in his or her own way. Some may wash their hands, others may splash their faces with water, and others may simply place their fingertips in the water. After this symbolic experience of cleansing, worshipers move to find a seat in the sanctuary.)

General Worship

The Meditation
(After congregants are seated, the musician moves in a processional on the main aisle leading the congregation in the meditative prayer songs of Taize that have been rehearsed. After the musician takes a place at the front of the worship center, another leader processes down the center aisle swinging the incensor and filling the room with incense that offers a visual reminder of the sacredness of this space and a scented invitation for congregants to worship God with their entire beings. Throughout this time of meditation, worshipers spontaneously partake of the sweet assurance of God's resourceful companionship symbolized by the availability of bread and honey. In advance of the service, ask worship leaders to model moving to the table and partaking the elements.)

The Attestation of Faith
What is it when you want something so bad, and there it is? What is that? Hope? No, it's more than hope. When you've just worked out and your clothes are clinging to you and your legs are shaking, your mouth is dry and your throat is parched, and you're reaching for that bottle of ice cold water. . . . What is that? Is it anticipation? No, it's more than anticipation. You've been outside in the dead of winter and you can't feel your toes, and where your toes connect to your feet, it hurts, and you come inside, pull off your boots and the two layers of socks and stretch your feet out to the fire . . . ahhhhhh . . . . What is that? It is more than anticipation, isn't it? Fulfillment, maybe? Satisfaction? Gratification? Hmm, gratification may be the closest word we've got, but—well, gratification is only a word. It's perfect, perfect. It's when you first put on glasses and the blur became a beautiful clarity. . . . It's when you realized for the first time that church wasn't something you did for your parents or your Sunday School teachers or your youth minister, but something you needed—something you wanted for your well-being, and the Lord's Supper for the first time became nourishing—sustenance. . . . It's when you asked him to marry you, and he said yes. . . . It's when you looked into the eyes of your newborn child for the first time to see a new image of God—breathing—it is so good. . . . It's when you realized that

ministry wasn't an option for you, but a sacred calling. God calling you, and you said yes. . . . It can be as mundane as hitting the shot with a seven iron and watching the ball arc into the sky. . . . It's when you can't imagine anything being better. . . . It's a click deep, deep down inside as two pieces you may not even have known needed to be connected fit together. . . . It's a connection, a fit, a belonging. It's a sigh, a moan too deep for words . . . no words—no words. It's perfect—too much for words. How do you preach that? How do I preach that? How do I use words to evoke something beyond words? Tell my people something they haven't experienced or don't know? What many of them can't even imagine? How do I preach that? I don't. I don't. I find the deepest dreams, the richest hopes, the needs most true to who we are as people created in the image of God, and I know that there, there God is at work. There, God is to be found. I don't preach; it's those longings that preach, that resonate in a person's soul, that ring true. It's God at work in the truths of a person's soul who preaches. Never forget that, I remind myself over and over.

So to those who were slaves in a foreign land, I say the day is coming when they will be neither slave nor free, Jew nor Greek, male nor female. To those wandering in the desert, I say there's a land of milk and honey—or maybe, living waters flowing through desolate wastelands. To those shivering over an open grate on a big city sidewalk I say, there shall not be cold or frost. To those whose cynicism allows them only to be against and not for, there will be an integrity within enthusiasm and exuberance. To those who can't see, there shall be no more darkness. To the lame, there shall be dancing—no more tears. The outcasts will be gathered in and their shame changed into praise. The lonely will be embraced. The day is coming that when one suffers, all will suffer. When one rejoices, all will rejoice. And the trees will clap their hands for joy; the lion will cavort with the lamb. The very rocks will sing. The mountains will drip wine, and even the dead, dry branches of yesterday will blossom and bloom in glorious color. The whole earth will shine with glory.

There will, in fact, be a new heaven and a new earth, and you, you shall be called by a new name—your true name. Rejoice! Rejoice and exult! The day is coming—a day of everlasting joy when we will all be welcomed home, and there will be praise, and there will be thanksgiving in the voice of song—a sigh too deep for words.

How do I preach it? I listen. And I tell them it's like ice cold water after an intense workout—like a warm, warm fire on a cold, cold night—like asking her to marry you and having her say yes—like putting on glasses for the first time.

I tell them it's a click deep, deep down inside, as pieces that have been apart that belong together—fit. I tell them these are the promises of God. We're going to the promised land.

And now is not the time. It's not the time to say this was a land of plenty, with food enough for all—room enough for all—not the time, now, to point out that those who won't see, their darkness too, will disappear. Now is not the time to say that the outcasts will be gathered when we include them—that their shame will be turned to praise when we love them. It's not the time to say that oppression and injustice cannot be where we do not permit them to be—not the time to say that all will suffer when one suffers when we choose to live that way—when we dedicate our living to such a loving. That's for me to know.

My people don't want to hear: we're growing to the promised land—as true as it may be—don't want to hear that our growth has been stunted—that we are not the wonderful, beautiful, glorious growth we ought to be—that there is too much of death about us. We're growing to the promised land? They don't want to hear that—as true as it may be.

And the truth of the matter is that the dry and dead branches of our yesterdays do bloom and blossom in the glory of the presence of God. We are going to the promised land!

(JB)

(After the worship leader concludes reading the Attestation of Faith, the presiding leader of worship speaks again. The prelude to joy is the culminating climax to this service of worship. It is during this meditative musical experience that all the components of worship come together to create our sermon. This musical composition is designed for the listener to experience the natural movement of a worship service. Listen and meditate as the organist recreates this glorious offering.)

The Prelude to Joy — C. Franck
Chorale in A Minor

(If this piece of music is unavailable, select a composition that is designed to usher worshipers through the natural movement of worship with an air of celebration.)

The Benediction
>Leader: To look through the eyes of God is to see differently.
>**People: It is to see the strength the world deems weakness, and the glory the world calls shame. It is to see the death that can fill life, and the life that transcends death.**
>Leader: By God's grace we move from believing what we see to seeing what we believe,
>**People: and the love of God rearranges our world and reevaluates our priorities and changes what will be and who we'll be,**
>Leader: in the marvelous topsy-turviness of God incarnate. To look through the eyes of God is to see differently.
>**People: It is to have God shining brilliantly through our eyes. It is, therefore, to be seen differently.**
>**All: Thanks be to God.**

(JB)

THE WORSHIP OF GOD
The Visions of Worship

Isaiah's experience of worship in the ancient temple in Jerusalem long has been considered a model for the worship of God in all times and places. The components of the following service encourage a careful exploration of and personal identification with each of the visions that comprise a worshipful experience with God.

The Prelude
(As people enter the sanctuary, an usher or another worship leader hands each person a round black stone, symbolizing the "coal" in the Isaiah passage, and a kazoo. Each worshiper also receives a printed order of worship that contains musical scores of the Taize meditations to be used in the service. During the prelude, actions at the altar indicate the holiness of this space in which worship will occur. These actions include: covering the communion table with a celebrative cloth [ex: white damask fabric]; clipping the wicks of all the candlesticks on the communion table and igniting the flame on each one, touching up floral arrangements at the front of the sanctuary, opening the Bible at the lectern or pulpit, and marking the space with the use of incense.)

The Prologue
  Leader: And God looked upon all the things that had been created—the sun, the moon and stars, the earth and all the living things upon it,
  People: And God said, "That's good!"
  Leader: When we retreat into the wild places and surround ourselves with things God made, our spirits are healed, freed from the deafening noise that humans make.
  People: We feel the stillness of a million summers, the peace that settles into our troubled hearts. We can hear the still, small voice of truth in the falling of a single leaf. And we say silently in our hearts, "That's good!"

Leader: When we see something naturally beautiful—a surprise splash of butterfly wings, the mystical, fleeting theophany of fireflies in the night, the majestic streak of brilliant color in the evening sky,

People: We feel the power and glory of God, and we cry out with laughter to the trees and clouds and insects, "That's good!"

Leader: When we realize what we have done to the planet God fashioned for us, we feel anger and cynicism.

People: We point our fingers at each other and accuse, for we cannot say this is good.

Leader: Our word from God today is a hard saying. It is that we have been unfaithful stewards. We are the ones who clutter the earth with our refuse, by clinging to our small comforts.

People: We have beaten our sister the earth and left bruises and gashes; we have raped her; we have neglected her and caused starvation and disease.

Leader: We have dabbled in her resources and used them without adequate knowledge; we have used them irresponsibly. We have covered her face with our own masks. Even now we hold a loaded gun at her head.

People: What can we do? Once again we long to hear God say, "This is good."

Leader: Our God is the Maker of second chances, our God is the great Healer. With God's help we can make amends to our sister. We can do even small things to bind up her wounds. We can restore her dignity.

People: With God's help, and with each other's support, we can heal and nurture our sister the earth. We now, before God, pledge to each other, to God, and to the earth, that we will again receive this precious gift, and we will do all that we can to cherish it.

All: So that we all can say, as God said in the beginning about the earth and the heavens and all the living creatures, "It is good."

(LKC)

General Worship

The Meditation
(The organist plays an improvisation of a contemporary, avant-garde composition characteristic of New Age sounds. While this music is played, slides of the universe flash on a screen depicting images of galaxies, bursts of starlight, cosmic formations, and other facets of the mystery and grandeur of the heavens.)

The Call
Leader: Holy, holy, holy is the Lord of hosts; the whole earth is full of God's glory.
People: Splendor and majesty are before him; declare his glory among the nations, his marvelous deeds among all people.
Leader: Sing to the Lord a new song, for He has done marvelous things; the Lord has made his salvation known and revealed his righteousness to the nations.
People: Glorify the Lord with me; let us exalt his name together.
(Compiled from the Hebrew Scriptures)

The Introit   Songs and Prayers from Taize
Confitemini Domino
"Come and Fill"
(The congregation sings in unison.)

The Invocation
God of Brother Sun and Sister Moon, Sister Water and Brother Fire: Come to us this morning and dwell with us. Restore our sense of wonder and awe. Restore our joy in knowing you and exulting in the simple surprises you have placed all around us. May we never fail to see what you want us to see: the world in need or the random beauty. Amen.
(LKC)

The Exultation   Songs and Prayers from Taize
Adoramus Te Domine
"We Adore You"

The Lesson   Isaiah 6:1-3

The Hymn of Response   Nicaea
    Holy, Holy, Holy

The Sermon I
    "Vision of God"
(The text for each sermon part appears on pages 8-12 in volume 3)

The Recognition of the Presence of God
    (Congregants sit in silence to reflect on the presence of God).

The Hymn of Response   LASST UNS ERFREUEN
    All Creatures of Our God and King
(Worshipers sing verses 1 and 2, verse 2 being the traditional Doxology.)

The Lesson   Isaiah 6:4-7

The Meditation   Songs and Prayers from Taize
    Nada Te Turbe (Nothing Can Trouble)
    O Lord, Hear My Prayer
    Wait for the Lord

The Silent Confession

The Sermon II
    "Vision of Self"

The Hymn of Response   MY SAVIOR'S LOVE
    I Stand Amazed

The Call to Confession
    Like our predecessors in faith, we have sinned. We identify not only with their wrongdoing, but also with their words of confession. Let us speak to God about the reality of our sins and our desire for forgiveness.

                                                                   (CWG)

The Prayer of Confession
    "Woe is me! For I am lost; for I am a person of unclean lips; and I dwell in the midst of a people of unclean lips." "Have mercy on me, O God . . . blot out my transgressions. Wash me thoroughly from my iniquity, and cleanse me from my sin! For I know my transgressions, and my sin is ever before me.

Against thee, thee only, have I sinned, and done that which is evil in thy sight . . . Purge me with hyssop, and I shall be clean; wash me, and I shall be whiter than snow. . . . Hide thy face from my sins, and blot out all my transgressions. Create in me a clean heart, O God, and put a new and right spirit within me." Amen.

(Isa 6; Ps 51)

The Touch
(Print in the order of worship: "During these moments of silent meditation, touch the black 'coal' to your lips and be reminded of God's great gift of forgiveness.")

The Words of Assurance
As surely as the coals have touched our lips in this moment, God has heard our prayers of confession and with steadfast love granted us forgiveness. Let us hold unswervingly to the hope we profess.

(Hebrews 10:23)

The Response of Absolution
(Print in the order of worship: "During the singing of the meditation, you are invited to bring the black 'coal' that has touched your lips and place it on the chancel as an outward sign of release from guilt and a confirmation of the forgiveness of sin.")

The Meditation   Songs and Prayers from Taize
Bless the Lord, My Soul
In the Lord

The Attestation of Faith   R. Courtney
"The Leper"
From *Bright New Wings*[3]

The Sermon III
"Vision of Ministry"

The Response
(Worshipers quietly meditate, envisioning their calls to service and reflecting on the total impact of this encounter with God.)

The Recessional Hymn   HYMN TO JOY
   Joyful, Joyful, We Adore You

(Print in the order of worship: "You are invited to join in the recessional as we move through the nave of the church.")

(The organist plays the first three bars of the recessional hymn and stops. A worship leader at the front of the sanctuary repeats the notes using a kazoo. After the organist plays three more bars of the recessional hymn, the same worship leader responds again repeating the notes in those bars using the kazoo. The recessional hymn continues with the organist playing the organ and all worshipers playing kazoos as they depart from the sanctuary.)

NOTES

[1] Used by permission, Garth House, *Litanies for All Occasions* (Valley Forge PA: Judson Press, 1989) 17-18.

[2] See *Songs and Prayers from Taize* (Chicago IL: GIA Publications, Inc., 1991).

[3] A dramatic monologue spoken by the leper in *Bright New Wings*, Courtney/Clawson/Red (Nashville/New York: Triune Music, 1977).

Seeing truth and experiencing praise; a visual interpretation of Psalm 147

Advent

THE WORSHIP OF GOD
First Sunday of Advent

Advent is a spiritual call to pilgrimage; Christmas is its destination. The journey is inspired by and begins with hope. The following service unveils the mystery of God's love made known in the Christ. The mood of this experience is one of patience blended with expectation.[1]

The Carillon Prelude   arr. D. H. Clark
    Paraphrase on *Divinum Mysterium*

The Opening Voluntary   J. S. Bach
    Sheep May Safely Graze

The Prologue   Prudentius
    Divinum Mysterium, Medieval Sanctus Trope
(To contribute to the mood of mystery and the advancing realization of hope, the choir begins singing the Prologue from a removed chamber, such as the narthex, and advances the sound into the room where worshipers are gathered. As the choir sings, an elderly woman enters the sanctuary carrying a flaming candle and moves to the Advent wreath to light the candle of hope.)

The Call to Advent
    Advent is an adventure—a spiritual journey to a manger in Bethlehem, a personal pilgrimage to find Christ in our town.
    Advent is a period of waiting—a time for pondering God's promises of the past, a season for contemplating the fulfillment of those promises in the present.
    Advent is an occasion for preparation—getting ready to celebrate God's invasion of history in Christ, making plans for the moment when God will do it again.
    Advent begins today. So, we set our faces toward a star in the East or toward whatever bit of light we can find, and we start moving in the direction of the last sighting of the Messiah. We strain to keep our thoughts centered on what God has already told us, while bending forward so as not to miss a single word God may speak today. And we try to make preparations for nativity celebrations.

Here at the beginning of Advent we need messengers from God, or at least one. Send your messenger to us, God. We promise to welcome her, to encourage her, even to bless her. As we travel toward the light, we need someone you call to comfort us, to inspire us, to correct us, to bring us to Christ. God, open the altar built for worship. Remove any veil that keeps us from fellowship with your presence. Call us to communion again.

It's Advent. Act, God. Come, Lord Jesus.

(CWG)

The Response   J. Rutter
II. from *Gloria*

(While the choir sings the "Gloria," a liturgical dancer interprets the revelation of Christ in a response to the holiness of God. The visual creates a tension of anticipation as the dancer moves around the communion table on which the elements are mysteriously veiled by a piece of sheer purple fabric. As the Rutter text centers on Christ, the symbolism of the table becomes more important as does the dancer's concentration on the table. During the musical climax, with the choir singing about Christ the King of Heaven, the dancer dramatically lifts the veil from the table confirming the awesome reality of Incarnation—the newborn King. Clearly, it's Advent.)

The Call to Pilgrimage

    One: And now we begin the waiting. The coming that we anticipate is foretold by the prophets of old:

    Many: **"And there shall come forth a rod out of the stem of Jesse, and a Branch shall grow out of Jesse's roots; and the Spirit of the Lord shall rest upon this chosen one;**

    One: "And when this happens, the wolf shall lie down with the lamb, and no harm will come to them, and a little child shall lead them all;

    Many: **"They shall not hurt anyone nor destroy anything in all of God's Holy Mountain; for the earth will be full of the knowledge of God, as the waters cover the sea."**

One:	"For unto us a child is born, and unto us a son is given." It is for this coming that we wait.
Many:	**Into our darkness a light has shone. We wait to see it shine once more.**
One:	Into our hearts a hope is born, that joy will return to our lives, that peace will be restored in all the earth.
Many:	**It is for this joy, this hope, this peace that we wait.**
One:	Advent is a time of waiting, but it is also a time for reaching out beyond ourselves.
Many:	**For Advent is Christ incarnate in the face of the poor one;**
One:	Advent is Christ in those who are hungry and cold, homeless and imprisoned, lonely and in despair.
Many:	**Advent is also Christ . . . in me.**

(LKC)

The Introit   R. Proulx
Veni, Veni Emmanuel

The Prayer of Praise and Adoration
Eternal and Everlasting God, it is in you that we find hope. We acknowledge that all things are given to us full of your good grace. Our lives are favored because of your promised love. We praise you, O God, who gives us faith and who keeps our lives secure. We trust that in every dark place there awaits a dawn. Replace our fear with your strength and courage. Even now, O God, our souls wait. Our hope is in the One who gives life in our death and who comes to bring peace to our distress. Come Almighty to deliver. Come and fill us full of light. You, only you eternal God, can change our despair into joy and our weakness into strength. God, you alone are our hope and in that mystery we wait secure. We rest, O great Comforter, in the truth and knowledge that you will never let us go. Through Christ our Redeemer, who comes to reveal your grace and raise us to heaven's glory we pray. Amen.

(DWN)

The Processional Hymn	HYFRYDOL
Come, Thou Long-Expected Jesus	
The Old Testament Lesson	Isaiah 2:1-5
The Meditation	P. Manz
E'en So Lord Jesus	
The New Testament Lesson	Romans 13:11-14
The Hymn	MELITA
The Word Made Flesh and Come to Dwell	

The Pastoral Prayer

    Everything is going too fast, God. Was it not just a few days ago that we welcomed the new year? Have we not only recently celebrated Easter and enjoyed the days of summer? Could it be the beginning of Advent again already, when we are so unready?

    We have to have something to hold on to, God; something to give us stability, something around which we can gain a sense of orientation, a place to stand in which we can touch, or be touched by, a bit of peace. Negotiating our days is like living in free fall. We hardly have time to know where we are, much less who we are and what should come next. Even before we think too much about that, everything has changed—there's another job to do, another engagement to keep, another person who wants our attention. God, forgive us for asking if forgiveness is needed for raising these questions, but where is the sense in all this? What's the purpose of this frantic way of life? Surely there must be a time for silence, an occasion for rest, a moment for love, a source of hope?

    God, help us. Right now we would not know when time is fulfilled and days are accomplished. One time looks just like another, and promise seems out of sight. God, help us. Right now we would not see a star in the East because we rarely look up anymore. God, help us. Right now we would not likely hear an angelic chorus of good news because our ears are tuned to hear only those sounds that fill us with criticism and fear. God, help us.

Will you come into our preoccupied lives, God? Will you bring comfort when we do so little to make life peaceful for ourselves or offer comfort to others? Will you engage us with permanent joy though we are so addicted to passing flings of happiness?

Come to us, God. We would like to say, "Hurry." But that would betray our desire to make you like us rather than to open ourselves to you and let happen whatever happens when you enter our lives. Come to us, God. O come, O come Emmanuel, not this time to deliver ancient Israel, but this time to deliver us. Come on, God. Come on. O come, O come, Emmanuel. Amen.

(CWG)

The Proclamation   K. Jennings
In the Beginning

The Gospel Lesson   Matthew 24:36-44

The Anthem   A. Thomas
Keep Your Lamps!

The Sermon
"The Journey Begins"

The Offering of Our Lives and Labors unto God

The Service of Holy Communion

The Call to Confession   J. Van
Psalm 131

The Prayer of Confession
Your coming into our troubled world has brought hope to all people. Your death on the cross reinstates our reconciliation with God. Cleanse us from every sin. Renew our hopes so that we can share good news with those who struggle on the journey of life. Forgive our weak faith and our failure to believe fully. Fill our lives with such confidence that we might convey our belief that "with God all things are possible." Our hope and peace rest in you, O God.

(DWN)

The Assurance of Forgiveness
To those who wait upon the Lord, their strength shall be renewed. God's revelation restores light to those who sit in darkness, to those who long for hope. Rejoice, for Christ comes to heal your broken spirits and to turn your nights into day. Give thanks to God who lifts your fearful hearts to new hope.

(DWN)

The Communion Prayer
Leader: God of Abraham and Sarah, of Isaac and Rebekah, of apostles and prophets: In every age, you have chosen a people.
People: Since you have called and chosen us, O God, lean us into hope, that the church may rise and flourish with new vitality among us and through us.
Leader: Hope's call is to reenter life, with a new birth of all that is liberating. So come, Hope, to fill us with courage and imagination. Come, O God of new beginnings. Envelope, invigorate, and free us anew.
People: From living the past, free us. From clinging to our complacent religious practices, free us. From the frustration of trying to get our old wineskins to hold our new wine, free us.
Leader: And give us hope, O God, a hope that is always looking forward.
People: Looking forward to the hungry being fed, to the homeless being housed, to a new day of justice.
Leader: For hope sees beyond the obstacles at hand to the possibilities to come. Hope is willing to stake the hard work of the present on the promise of the future. Hope rejoices in all that has been, but also rejoices in all that will be.
People: With hope, we journey to a land we have not yet seen, by way of a road we do not yet know.

Leader: Hope does not give us concrete guarantees, only whispers in the night. Hope does not give us detailed road maps, only a deep yearning in our hearts. God of hope, lead us on our journey to this table and beyond. Amen.

(KMF)

The Distribution of the Elements

The Meditation   J. Martin
Canticle of Hope
(The choir sings as worshipers celebrate communion.)

The Recessional Hymn   DIX
God of Mercy, God of Grace

The Commission and Benediction
Go now with patience born and nurtured by the hope inspired by the God who makes and keeps promises. Set your face toward Bethlehem and walk steadily toward Christmas Day. As you depart from this place of worship to wind your way through the parties, shopping malls, concerts, and special programs of this season, move with assurance that God continues to come to this world. Knowing that the One whom we journey to Bethlehem to meet waits and wants even now to be born in us. Live with expectation. God is with us. Amen.

(CWG)

The Benediction   David White
Comfort, Comfort Ye My People

The Closing Voluntary   J. Ness Beck
Come, Now, Savior of the Nation

The Pealing

THE WORSHIP OF GOD
Second Sunday of Advent

The pilgrimage of Advent leads to the need for peace among individuals and nations and the reality of peace as a gift from God. But do we experience God's provision in our tumultuous lives? The following service seeks to sensitize worshipers to the theological truth and practical reality of God's peace now.

The Prelude   Goeffrey Shaw
        Variations on *Puer Nobis*

The Prologue   arr. Furguson
        Let All Mortal Flesh Keep Silence

(Six readers scattered throughout the sanctuary stand sequentially, open a newspaper [one from each day of the previous week], and read major headlines. The readings proceed at a rapid pace, creating a cacophony of disturbing announcements. The headlines blare the need for peace now. Worshipers are jolted as the distress fomented by this news is interrupted by the choir's ancient, haunting chant affirming that with the advent of Christ come comfort and peace.)

The Call to Worship
    Leader: Comfort my people, says the Lord. Speak unto them words of deliverance.
    People: **God will break the chains of the bound.**
    Leader: Comfort my people, says the Lord. Speak unto them words of peace.
    People: **God will cast out the fears of the troubled.**
    Leader: Comfort my people, says the Lord. Speak unto them words of order.
    People: **God will hallow the cause of the righteous.**
    Leader: Comfort my people, says the Lord. Speak unto them words of assurance.
    People: **God will raise the eyes of the hopeless.**
    Leader: Comfort my people, says the Lord. Speak unto them words of blessing.

Advent

People: "Lord, give us faith and strength the road to build, to see the promise of the day fulfilled, when war shall be no more, and strife shall cease upon the highway of the Prince of Peace."

(Everett Tilson and Phyllis Cole[2])

The Introit   Y. Yarrington
Fling Wide the Door

The Processional Hymn   MENDELSSOHN
Hark! The Herald Angels Sing

The Prayer of Praise and Adoration

We come aside from the chaos and conflicts that surround us and seek rest in your arms, true rest like that of a sleeping child. But anger and threats of violence disturb our worlds, great Prince of Peace. As we sit beside the manger and rock it ever so gently, we begin to grasp a glimpse of your gift of peace. Dear God, in this quiet moment we realize what love you entrusted to us in Jesus Christ, what peace you extend to this world reaching far beyond our limited understanding. But Great God, it was enough then, and it is enough even now.

Sometimes, O God, we wish you would silence that which threatens peace. Yet, when we ourselves become silent, we realize that your power gives birth to a peace, an inner peace that cannot be conquered by threats or force. May we make a home for you, O grantor of peace. May we find room in our hearts for the one who offers harmony. May those who are oppressed find the peace that sustains throughout life, even the peace through Jesus Christ our Lord. Amen.

(DWN)

The Response   PAX IAM
Peace in Our Time

The Old Testament Lesson   Isaiah 9:1-6
    Leader: This is the Word of the Lord.
    People: Thanks be to God.

The Contemporary Lesson
(Select an article from a local newspaper and read a section of it that describes the need for peace in your community or invite comments from a person who questions either the existence or the possibility of peace in today's world.)

The Meditation   F. Schubert
Dona Nobis Pacem

The New Testament Lesson   Revelation 12
Leader: This is the Word of the Lord.
People: Thanks be to God.

(As the lesson is read, the steady beat of a timpani is heard, creating tension and signaling the onslaught of evil. Immediately after the congregation says, "Thanks be to God," children placed throughout the room with noise-making instruments rise to join the beckoning of the timpani, sharpening anticipation among worshipers.)

The Lighting of the Candle of Peace
(Four teenagers move through the sanctuary, each bearing a lighted candle. They move to the Advent wreath and ignite the candle of peace. As the candle takes flame, the noises in the room fall silent.)

The Silent Prayers of the People

The Pastoral Prayer
Dissonance, not harmony; jagged edges, not smooth plains; disjointedness, not unity—that's what we see, hear, and feel.

Two candles burning in the Advent wreath are better than one, God; but can these flames survive the heavy wind gusts that are storming through our lives?

We want to hear your Word, God. Honestly we do. We need to hear your Word. But there are all of these other words: people telling us bad news, insisting on conformity, discouraging risk, counseling the status quo.

And we are left thinking what might have been and what could be, trying to make sense of the relationship between morality, responsibility, and spontaneity, asking, "Why not?" confessing disappointment, pleading, "Help us, God."

So, our words and other words almost drown out your Word. On the second Sunday of Advent some of us are joyful, and some of us are profoundly sorrowful; some of us hopeful, and some of us discouraged; some of us laughing, and some of us hurting; some of us feeling more alive than ever, and some of us sensing an onslaught of depression.

    Maybe it's not the way we should be, God, but it's the way we are. And maybe this is the way we have to be. If we hear, see, touch, taste, and smell nothing else in this hour, let us know your comfort. Comfort us, God. Comfort us and make us comforters. In the name of the Prince of Peace. Amen.

(CWG)

The Hymn   HYFRYDOL
God of Justice, God of Mercy

The Anthem   R. Nintz
The Questions Asked

The Sermon
    "Apocalypse Now: Come Peace of God"

The Offering of Our Lives and Labors unto God

The Meditation   E. Butler
Come, Peace of God

The Invitation

The Commission
    Historically, Christians have greeted each other by passing the peace of God. One believer says, "May the peace of God be with you" and another responds saying, "And also with you." Before reentering our noisy, chaotic existence in the world, assure one another that you take from this place God's peace.

(CWG)

The Recessional Hymn   SINE NOMINE
Great God, Whose Will Is Peace

The Benediction   Walter Pelz
Peace I Leave with You

The Closing Voluntary   J. S. Bach
Come Now, Savior of the Nations

THE WORSHIP OF GOD
Third Sunday of Advent

The pace of Advent quickens in the following service. As we move closer to the manger, quiet whispers of hope and somber prayers for peace give way to explosive expressions of joy evoked by the birth of Jesus. However, various opportunities for exultant joy in the service do not occur apart from realistic acknowledgements of elements of life that make joy difficult. Vibrant hallelujahs prevail, but not without serious challenges and good reasons.

The Preludes .... Dietrich Buxtchude
> *Nun komm den heiden Heiland*
> *Puer natus est*
> *In dulci jubilo*

The Prologue .... Randall Thompson
> *Nowell*
> from *The Nativity According to St. Luke*

(As the choir sings the prologue, a group of five children enters the sanctuary carrying a flaming candle, moves to the Advent wreath, and lights the pink candle—the candle of joy. Once the candle begins to burn, the quiet and somber mood with which the service has begun gives way to sounds of festivity and celebration as herald trumpets erupt into a fanfare signaling the joy of this Sunday in Advent. If trumpets are unavailable, create this same effect with the pealing of bells.)

The Call to Worship
> Leader: Rejoice, I say: rejoice!
> **People: What? Are you talking to us?**
> Leader: Yes! Rejoice! This is the happiest time of the year!
> **People: It usually is, yes. We really like Advent and all of the wonderful Christmas feelings. Usually. This year we don't much feel like rejoicing. It's been kind of a hard year . . . you know?**
> Leader: Yes, I know. I have felt your pain. But you can still rejoice. Have joy in all things.

People:	**How? How can we rejoice when we don't feel like it? You know that this is also the most difficult time of year for some people.**
Leader:	Yes, I know. I feel their loneliness, their pain, their loss.
People:	**Well, then, why are you telling us to rejoice? Even if we had no loss ourselves, these other ones are all around us. Do you expect us to dance?**
Leader:	Not all joy is boisterous. You know that.
People:	**Yes, we do. But—**
Leader:	You know that deep within you, in the silence, even in the tears, you have an undercurrent of peace. And you know that this Christ Child came for just this purpose—to become one with us in our pain.
People:	**Yes, we know that.**
Leader:	Isn't that cause for hope? And what is hope but the expectation of joy?
People:	**But how can we hope for joy when we are bleeding and broken?**
Leader:	You are not alone in your pain. You wonder sometimes if life is worth the aching and the bleeding. But you are not alone.
People:	**So, it is. It is worth it. So we can rejoice, just knowing that. We can raise our faces, wet with tears, toward heaven and laugh–out loud–and welcome this Christ Child, who joins us in our pain. Welcome!**
All:	O gentle Child of Bethlehem, help us to see beyond the sentimental pictures of your birth, to the real and holy purpose of your coming. Help us to know the hope that is the expectation of joy, even in our sorrow. Help us to celebrate the light, even in our seasons of darkness. To you, the one who joins us in our pain, we pray. Amen.

(LKC)

The Introit L. Pfautsch

Torches

The Response
> Leader: Come let us give thanks and sing praises for God's gift of love.
> **People: We celebrate God's revealed truth and rejoice in God's love.**

The Processional Hymn   MIT FREUDEN ZART
> *Sing Praise to God, Our Highest Good*

The Prayer of Praise and Adoration
God of Joy and Delight: This is almost too much for us. Certainly it is more than we can contain. Once we begin to see the importance of Christ's light in our lives, we want it for everyone—we want him for everyone.

    Spread the light that emanates from the manger, O God. Surely you can do it. You lift the sun into the sky every morning so that even on a cloudy day there is enough brightness for us to know that behind the clouds the sun is shining. You can take the light that comes from one candle of truth and turn it into a luminary that covers the whole earth with bright promise. If you need us to help, we will.

    Use us as candle-lighters, flame-bearers, light-spreaders. Use us in a ministry of light that exposes untruths, gives guidance for people who have lost their way, highlights grace, melts away fear, warms our ability for affirmation and acceptance.

    Strengthen us as we serve you with light. Enable us to spark enough light in this world that Christ will never again have to come in darkness, and that every time he comes people will know who he is.

    Fill us and our world with the light who started to shine in Bethlehem, the one who gives us light, the one who understood himself as the Light of the World. Amen.

(CWG)

The Old Testament Lesson   Isaiah 11:1-5, 10, 11, 16; 9:6b-7
> Leader: The Word of the Lord.
> **People: Thanks be to God.**

Advent

The Meditation   R. Vaughan Williams
                        Epilogue
                       from *Hodie*

The Gospel Lesson   John 1:1-14
    Leader: The Holy Gospel of Our Lord Jesus Christ.
    People: Praise be to thee, O Christ.

The Hymn   GOD REST YE MERRY
                  God Rest Ye Merry Gentlemen
           (Substitute the word "Christians" for the word "gentlemen.")

The Gospel Lesson   Luke 2:1-7
    Leader: The Holy Gospel of Our Lord, Jesus Christ.
    People: Praise be to thee, O Christ.

The Response   Traditional
                    Sweet Little Jesus Boy
                            (Solo)

The Contemporary Lesson
    I have held you, little one, cradled in my arms, astounded at the wonder of you who has been exuberantly and painstakingly knitted from encoded, colorful strands of DNA that had their initial shaping in the mind of God even before the Milky Way was a spinning wheel.
    The curve of your perfect little lips, the little delicate blue veins on your translucent eyelids, the noble expanse of your sweet brow waiting to be kissed are direct signs from the Life Maker of the incomprehensible value of your new life. After an outlay of ecstasy, patience, and pain (a fair price for such a treasure) your little life was entrusted into my arms for a short while. Your sleeping form melded with my heart. Your face mirrored my face, and I wept looking there to see those little features that were in reality the seal of the living God set there, an emblem of ownership by the very one who had so carefully formed you in the sanctity of your mother's womb and in His image.
    As I held you, I felt the Father God lift me up out of this reality and cradle me, humming a lullaby as a reminder from

His Fatherheart to me, His prodigal son, that I, too, have been set with a seal. Such love. Such security. Such peace.

(RC)

The Anthem   G. F. Handel
Hallelujah Chorus

(Prior to the service, the musician and the proclaimer agree that the "Hallelujah" chorus will be interrupted by the introduction to the sermon. No other participant in the service is aware of this plan so that all present can experience the shocking surprise and the comforting truth that follows. Shortly after the choir begins to sing, the preacher stands, asks the choir to stop singing, and moves into the pulpit to speak.)

The Sermon

        "A Question about Hallelujahs"

The Anthem   G. F. Handel
Hallelujah Chorus

The Offering of Our Lives and Labors unto God

The Peoples' Prayers of Joy
(Prior to the service, select four people to contribute elements of praise to this prayer of joy.)

    Leader: Having heard the good news and felt again the exultation of joy that comes from God's revealed truth, let us speak to God and to each other of the joy with which we depart from worship.

The Invitation

The Commission
    Leader: Wake up, O world. The dawn of ages is shattering the night. The kingdom of God is coming down. Wake up, O world. Shake off the slumber of the night. God did not let us go. God's love has made a way. Rejoice and sing.

People:	**The news is good. Dawn breaks forth. Our darkened world is filled with marvelous light. At last we can find the way.**
Leader:	Celebrate the good news; step into the radiance of the divine. Sing and let all the earth share in the glory of Christ's coming.
People:	**We will no longer sit in the gloom of darkness. We will dance in the joy of this new day. God has turned our darkest night into morning's light. We will lift our voices with the song of the heavens. We will turn towards the Light. We will follow the Way.**

(DWN)

The Recessional Hymn   IN DULCI JUBILO
Good Christian Friends, Rejoice
(Ask worshipers to be seated for reflective meditations on joy during the offering of the closing meditation.)

The Meditation   P. Doyle
Non Nobis Domine
(from Psalm 115:1)

The Benediction
May the God who changes everything change you and give you strength, comfort, and joy for the struggle of change. May you be refreshed and enriched in ways that will draw the world toward reconciliation with God.

(CWG)

The Pealing

The Closing Voluntary   J. S. Bach
In Dulci jubilo

THE WORSHIP OF GOD
Fourth Sunday of Advent

Familiarity deadens sensitivity. The following service turns familiarity upside down and seeks to create a level of attentiveness to the truth of God's love that causes worship to occur as if for the first time. Note that, with the exception of the words of welcome, the order of this service proceeds from the end to the beginning of a traditional order of worship.

The Words of Welcome
(After greeting and welcoming worshipers, a worship leader explains the nature and purpose of this service and the order of it. The statement printed above can be used in this explanation.)

The Postlude   J. F. Wade
Lo! He Comes with Clouds Descending

The Benediction   G. F. Handel
Hallelujah Chorus

The Commission
    Leader   The God of love sends us from this place to share the gift revealed.
    People: **We will go into the world celebrating the good news of this day. Our journey shall be filled with joy, for our spirits have found soul's peace.**
    Leader: Carry to all the world the light you have witnessed. Tell of love-made-flesh and grace-offered-freely. Receive and repeat the glad tidings to all you encounter.
    People: **We will rejoice and be glad. Our hearts shall be filled with song. God's own child comes to smooth the crooked way and bring dawn to salvation's day.**
    All: **Let our joy know no end. Hallelujah!**

(DWN)

The Hymn of Response   ANTIOCH
Joy to the World!

The Offering of Our Lives and Labors unto God

The Words of Advent

"I never knew how much you loved me," I said in my troubling dream. Your mouth dropped open in incredulity while your eyes narrowed in disbelief like they did when you were alive—an accusing look, implying stupidity on my part. "See," I wanted to say, "That expression on your face makes me wonder."

"No, you see!" you loudly replied, pulling out the letter. It was on lined paper (I believe on Big Chief Tablet writing paper) with several smudges leaving gray clues where a rubber eraser nearly rubbed holes in the rough paper, verifying that you had wrestled as you tried to say it just right. You didn't. But you tried. And holding up the white page like a flag of surrender, torn from an inerrant book of love, you frantically waved it.

"See!" you said in my dream, bridging that chasm for the second time since you died, "I told you that I loved you, and here is the proof." You exhibited that smudged, illegible schoolboy paper as tough as if it were a royal sealed testimony, allowing me to finally see . . . us. And then I knew.

(RC)

The Silent Communion
(Print in the order of worship: "Following the contemporary reading, you are invited to touch and to taste the love of God as you silently receive God's gifts of bread and wine.")

The Anthem　　　　　　　　　　　　　　　　　　　　　R. Thompson
Alleluia

The Sermon
　　　　　　　　"Let's Do Christmas!"

The Response　　　　　　　　　　　　　　　　　R. Vaughan Williams
Choral
from *Hodie*

The Apocalyptic Lesson					Revelation 19:1, 3-4, 6-7
    Leader: This is the Word of God.
    People: Thanks be to God.

The Response					R. Young
    To Him We Sing

The Litany
    Leader: We are called to prepare a way,
    People: God's way on earth. We are called to make it smooth—to make it straight,
    Leader: which means our ways will not be smooth—or straight.
    People: We struggle to incarnate our God—to allow the Words of God to take our flesh—to birth this strange and beautiful way of living.
    Leader: We believe that Christmas is preparing us for you,
    People: that your paths might be made clear, and all mouths be filled with laughter as every tongue tastes your joy and as all flesh sees the salvation of God.

                                                                   (JB)

The Hymn of Advent					VENI EMMANUEL
    O Come, O Come, Emmanuel

The Prayer of Advent
    Loving God, you know that feeling we have when we stand on the edge of a cliff and peer downward into a gaping chasm. Insecurity and a sense of danger interact with excitement and a sense of wonder. That is sort of how we feel this morning, standing at the edge of Christmas this year. We sense a vast, gaping chasm separating a realization of the biblical message of this season and the texts of news scripts that describe the content of our days.

    Isaiah dreams of peace, Matthew writes of a star of hope in the east, and we watch missiles of destruction blast against their targets in the east. Luke tells of the birth of a baby, and an obituary enumerates key events in the years of a loved one who has died. Angels sing of glory, and a friend anxiously awaits the results of a biopsy. Messengers from God instruct the people of God not to fear, and we wrestle with our multiple fears like Jacob fighting with that stranger at Jabbok Ford. The apostle Paul looks at the birth of Jesus and thinks of grace, and we look at the birth of Jesus and unleash harsh judgments.

O God, help us. As members of a fragmented society, we are teetering on the edge of a precipice, in danger of falling into a chasm, while singing, "Joy to the World." Save us, God. Save us from segmentation and compartmentalization. Make us uncomfortable in our efforts to affirm your vision of the world in celebrations of Christmas while vigorously pursuing our self-interests in the world most of the rest of the time.

Come here, God. Come now. Be born among us. Take up residence in us. Turn our hearts into mangers that you may turn our lives into instruments of your peace and media of your love. Please come here, God. Amen.

(CWG)

The Response					Ryan-Wenger
In the Beginning
(During the singing of the response, a family enters the sanctuary carrying a flaming candle, moves to the Advent wreath, and lights the fourth candle—the candle of love.)

The Gospel Lesson				Luke 2:16

The Proclamation				R. Vaughan Williams
Epilogue
from *Hodie*

The Hymn of Praise				ADESTE FIDELES
O Come, All You Faithful

The Call to Worship
    Leader: We want to raise our hearts in love, but we must confess, our God, that love is difficult—

People: **that it's easier to keep others, and to keep you, at somewhat of a distance—a distance we determine and maintain—that we're in control of.**

Leader: It's easier not to work at the interconnectedness—the interdependence.

People: **But this is the irrational season, and we confess, too, that it is love that fills our days with brightness—our lives with joy and peace.**

Leader: We confess that the easiest life is not the richest life,

People: **and we commit ourselves to you—integrated more fully into our day-to-dayness—exploring love in all the dimensions of our living.**

(JB)

The Prologue   arr. P. Wohlgemuth
Of the Father's Love Begotten

The Meditation

The Prelude to Witness   J. S. Bach
Wachet aug, ruft uns die Stimme

NOTES

[1] See pp. 296-98 for suggestions on visual enhancements for the four Sundays of Advent worship.

[2] Everett Tilson and Phyllis Cole, *Litanies and Other Prayers for the Common Lectionary*, Year B (Nashville: Abingdon Press, 1990) 18.

THE WORSHIP OF GOD
Contemporary Advent

The season of Advent pulsates with the familiar themes of hope, peace, joy, and love. But what do these themes mean in our world? What is the nature of hope, peace, joy, and love among people who live two thousand years after the arrival of the Messiah? This worship service, intended for use early in the season of Advent, enables worshipers to explore the nature of God-inspired hope, peace, love, and joy today.

The Prologue   Monroe, Louisiana
"The Real Picture"

(As worshipers enter the building, they are confronted with an astonishing mixture of sights and sounds. The narthex includes a man hammering nails into lumber that will go into a house constructed by Habitat for Humanity, a young woman playing "Ode to Joy" on a cello, a table that displays paraphernalia confiscated from gangs in the local area, a law enforcement officer displaying a variety of drugs taken in recent drug raids in the community, and an old movie projector clacking as it throws onto the wall images of hopeless situations throughout the world. Here is the context in which we must celebrate Advent. This is the kind of world into which Jesus comes today. A worship leader joins the worshipers who have gathered amid the cacophony of sounds to summon worshipers to move away from this noisy, somewhat disturbing environment and enter into the quietness of the sanctuary.)

The Call   Veni Emmanuel
O Come, O Come, Emmanuel
(verse 1)
(This carol is sung while worshipers remain in the narthex.)

The Processional Hymn   STUTTGART
Come, O Long-Expected Jesus
(As worshipers begin to sing this carol, worship leaders start a spontaneous processional into the worship center where people take their seats. The choir remains in the narthex to support the singing of the carol. After all other worshipers are seated, the choir processes into the choir loft.)

Hope

The Lesson   Romans 8:19-23

The Meditation   D. Besig
                    Will We Know Him?

The Revelation of Hope   John 1:1-1

The Response   Ryan-Wenger
                    In the Beginning

The Reality of Advent
    (A law enforcement officer, social worker, or court official describes people in the community who live in seemingly hopeless situations.)

The Meditation   K. Medema
                    "I Was Hungry"
                  from *The Gathering*

The Attestations of Hope
    (Persons who have found hope in hopeless situations tell their stories. A man describes his experience of hope while undergoing chemotherapy to treat a malignancy. A woman relates her journey into hope while trying to raise a family in substandard housing. A young person speaks of hope in relating to peer pressures in school.)

The Response   Manz
                  E'en So Lord Jesus

The Prayer of Hope
    God of Life and Death, Crèches and Crosses, Whimpering Babies and the Sighing Elderly, Great God:
        Some of us have trouble with this season. The more joyful the celebrations around us, the more severe a sense of desperation within us. That which brings other people pleasure brings some of us pain. Singing makes us want to weep. Parties send us in search of solitude. Galas threaten us with depression. We hope, God, how we hope. We hope for the discovery of a peace and joy that can sustain us in the face of loneliness, disappointment, and unrealized dreams. We hope, God.

Some of us are too busy for this season. All that we have to do in the name of celebration obliterates the meaning of the event to be celebrated. Festive occasions become items on a list to be checked off as "done" before we move on to the next activity. We hope, God, how we hope. We hope to claim the promise of revelation that resides at the heart of this season. We hope, God.

Some of us will miss this season because of a preoccupation with hunger, a distortion of reality perpetrated by drugs, a lack of sensitivity brought on by senility, a spiritual void dug out by constant threats and violence. That, too, is a factor in the human family. We hope, God, how we hope. We hope that as the content of Advent grips our lives, we will be moved to make a difference in the lives of those who are homeless, drugged, senile, worn out by threats, or shattered by violence. We hope, God.

And, of course, there is more. Our hopes are our prayers, God. Amen.

(CWG)

The Challenge

Little homeless family huddled in an old car, the night air is not filled with angelic voices—rather, politicians yelling until they are hoarse about family values. And you, little holy family, shiver as your breath forms frost on the car windows. The dash is not littered with gold, frankincense, or myrrh—rather empty, fast food boxes.

And there wrapped in an old blanket, nestled close to his mother's heart the least of these sleeps, waiting for wise men to read the prophecy and see what they should do about this newborn promise.

(RC)

The Anthem   W. Dawson
There Is a Balm in Gilead

The Lesson   Isaiah 61:1-3
The Carol   HYFRYDOL
Come, Thy Long-Expected Jesus

Peace

The Lesson
    (Read the Hebrew prayer from *The Gates of Heaven* [New York: Central Conference of American Rabbis, 1997, pp. 692-693].)

The Meditation   R. Nimt
    "The Questions Asked"

The Attestation of a City in Need of Peace
    (A community leader describes the family conflicts, the gang warfare, and other forms of physical and emotional violence that feed a longing for peace among people in the local community.)

The Prayer for Peace
    Leader: We have, our God, become accustomed to so much pain.
    People: We have become accustomed to our privilege.
    Leader: (from newspaper headlines)
    People: We have become accustomed to independence and the idea of self-sufficiency.
    Leader: (from newspaper headlines)
    People: We have become accustomed to violence, injustice, hunger, and pain.
    Leader: (from newspaper headlines)
    People: We have become accustomed to too much; we have become accustomed to our world.
    Leader: Help us, our God, become unaccustomed,
    People: that we might see again with your eyes, your world, and commit ourselves to the peace that should be . . . to the peace that still can be!
    All: Amen.

                                                                                            (JB)

The Meditation   A. Burt
    Some Children See Him

The Truce
    Leader: We have heard of the warfare. We have prayed for peace. We have witnessed God's call for us to be

peacemakers. Let us pray that God will give us the will to proclaim the message of peace and to do the work of peace.

The Blessing   J. Rutter
Gaelic Blessing

Joy

The Challenge   Peter 1:8-9
James 1:2-3
Luke 2:10

The Meditation   M. Hayes
And the Father Will Dance

The Attestation of Joy   Lisa Hawkins
(A modern liturgical dancer performs an original program that spells out the name "Jesus" to call worshipers' attention to the importance of the one who comes in this season to bring joy.)

The Prayer of Thanksgiving and Joy
God of good news, gladness has filled our souls. We cannot contain the joy that Christ brings to our lives this day. Our hearts want to sing. Our longing has found promise. Our desert places spring forth with everlasting joy. Your transforming realm comes to us and offers wholeness and peace to our broken worlds. Almighty God, with all the heavens, we offer unto you our praise and thanksgiving. Glory to God in the highest. Joy to all the world, for God is come. Amen.

(DWN)

The Celebration
Hilariter   K. Lee Scott
Masters in the Hall   J. Miller
This Night Did God Become a Child   M. Sedia
Sing We Noel   N. Goemanne
Sing We Now of Christmas   F. Prentice

Love

The Revelation of Love   John 3:16-21

The Reflection   R. Young
             To Him We Sing

The Lesson   John 15:9-17

The Meditation   H. Friedell
             Jesus So Lowly

The Attestations of Love
   (A doctor speaks of her experience of love in the life of this congregation of believers. She reflects on the support she has felt both professionally and personally, in her daily work and in times of crisis such as the loss of her mother. A recent recipient of a house from Habitat for Humanity relates her feelings of love in watching people build a house for her and her family.)

The Meditation   H. Hopson
             The Gift of Love

The Prayer of Love
   Love with flesh on it, God. Wonder of wonders; what a gift! As we look once more at a distant manger, we see—and feel—love that touched people and spoke well and intended well for people.
   Thanks be to you, O God, for love that rubs tired feet, that cools a fevered forehead, that clothes a naked back, that picks up a hammer and builds a shelter for the homeless, that writes a letter to the newspaper challenging prejudice, that lifts a drugged teenager who has fallen, that makes and distributes soup to people who are hungry, that halts the mean advance of warring groups, that embraces a stranger as well as hugs a lover.
   As we worship the love in flesh of the Christmas baby, enable us to embody love in the flesh of our lives that the promise of this season may be realized throughout every day of the year. Amen.
                                                          (CWG)

Advent Today

The Question   Matthew 25:31-42

Advent

The Invitation　　　　　　　　　　　　　　　　　　　　　G. Holst
　　In the Bleak Midwinter

The Commission
　　(When the musical invitation concludes by urging people to give their hearts to the Christ, a worship leader immediately challenges congregants to live as agents of hope, peace, joy, and love in their community even as they celebrate these divine gifts during this liturgical season.)

The Response　　　　　　　　　　　　　　　　　　　　　　Pierce
　　Fanfare for Tomorrow

The Postlude　　　　　　　　　　　　　　　　　　　　　J. G. Barr
　　Reflection on "Veni Emmanuel"
　　(Print in the order of service: "The congregation is asked to remain seated until the conclusion of the postlude.")

The Pealing

Third Sunday of Advent;
Joy heralds the good news

*First Sunday of Advent;
Hope Springs Forth*

*Second Sunday of Advent;
Visions of Peace*

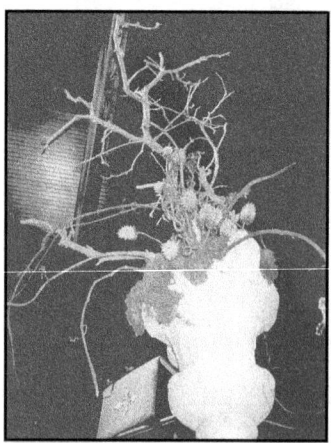

*First Sunday of Advent;
The root of Jesse brings
forth new hope*

*Fourth Sunday of Advent;
Love in Full Bloom*

Christmas

THE WORSHIP OF GOD
Christmas Eve

The traditional Oxford service of lessons and carols inspires and informs the following service built around familiar lessons from the Hebrew and Christian Scriptures and the texts of beloved carols. We suggest not using a choir for this service so that all participants can sit with family members and friends.

The Organ Voluntary   T. Adams
Adeste Fideles

The Processional Carol   IRBY
Once in Royal David's City

The Call to Worship
- Leader: It's the eve of wonder.
- **People: Angels are singing again; children can't sleep; the wise look to the heavens.**
- Leader: Parents are piecing together what they hope will fulfill the dreams of their loved ones,
- **People: and everyone hopes that tomorrow, somehow, their deepest dreams will be met.**
- Leader: It's the eve of wonder.
- **People: God is at work, birthing into our experience the potential for the blessedness for which God created us.**
- Leader: Angels are singing again,
- **People: and the wise look around to see God being born.**
- Leader: Our deepest dreams surround us waiting to be recognized and embraced.
- **People: Angels are singing again, and the wise see.**
- **All: Glory to God in the highest, and on earth . . . peace. Alleluia!**

(JB)

The Carol   DIVINUM MYSTERIUM
Of the Father's Love Begotten

The Lessons of Prophecy

Isaiah 40:1-8; Jeremiah 23:5-6; Zechariah 9:9-10

The Carol   ES IST EN' ROS'
Lo, How a Rose E'er Blooming

Micah 5:2-4

The Carol   ST. LOUIS
O Little Town of Bethlehem

The Evening Prayer

    Tune our hearts to hear your music, God, ancient music that so long ago called a world into being—called life into being. Glory to God in the highest, and on earth—peace. Music that has echoed through the ages offering an alternative to the noise of the world, reminding all of what creation is to be; music made flesh in a stable; music made flesh in your children; music made flesh in us . . . May the music that surrounds us comfort us, heal us, challenge us, invite us to be a part of it.

(JB)

The Coming of Christ

Luke 1:26-35

The Carol   GABRIEL'S MESSAGE
The Angel Gabriel from Heaven Came

Matthew 1:18-25

The Carol   LIEBER/MEIN
Gentle Joseph, Joseph Dear

Luke 2:1-8

The Carol   MUELLER
Away in a Manger

Luke 2:8-12

The Carol   THE FIRST NOWELL
The First Nowell

Christmas

Luke 2:13-14

The Carol   GLORIA
Angels We Have Heard on High

Luke 2:15-20

The Carol   GREENSLEEVES
What Child Is This?

The Revelation   John 1:1-14
  Leader: This is the Word of God.
  People: Thanks be to God.

The Lighting of the Christ Candle
(In the awesome silence created by the astounding truth of the word becoming flesh, someone least expected to serve as a worship leader enters the sanctuary bearing a flaming candle, walks to the Advent wreath, where all four of the Advent candles are burning, and touches the flame to the large white candle that stands in the center of the Advent wreath—the Christ candle.)

The Homily
  "On Being Light"

The Carol   STILLENACHT
  Silent Night, Holy Night
  (verse 2)

The Service of Holy Communion

The Communion Prayer
  Holy God: On this night of wonder and mystery, we give you thanks for love in the flesh—warm, sensitive, cooing flesh—and for the ministry of the body we remember and celebrate in drinking the fruit of the vine and in eating broken bread.
  We praise you for the opportunity to meet at a table and enjoy your good gifts even as we pray for those who cannot get to a table and for those who have no table. Surely if you would come to a manger in a cattle stall, you will visit a shelter for

the homeless, a refuge for the abused, a soup kitchen for the hungry, a home for the elderly.

Surely if you would abide with Mary and Joseph amid their anxiety and controversy, you will stay among persons stung by criticism, hurt by schism. Surely if you would welcome shepherds to your side, you will reach out to those who are away from home tonight and to those who cannot share these hours with the ones they love.

Welcome to our world, God. We want you here, though we don't always act like it. We join you now in the meal that you lovingly provide for us. Allow us to taste not only wine and bread, but also grace and peace.

We pray in the name of Emmanuel who does indeed come to us. Amen.

(CWG)

(Request worshipers to come forward where worship leaders are serving communion. A worship leader also stands beside the Christ candle and hands a votive candle to each participant in communion who in turn lights the votive from the Christ candle before returning to his or her seat.)

The Commission

The light you make together here is beautiful. But we cannot stay here. This light can change the world. Go into the darkness and share your light even as you share the good news of the birth of Christ. Rejoice and be glad for Christ has come.

(CWG)

The Recessional CarolIN DULCI JUBILO
Good Christian Friends, Rejoice

(Print in the order of worship: "As you depart with your lighted votive candle, please place the burning candle along the walkway leading from the sanctuary representing to the world our celebration of the Light that has come.")

The PostludeA. Fedak
Joy to the World

THE WORSHIP OF GOD
Christmas Day

Occasionally, Christmas Day falls on a Sunday. However, no day on the Christian calendar or civil calendar merits a corporate worship experience more than Christmas Day. The following service, intended for mid-morning on Christmas Day, is designed as a simple expression of gratitude to God for the unspeakable gift of Incarnate Love.

The Prelude   A. Jordan
Gloria for the Flutes

The Prologue   R. Thompson
"Nowell"
from *The Nativity According to St. Luke*

The Call to Worship
- Leader: In this region we have been doing our Christmas shopping, going to our Christmas parties, and singing our Christmas songs. And we are filled with the hope that this time we will unwrap the promises of God, and live so that what it feels like is what is supposed to be.
- **People: But at this time and in this region, while we celebrate the birth of the one who was to have brought peace, we read our newspapers and try not to be confused.**
- Leader: In this region and at this time we struggle with our loneliness—with our sense of emptiness,
- **People: And we're not sure how to reconcile who and what we claim has been born, with what we do, and how we feel, and what we see—all around us—in this region . . .**
- Leader: In that region there were shepherds living in the fields, keeping watch over their flock by night. Then an angel of the Lord stood before them, and the glory of the Lord shone around them, and they were

terrified. But the angel said to them, "Do not be afraid; for see—I am bringing you good news of great joy for all the people: to you is born this day in the city of David a Savior, who is the Messiah, the Lord. This will be a sign for you: you will find a child wrapped in bands of cloth and lying in a manger." And suddenly there was with the angel a multitude of the heavenly host, praising God and saying, "Glory to God in the highest heaven, and on earth peace among those whom he favors!" When the angels had left them and gone into heaven, the shepherds said to one another, "Let us go now to Bethlehem and see this thing that has taken place, which the Lord has made known to us." So they went with haste and found Mary and Joseph, and the child lying in the manger. When they saw this, they made known what had been told them about this child; and all who heard it were amazed at what the shepherds told them. But Mary treasured all these words and pondered them in her heart. The shepherds returned, glorifying and praising God for all they had heard and seen, as it had been told them. . . . And we are grateful for what has been told us—again. We treasure these words and ponder them in our hearts, for God has taken the initiative. God began a work we continue.

People: And it is in the process of our work with God that we find peace, glorifying and praising God for all we hear and see, by the grace of God—fully revealed in Christ Jesus. Amen.

(JB)

The Introit   M. Sedio
This Night Did God Become A Child
(The choir sings from the rear of the sanctuary.)

The Processional Hymn   ADESTE FIDELES
O Come, All Ye Faithful

The Psalm   Psalm 98
> Leader: The Word of God.
> **People: Thanks be to God.**

The Meditation   J. Mochnick
> *Companions, All Sing Loudly*

The Morning Prayer
> Here is this news, God, and we're not sure how to respond either to it or to the one whose birth is announced by it. How do we welcome the baby Christ? Rattlers and lace gowns don't seem appropriate. He already has some clothes or wrappings that serve as clothes, and we're not sure he would like a rattler. Honestly, not even gold, frankincense, and myrrh make much sense as gifts. What can a baby do with such extravagance? Besides, those things seem out of place in a stable.
>
> How do we welcome the infant Messiah? It seems a bit awkward to talk of hopes that he will do well in the world. We know too much. And babbling about his beautiful eyes or the shape of his nose—well, that's not for us.
>
> God—Parent of the Christ and of us all: We welcome your son, our elder brother, the would-be Savior of the world. Forgive us, if we don't do it right, and help us to do it better.
>
> We welcome Christ into our world, praying that we will always prefer seeing him stretched out in a manger or on a pallet rather than on a cross.
>
> We welcome Christ into our society, praying that we will do more than admire his wise teachings, working to make his truth incarnate in people's lives.
>
> We welcome Christ into our church, praying that he will continue to shape our identity according to his likeness.
>
> We welcome Christ into our lives, accepting him as Savior, exalting him as Lord, loving him as Friend.
>
> Welcome Christ! O come, O come Emmanuel. Welcome. Welcome. Amen.
>
> (CWG)

The New Testament Lesson　　　　　　　　　Titus 3:4-8; 2:11-15
　　Leader:　This is the Word of God.
　　People:　Thanks be to God.

The Meditation　　　　　　　　　　　　　　　　L. Pfautsch
　　　　　　　The Wondrous Mystery

The Gospel of the Nativity　　　　　　　　　　　　Luke 2

The Contemporary Lesson
　　Hawkers and mockers, believers and deceivers, brick-a-brack and knickknacks, children selling olive branches for a dollar, prerecorded call to prayer for faithful Muslims from multitudinous minarets, the drone of Jewish men groaning prayers at the Wailing Wall, the bleating of the herds of wide-eyed Christian pilgrims darting wherever their rent-a-shepherd leads them . . . The tumult of frantic traffic, the continued digging of archaeologists—like scarab beetles burrowing in dung, like maggots in holy carrion—bombard us.
　　We bow to enter the church of the Nativity as a stout woman with no sense of decorum or civility presses a group of Asian pilgrims to the front of the line. (The last shall be first.) Other busy guides chat their endless litany of: "It is believed . . ." or, "Tradition has it . . ." to the mesmerized flock, as the clock determines what time is available before the next group is due.
　　On every wall and over the altar are faces of the Virgin and the Child—variations on the theme. The silent two seem to peer through the haze of candle soot, dust, incense, and the damp breath of murmured prayers. Her eyes are unfocused as she sits posed and poised waiting for all the pandemonium to pass.
　　Is she remembering an earlier time, when she held that tiny, newborn infant to her virgin's breast offering warmth, succor, and as much protection from the world as innocence and love can afford?

Oh, Divine Incarnation, we worship you in a temple far away from peddlers of postcards and religion. We worship you in the Holy of Holies of our hearts as we marvel the meaning of the name, Emmanuel.

(RC)

The Anthem   G. Young
Cradle Hymn

The Sermon
"Whispers of Christmas"

The Offering of Our Lives and Labors unto God

The Instrumental Meditation   T. Ripper
Puer nobis nascitur
(You may use an alternative instrumental meditation that moves the service from our offerings to God to a celebration of God's supreme offering to us.)

The Service of Holy Communion

(Note the absence of prayers of confession. This is a day for a singular focus on joyous gratitude.)

The Communion Prayer

God of body, God of blood, Word made flesh in our midst: speak to us. God of body, God of blood: speak through us words of transformation, words of healing and love, words for each one here, words for our community, words for our world, words made flesh in our ministry and in our love as we grow in our faith.

God of body, broken for all; God of blood, shed for all: prepare us for our breaking, that of our bodies and of our blood your word might anoint all your children to proclaim the time of God's favor, to proclaim freedom and justice for all, and we might once again hear the sound of God walking in our midst and joyfully and thankfully choose to walk humbly with our God. Amen.

(JB)

The Distribution of the Elements

The Invitation

The Commission
"Come, Lord Jesus!" people prayed. And you did! Go now to enjoy a celebration of Christ's birth and to engage in a demonstration of God's love. Go to live as people visited by God. Go to live as the people of God. Christ the Savior is born! Thanks be to God! Amen and amen.

(CWG)

The Recessional Hymn   ANTIOCH
Joy to the World!

The Benediction   F. Prentice
Sing We Now of Christmas

The Pealing

THE WORSHIP OF GOD
First Sunday after Christmas

Soon after Christmas Day, many people begin to talk about getting life back to normal. A more biblical response to Christmas Day is a resolve to be sure that life never gets back to normal. The imagery, themes, music, and surprises of Christmas Day inspire grand expectations related to the possibilities of every day—dreams and visions of a different kind of world and people who appear as new creations. The following service affirms the importance of dreams and visions and encourages dreamers and visionaries.

The Prelude   J. S. Bach
    Vivace

The Prologue   Jeffery Honore
    Creator of the Stars of Night

The Contemporary Reading   Cynthia Rulant/Barry Moser[1]
    The Dreamer
(A worship leader reads aloud this children's book against a backdrop of images flashing across a screen. As each day of creation unfolds in the text, slides of contemporary pictures enhance and reinforce the message of the text. Show slides of the cosmos, terrain, ocean, and mountains along with a variety of pictures of humankind. As the story focuses attention on the children of God, display images of people of all races and cultures that slowly narrow to people with similar faces, then to the faces of people well known locally, and then to the faces of people within the church family.)

The Call to Worship   T. Fettke
    The Majesty and Glory of Your Name

The Prayer of Praise and Adoration
    Dreamer God, Giver of life and Creator of all time and space, we come before you in awe. Words cannot express the deep gratitude and thanksgiving our souls ache to convey. Your love and your grace are overwhelming. You have imagined and created for us a world that is beyond our thoughts. You designed

us to be far more than we have conceived or attempted to fulfill. You dream for us a life of goodness and joy. We have not believed in the possibilities of your creativity. Reveal your visions to us, O God. Come to us in refreshing ways and renew the courage and faith that we need to live as your children. Breathe into us once again the breath of life so that we can become fully alive.

(DWN)

The Call to Celebration
> Leader: Rejoice and be glad. The Dreamer has once again touched the earth. Search through the heavens and follow the star. Hasten to the place of revelation. Discover anew the glory of God's creative love.
>
> **People: We will believe and celebrate the miracle of this day. God comes to bring salvation to all people.**
>
> Leader: The Creator of light comes to bring a new world.
>
> **People: With alleluias and songs of praise, we will greet this new day.**

(DWN)

The Introit   J. S. Bach
Break Forth, O Beauteous Heavenly Light

The Processional Hymn   SUSSEX CAROL
On Christmas Night All Christians Sing

The Hebrew Lesson   Isaiah 60:1-4a

The Meditation   R. Thompson
Choose Something Like a Star

The Morning Prayer
> O God, we want to be able to "really see" beyond that which we actually can see. We pray that you will give us visions and fill us with dreams. But honestly, God, all too often we are way too weary even to lift our heads to look at what is around us much less to perceive with our souls that which is beyond us. Then, too, anxieties play havoc with our concentration; we

can't even sleep much less dream. We also have to contend with a cynicism, born of disappointments, that shrouds our spirits' sensitivity to visions like thick cataracts block the eyes' awareness of light.

O God, please give us rest—the kind of rest from which dreams emerge. Grant us the discipline of a single eye—the kind of focused attention that produces insights as well as sights. Fill us with hope—the kind of hope that enables us to cope with what is and nurtures visions of what can be.

Help us to see, God; help us to really see. We pray in the name of the visionary Christ. Amen.

(CWG)

The Response   Children's Choir
When You Wish upon a Star

The Gospel Lesson   Matthew 2:13-15, 19-23

The Hymn   SCARLET RIBBON
Who Would Think That What Was Needed

The Sermon
"Tell Me Your Dreams"
(As the sermon progresses, introduce the worshipers to a roll call of "dreamer saints." The preacher picks up an obviously aged photo album as he or she begins the introduction of each dreamer. As the first is opened, project a slide on to a screen that worshipers can see. Parallel the litany of names mentioned with the presentation of slides reproducing art works from the old masters. These visuals should aid the preacher's persuasion that God has dreamed through the lives of people and is continuing to do so.)

The Response   Leigh
The Impossible Dream

The Commission
One: Go out into the world and dare to dream the dreams of God.
Many: We go from this place inspired to live visions of holiness.

One: Follow God's leading into a new day. Stay the way even if it ventures from the well-worn paths of the known.
Many: In faith and courage we will journey toward the joy and mission of God's dream.
One: May God's eternal light fill your heart with joy as you realize the imaginable truths of God's dreams. Go and be dream catchers and vision makers in the world.

(DWN)

The Retiring Procession — DIFFERENT SONG
Sing a Different Song

The Benediction — M. Ryan-Wnger
In the Beginning

The Postlude — McCleery
Toccata in A-Minor
Handbells

NOTE

[1]Cynthia Rulant and Barry Moser, *The Dreamer* (New York: Blue Sky Press, 1993).

Garlanded images of creation's revelation

Epiphany

THE WORSHIP OF GOD
Epiphany Sunday

For congregations unfamiliar with the season of Epiphany, the following service introduces both the spirit and substance of this special time in the Christian year. The themes affirmed in and the mood inspired by the message of Epiphany appear in various components of the service. This experience moves worshipers to recognize the universal implications of the nativity of Jesus and their roles in sharing with the whole world the good news emanating from that nativity. Though this particular service focuses on the visit of the magi—the presentation of Christ to the Gentiles—Epiphany Sunday worship can also center on the baptism of Jesus or the first miracle of Jesus.

(Prior to the service, place in each printed order of worship a blank piece of paper the size of the order of worship. This service begins in virtual darkness; no artificial lighting can be seen—"the world waits in darkness.")

The Prelude												P. Manz
Three for Epiphany
(During the prelude, a procession of children enters the sanctuary carrying hanging candles shaped as stars with silver streamers. A dancer, perhaps an adult or an older youth, carries the largest star. Those in the procession take "the light"—the candles (stars)—to the chancel to bring light to the altar and form a backdrop against which the service proceeds.)

The Prologue											Ron Nelson
Where Is the Newborn King of Israel?
from *The Christmas Story*

The Call to Worship
    Leader: As we settle back into our ordinary lives, remind us of the extraordinary life you lived on this earth.
    People: **When we are tempted to follow only our daytimes, send us a star to order our lives, and lift our heads up that we may see it.**

Leader: Grant us the persistence to follow that star until it leads us to you.
People: May we find you right now in this service of worship.
Leader: Let us experience a sense of newness in our lives because of your presence here with us today.
People: And let us live our ordinary, everyday lives as extraordinary new creatures made over in the image of Jesus.

(JWC)

The Meditation   D. Mengel
O Splendor of God's Glory Bright

The Prayer of Praise and Adoration
God of the star and of those who followed its journey, lead us beyond our knowledge and suspicions. Give us grace to trust and strength to follow. Give us discernment to see and hear you with eyes and ears of faith. Be the goal, the guide, and the guardian of our journey. Open our lives to your compelling companionship. We pray in the name of your incarnation, Jesus the Messiah. Amen.

(PR)

The Introit   M. Practorius
This Day Is Born, Immanuel

The Processional Hymn   SINE NOMINE
All Praise to Thee, O Christ

The Old Testament Lesson   Isaiah 60:1-6
Leader: This is the Word of the Lord.
People: Thanks be to God.

(During the reading of the text, a worship leader enters the room carrying a large lighted candle representing the Christ child and moves to place this "Christ light" on the chancel where all can see it.)

The Response   D. Danner
Arise, Your Light Has Come

Epiphany

The Gospel Lesson   Matthew 2:1-12
    Leader: This is the Word of the Lord.
    People: Thanks be to God.

The Meditation   H. Willan
Three Kings
(During the singing of the meditation, three persons—three because of tradition—enter the sanctuary carrying three large vessels that they place in highly visible locations around the room. Each vessel has been wrapped with large trains of fabric and filled with a floral interpretation of the gifts of the magi. It is important to use fabrics in a variety of colors and textures. Each piece of fabric should represent a different part of the world to which the Christ is being made known. Use more than three vessels if you wish, but if you do, include humble vessels wrapped in rough, unrefined fabric along with pieces of a regal nature.)

The Morning Prayer
O God, it's so cold here; the weather, not the fellowship; the air, not our spirits. Of course, it's nowhere near as cold here as it is in other places. But that realization brings us no warmth. In such unusual weather we find it difficult to think about much else—it's cold, and it may get worse.

But now a moment for worship has arrived—a time to focus our thoughts on you, to look at our lives from the perspective of our relationship with you, to sense the lure of your love, to ponder the meaning of obedience to your will. Can we encounter you amid our thoughts about the weather? Yes, God, please help us. Must we shut out thoughts about what's around us to know you are among us? No, God, please help us.

We pray for people for whom the cold threatens health, even life. Giving thanks for individuals and institutions that provide warm shelter for homeless or ill-clad persons, we offer ourselves in such service. Offering gratitude for the warmth we enjoy in our clothes and places of residence, we ask for insight into the lives of people with whom we need to share.

We pray for people who are cold regardless of the temperature of the air; persons who are cold inside—insensitive to others, filled with icy resentment, frozen in cynicism, frigid due to anger, resistant to warmth because of a fear of vulnerability, rigid lest they be known. Wrap these people in the blanket of your love and warm them until their cynicism, resentment, and anger melt, leaving them open to the possibilities of faith and the formation of healthy relationships. If we can be bearers of those blankets, use us in this work, O God.

Fix our focus. Open our minds. Touch our emotions. We have come to worship you in a manner that brings you pleasure and transforms our lives. Help us God even as you help others. We pray as we meet, in the name of Christ. Amen.

(CWG)

The Hymn   DIX

As with Gladness Those of Old

The Litany
    Leader: Come traveler, wanderer, and all who search for truth. Your darkest night is ended. Love's mystery is revealed.
    People: **We have come from different places, each seeking the one whom heaven makes known.**
    Leader: With joy and gladness enter into this place. Your desire is made flesh. Come, gaze with deep wonder. Here, look into the face of God.
    People: **Our spirits have longed for this journey's end. Our souls are awakened—God's presence transcends.**

(DWN)

The Anthem   H. Friedell

The Song of Mary

The Sermon

    "The Challenge of Epiphany"

The Offering of Our Lives and Labors unto God

Epiphany

The Meditation　　　　　　　　　　　　　　　　　　　　　　Massenet
Meditation
(violin solo)
(During the meditation, invite congregants to create a representation of the greatest gift they can offer to the Christ child. Using the paper provided in each order of worship, worshipers should fold or tear the paper to create a symbol of their gift.)

The Invitation
On this Epiphany Sunday, let us join those of old who worshiped the Christ child with costly gifts by offering our own best gifts to him. Let us lay before the Christ candle our symbolic gifts even as we offer the entirety of our lives to this illuminating incarnation of love.
　　　　　　　　　　　　　　　　　　　　　　　　　　　　(CWG)

The Commission
Jesus said of himself, "I am the light of the world" (John 8:12). Jesus also said to us, "You are the light of the world . . . let your light so shine" (Matt 5:14, 16). So, as Isaiah said, "Arise, shine, for your light has come, and the glory of the Lord rises upon you" (Isa 60:1).

The Recessional Hymn　　　　　　　　　　　　　　　　FESTAL SONG
Arise, Your Light Is Come

The Benediction
As you go, be alert, as was Jesus, to hear the blessing of God; be attentive, as were the disciples, to listen to the Teacher's words and deeds; be alive, as the saints of all ages must be, in the Spirit that God sends to strengthen and to comfort.
　　　　　　　　　　　　　　　　　　　　　　　　　　　　(PR)

The Response　　　　　　　　　　　　　　　　　　　　H. Schroeder
Let Our Gladness Know No End

The Closing Voluntary　　　　　　　　　　　　　　　　　D. A. White
Brewer's Trumpet

THE WORSHIP OF GOD
First Sunday after Epiphany

The liturgical season of Epiphany centers on the presentation of Christ to the Gentiles—indeed, to the world. We know how that was done back there and then, but what about now? How do we present Christ to the world today—present Christ in a manner that enables the world to understand his identity and to desire his ministry? The following service takes form around the art and work of live theatre, borrowing words, images, and dramatic actions that serve as effective media for conveying the meaning, the message, and the ministry of Christ to our world.

(Prior to the service, create the environment of Broadway and Times Square in New York City. Place five large posters advertising Broadway plays across the chancel and outline each poster in running lights.)

The Prelude   V. Klaus
Vie schon leuchtet derMorgenstern
(As the instrumentalist begins the prelude, play an audio containing sounds of the city—loud conversation, horns blowing, a siren screaming, buses moving.)

The Call to Worship
(Near the conclusion of the prelude, the preacher for the day walks on to the chancel and begins to turn off the running lights. The sounds of the city cease. When the prelude ends, the preacher voices the call to worship.)

At its best, worship is high drama—not a performance, not entertainment, but high drama; a dramatic offering to God.

An encounter with God takes your breath away. The rituals that facilitate our worship of God—moving us across a vast spectrum of emotions, challenging our minds to stretch enough to embrace new ideas, engaging us in awesome mystery—are as dramatic as the truths to which they point.

Epiphany

Since those wonderful days in Christmas when we celebrated the coming of the Savior, we have been pondering how best to present Christ to the world.

We do not have to do Epiphany. We get to do Epiphany. It is not with a heavy sense of duty but with a light sense of joy that we explore new ways in which to share the good news of Christ with all people.

Today, the medium for our celebration of the gospel is drama. We give ourselves to a new epiphany, an epiphany that enlightens us and glorifies God.

(CWG)

The Processional Hymn   NETTLETON
Come, Thou Fount of Every Blessing

The Prayer of Praise and Adoration

Gracious God, who invites our searching, who finds us before we know even to look for you, take us on your pilgrimage. Though we have found, keep us seeking; though we have known, keep us learning; though we have experienced, keep us growing. Make your mercies new every morning. Through Jesus, who came to seek and to save. Amen.

(PR)

The Old Testament Lesson   Exodus 3:1-6; 6:2-8; 33:12-23
Leader: This is the Word of Truth.
People: Thanks be to God.

The Meditation   C. M. Schonberg
I Dreamed a Dream
from *Les Miserables*

The Morning Prayer

O God, we live somewhere between Fantine's haunting, plaintive musings in the opening of *Les Miserables* and the exciting certainty of an oracle recorded in Hebrew prophecy. We know both lofty visions and developments that are not the dream we dreamed. Most often we feel your presence at the time of vision and sense your absence when the substance of the vision fails to materialize. We need you in both moments as well as in all of the moments in the middle.

Even as we thank you for sights and insights that have stretched our minds, excited our spirits, and motivated us to action, we request of you help when we cannot lift our heads to look at what is immediately in front of us much less entertain visions in our minds that touch the depths of our souls. Whether filled with insight or searching for sight, keep us doing what you call us to do—to take care of people who hurt, to obstruct the paths of people who inflict hurt, and to challenge people who don't seem to care whether or not anyone else hurts, inflicts hurt, or offers healing.

O God, regardless of where we are in the realization of our dreams, make us the fulfillment of your dream. Amen.

(CWG)

The Hymn SWEENEY
More about Jesus

The Gospel Lesson John 3:16
Leader: The gospel of our Lord Jesus Christ.
People: Praise be to thee, O Christ.

The Meditation C. M. Schonberg
Bring Him Home
from *Les Miserables*

The Service of Holy Communion

The Call to Confession

To the discouraged, light brings hope. To the restless, light brings peace. To those in despair, light brings joy. And to those in darkness, light brings the love of a new dawn.

Light provides courage and confidence in places that sometimes frighten or alarm. Light's radiant glow often reveals truths and treasures beyond imagination. Yet we cling to the source of hope and shield light's rays from others. We choose to enjoy love's warmth and condemn those who sit in shadowy places. We have not offered the story of grace as God intended. Let us confess our own places of darkness and seek new ways to perpetuate the light.

(DWN)

The Prayer of Confession

Star Light, Star Bright, Source of Eternal Light: Clinging to the source of Light, we continue to stumble and fall. We have not held the light close enough; therefore, we search for direction. With our small minds, we assume that you will reveal your truth through ways we would expect. We force labels on those around us, and we assume that our love is extended to those we choose.

Forgive us, O God. Open our eyes to see your truths. Reveal to us the power of your light shining far beyond our provincial minds. Remind us that light was created before darkness. Remind us that light was intended to shatter darkness. Remind us that it is your radiant presence that creates the source of light. Help us to remember that your presence enters all places where you are received. Broaden our vision to sights far beyond the prescribed places and the appointed messengers we select. Challenge us to go where others would not venture. Take us to the shadows where others fear, and reveal to us light's presence–casting away darkness.

Great God. Give us eyes to see. Amen.

(DWN)

The Assurance of Forgiveness

In him was life, and that life became the light for all. For those who are willing to open their eyes and look into the light, he gives them the right to be a child of God. Rejoice and be glad for we have seen his glory full of grace and truth.

(DWN)

The Distribution of the Elements

The Anthem   S. Schwartz

Day by Day
from *Godspell*

The Sermon
"A Most Unlikely Epiphany"
(After the introduction to the sermon, the preacher speaks of people's boredom as sung about in the chorus "At the End of the Day." The choir responds with singing.)

At the End of the Day
(The conclusion of the sermon speaks of people singing a song of courage and faith in a manner that invites the singing of the Broadway chorus "Do You Hear the People Sing?" which the choir begins to sing.)

The Response M. Schoenberg
Do You Hear the People Sing?
from *Les Miserables*

The Invitation

The Recessional Hymn MENDON
Soldiers of Christ, in Truth Arrayed
(During the recessional hymn the choir moves to the front of the chancel, but does not recess out of the worship center.)

The Commission
Go from here with God's grace to nurture you, with God's love to fill you with the strength to serve as Jesus Christ did. Go with the words and spirit of Jesus echoing in your living, and take from this place the blessing that is the ever presence of God working for good in this world through you.
(JB)

The Response M. Schoenberg
Do You Hear the People Sing?
from *Les Miserables*

The Postlude C. M. Widor
Symphony No. 5 Toccatta
(Near the conclusion of the postlude the choir recesses through an exit to the worship center, thus signaling the conclusion of worship.)

THE WORSHIP OF GOD
Third Sunday after Epiphany

Epiphany—the presentation of Christ—is for all people. When responsive to the impulse of the Epiphany season, we often find ourselves in interaction with individuals or groups of people who make us uncomfortable. Epiphany throws light on the radical grace at the center of the gospel of Christ. By means of drama and other media, the following service confronts worshipers with the challenge even as with the promise of God's wild and marvelous grace.

The Prelude   J. S. Bach
Fantasy and Fugue in C

The Prologue   H. Hopson
The Gift of Love

The Call to Worship
    Leader: We want to raise our hearts in love, but we must confess, our God, that love is difficult—
    People: **that it's easier to keep others, and to keep you, at somewhat of a distance—a distance we determine and maintain—that we're in control of.**
    Leader: It's easier not to work at the interconnectedness—the interdependence.
    People: **But this is the irrational season, and we confess, too, that it is love that fills our days with brightness—our lives with joy and peace.**
    Leader: We confess that the easiest life is not the richest life,
    People: **and we commit ourselves to you, integrated more fully into our day-to-dayness, exploring love in all the dimensions of our living.**
                                                                                (JB)

The Introit   Paul Manz
E'en So, Lord Jesus, Quickly Come

The Processional Hymn   NICEA
Holy, Holy, Holy

The Old Testament Lesson   Deuteronomy 5:4-12
    Leader: The Word of God.
    People: **Thanks be to God.**

The Meditation   JESUS I COME
    Out of My Bondage, Sorrow, and Night

The Morning Prayer
    Pardon us, God. We snicker and almost laugh aloud watching and listening to other people's reactions to grace once they understand—really understand—the nature of grace.

    Some gasp. Others squirm. Occasionally people flash a smile. Eyebrows rise. Jaws drop. A few folks appear disgusted. Frequently, someone declares wistfully, "That sounds too good to be true."

    Of course, God, when we reflect on the situations in which the nature of grace becomes most dramatically apparent, our smiles fade quickly, and somber looks spread across our faces; laughter may even turn into sobs. We see a family torn apart by selfishness, a popular woman embarrassed by debilitating gossip, a teenager retreating into the hurt of failure, a man dismissed from his profession because of legal charges against him, a friend bowed under the shame of betrayal, a woman sitting in the shock that comes from seeing the results of the murderous rumor she has spread, and a banker flinching when hit with the label "cheater."

    O God, we praise you for the grace that brings understanding, love, forgiveness, restoration, and new beginnings —the grace that turns sinners into saints and causes saints to take care of sinners.

    Teach us about grace. Touch us with grace. Fill us full of grace. Make us dispensers of grace.

    We pray in the name of the one referred to by his beloved friend as "grace upon grace." Amen.

                                                                                   (CWG)

The Gospel Lesson   John 8:3-11
(As the reader reaches the end of the gospel text, a woman steps forward to exclaim the following words:)

"That's my story; let me tell you about it. Let me tell you what I learned about Jesus. I learned I am a whore saved by God's grace."

(Carrying a red shoulder bag, this woman is wearing heavy facial makeup, a red dress, and red shoes. Though obviously not the person she once was, evidences of her past still threaten to define her. She speaks with aggression and without refinement. The woman's monologue is taken from a work called *Rubies* written by Ragan Courtney. Following is a portion of her story.)

"But let me tell you what I have learned about Jesus. I learned I'm a whore saved by God's grace. Just as I was, I came to him . . . right out of the bed of sin to the feet of Jesus. All of us, the Bible says, have gone whoring after other gods. So really—now I don't mean to insult you—but what does that make us? All our sins are scarlet, all of us must pay the price of that sin; and that price is not a financial failure, or illness, or a sick child, or what have you. The price of sin is death! . . . It's just that everybody looks at my sin, and they feel better because they are not as wicked. After I met Jesus, I had an old customer try to do a little business with me. I told him in no uncertain words, NO. He offered me more money. 'No,' I said. 'Come on, Pearl, everybody has a price.' 'You are right,' I said, 'but you can't afford it. I've been purchased by the Lord.'"

The Anthem   S. Adler
                        How Sweet the Sound

The Sermon
              "Scandalous (or Hilarious?) Grace"

The Offering of Our Lives and Labors unto God

The Meditation   Menken/Schwartz
                      God Help the Outcast
                  from *The Hunchback of Notre Dame*

The Service of Communion

The Call to Confession

> The ruined priest stood there as brazen as a golden calf and broke the bread. I choked to think he would offer it, wondered at his shamelessness, but, after all, who was I to deny the gracious gift?
>
> I bowed my head. My chin rested comfortably on my chest, a position of defeat to which it had grown accustomed. Like pulling a sunken vessel to the surface, I strained, red-faced, sweating, veins distended, only to gaze in candlelight on the face of Judas, the betrayer, whose terrible countenance was formed and painted by hypocrisy: humility and hauteur.
>
> Had the mask been torn from his face, I could have borne his related humanity by recognizing the marks of pain etched in his flesh that I see daily in my own mirror, and understood that we are both betrayers, brothers, prodigals, twins.
>
> Dear God, how can I live if I cannot forgive Judas and me, even if he never removes his pitiful mask?
>
> (RC)

The Prayer of Confession

> O God of the poor and the oppressed, God of the rich and exalted: In our worship, we long to see your face. Let us see your vision of peace and wholeness and well-being for all of your children. Help us see it clearly. In our confession we acknowledge our sinfulness. Forgive us for shrinking from visions of ministry to those who have more than we do. Forgive us for denying basic necessities to those around us in need. Forgive our participation in all forms of oppression.
>
> (KMF)

The Assurance of Forgiveness

> We know that God accepts our confessions and forgives us. We know that God calls us to rise from our knees to get to work.
>
> (KMF)

The Communion Prayer and the Lord's Prayer
> You are light, God, and we are created in your image. But so often the circumstances of our lives and our world block the light, and we find ourselves in the shadow. You are light, God, in the midst of all our circumstances. Gather us around your table. Feed us. Remind us who we are—whose we are.
>
> As we partake of the bread and the cup, fill us with the light against which the darkness cannot prevail so that we might go from here to illuminate the circumstances of our lives and our world in the name of Jesus Christ our Lord, who taught us to pray . . .
>
> (JB)

The Distribution of the Elements

The Meditation   Jean Berger
> *A Rose Touched by the Sun's Warm Rays*

The Invitation

The Challenge
> Leader: Creator of silence: In mourning places we see sisters in prison; brothers without the warmth of home; parentless children immersed in violence; fathers and mothers devastated by poverty; young people wandering aimlessly in the streets; old people enduring the physical and emotional torment of loneliness and abandonment—mourners who wait for our coming.
>
> **People: Together we share a despair that sparks no words. And so we are silent.**
>
> Leader: Creator of living dreams: You have given life's breath to your sons and daughters, and you have placed within us dreams of peace and visions of justice. You have anointed us and empowered us, dreamers and visionaries all, to put our hands to holy task . . . giving sight to blinded eyes, release to those who are enslaved, light to those who dwell in dark places.

People: **The energy of our dreams—dreams that we thought had died—awakens hope within us.**

Leader: Creator of living hope: You have given us passion of spirit, and you have placed within us creativity and strength. Our hearts are in our communities; our feet are in the doors of our congressional representatives; our hands are working works of compassion; our voices are speaking words that heal and bless and sometimes convict.

People: **The energy of hope—hope that we thought had died—awakens faith within us.**

Leader: Creator of living faith: Even in the midst of human suffering, you have graced us with the ability to believe in ourselves, to trust ourselves, to have faith in what we cannot see. And so we enter those places we never thought we would enter, and we find those people we never thought we would find. Those who are poor and lost and hungry and sorrowful wait for us.

People: **The energy of faith—faith that we thought had died—awakens life within us.**

(KMF)

The Recessional Hymn   HYFRYDOL
   Christ Has Called Us to New Visions

The Benediction
   God go with you, as daughters and sons of the light, as pilgrims following its illumination, and as light-bearers to the world. Go in peace, having glimpsed the salvation of the world, ready to make it plain before all the faces of earth.

(PR)

The Closing Voluntary   Maurice Greene
                    Caprice

THE WORSHIP OF GOD
Transfiguration Sunday

The mood of the Christian year begins to change after this service. Meditating on Jesus' experience called "the Transfiguration," worshipers become aware of the underside of glory—the real possibility of condemnation and encouragement, the likelihood of a growing number of enemies and friends, and the specter of death and success. Just as Jesus moved from this awesome moment of affirmation in his life with a determination to travel to Jerusalem and engage people's hostile criticism, worshipers now move from the happy season of Epiphany into the somber season of Lent. The following service openly reflects the mystery and majesty of this "mountaintop" event in the life of Jesus and subtly points to the serious challenges that lay immediately ahead.

The Prelude   C. Callahan
Resignation

The Prologue   D. Schwoebel
Speak Lord in the Stillness

The Call to Worship
 Leader: Come again to the mountaintop and witness the splendor of the Almighty. Leave behind the confusion of this world and gaze into visions of holiness.
 People: **We long to be transformed into God's presence. We dream of ways to "be still and know."**
 Leader: Fears and doubts too long have bound the possibilities of the Eternal. The glimmer of God's imagination has yet to be fulfilled.
 People: **May the experiences we share this day reveal to us truths beyond what eyes have seen or ears have heard.**
 Leader: Contemplate the mystery of whose you are and search deeply for possibilities of penetrating the dream of God.

All: **Through the power of the Omnipotent One we open our lives to transforming love. Let us offer praise and worship to the God of salvation.**

(DWN)

The Processional Hymn ST DENIO
Immortal, Invisible, God Only Wise

The Prayer of Praise and Adoration

God of Mystery, God of Disclosure, you have revealed your love to your children through the ages. At times we hear your voice and choose your way. At other times we cannot see your image for the glorious splendor; we fear we are alone, and our faith wavers. Take us once again to the mountaintop. Appear to us, Great God, and remind us that we are your children. Speak to us in a clear voice that we might fully understand your purpose in each of our lives. Give new visions of grace so that, when we come down from this holy place, your shining face will be reflected to all of the world. We have come searching, O God; reveal your mystery to us this day. Amen.

(DWN)

The Hebrew Lesson Exodus 34:29

The Meditation Scott and Allen Koepke[1]
I Listened

I listened to the breeze today that cooled and cleaned the air. It whispered, "I'll be here with Mother Earth and Fire; we care. The peace we long for will be found; with faith, we can sustain. The seekers can stop searching then; with love, peace will remain. To plant and reap and share and know that there is never enough goodwill to give, never time to give up." If we don't hear the wind, then how will we see? If we're blind in our hate, can we hear what will be? We can't honor the earth when we don't look around. I listened to the breeze today, the wind of hope and change. I heard the laughing children while the cries of freedom rang.

Epiphany

The Contemporary Lesson
(From the movie *The Lion King*, show a clip or read an excerpt from the moment of "transfiguration" in the life of Simba, the central character. Rafiki, the wise one, takes the young lion for a holy visit alongside a pond on his "mountaintop." There, the "child" discovers his destiny. Whether using a video or reading an excerpt, secure permission from Disney Productions.)

The Reflection   S. Naylor Callaway
Beloved in Christ

The Gospel Lesson   Matthew 17:1-8

The Sermon
"A Mythical Conversation on a Mystical Mountain"

The Meditation   J. Rutter
Be Thou My Vision

The Commission
   Leader: Go from the mountaintop and live according to God's calling.
   People: We have seen the Eternal One. We have experienced a glimpse of holiness.
   Leader: Go from this place knowing that, as you journey, you are surrounded and guided by the mystery of God's grace.
   People: We will go forth challenged by the truth and visions of this day.
   Leader: God grant courage and confidence as you face the transforming experience of another week. May God's glory shine through you and upon your heart as you go.
   (DWN)

The Benediction   A. Pote
The Prayer of Peace

The Postlude   D. White
Brewer's Trumpet

NOTE

[1]Scott and Allen Koepke, *I Listened* (Chapel Hill NC: Hinshaw Music, Inc., 2000).

Epiphany—Fulfillment Revealed

Lent

THE WORSHIP OF GOD
Ash Wednesday

Lent begins with Ash Wednesday, a solemn penitential day of worship, dating back to the eighth century. Though many congregations in the Free Church tradition never have observed Ash Wednesday, those who have bear witness to its powerful help in preparing them for more meaningful observances of Holy Week and celebrations of Easter. The following service, which can be scheduled for any time of the day on Ash Wednesday, introduces worshipers to the penitential season, draws them into an honest confession of personal identity, and challenges them to live as disciples of Christ.

(Prior to worship, prepare the worship center for Lent. Expose only materials with natural surfaces. [For example, clay or wooden candlesticks or crosses are more appropriate than those made of shiny metal.] Create a sense of intimacy by assuring that the room is dark and quiet as congregants gather. Many religious bookstores supply the need for ashes. However, you can create your own ashes, as most worship leaders prefer to do, by saving the palm branches from the previous year's Palm Sunday service. [Should you want to create your own ashes and you do not have palm branches from the previous year, you can purchase Commodore Palms from most any floral supply dealer.] Dry the palm branches, and then burn them in a container. The collection of ashes will contain residue of palm stems that should be sifted away. Place the ashes in a dry, sealed container for later use. Place the ashes for this service in a simple container that sets on a black/grey, wooden or concrete pedestal near the front of the chancel.)

The Prelude   H. W. Davies
Solemn Melody

The Call to Worship
    Leader: We gather as children of faith, formed from the dust of the earth, yet created in the image of the Almighty.
    People: **Remind us, Eternal God, of the frailty of this life. Restore us to the confidence of true living.**

Leader: In seasons of time we will strive to be known by our Creator's design. We will gain skills for shaping clearer images of the Divine.

People: **May each of us choose this day to be known as your child.**

Leader: Time will soon pass away. Life's pleasures will all fade. Memories of temporary things will soon fall into dust.

People: **Though we are transient in this life, words of faith give us comfort and strength. Our spirits rest in the truth of the eternal grace of the Alpha and the Omega.**

(DWN)

The Tolling
(To simplify this service, you may choose the tolling of a bell over the sound of an organ prelude as people silently gather for worship.)

The Prologue   Mueller
Create in Me a Clean Heart

The Processional Hymn   BEACH SPRING
Come, Ye Sinners, Poor and Needy

The Invocation

The course of living tends to dim our light, tends to make bland the wonderfully individual flavors of our lives. It's the tendency toward conformity, the process of living that takes so much out of us—it is such an investment. Restore to us the joy of being who we are: your creation in relation to you, your people gathered to be you for each other and our community. In the course of our living may our light shine brighter. May our individuality be celebrated and renewed. Make us salty. God make us bright in Jesus' name. Amen.

(JB)

The Psalm   Psalm 51:1-12

Lent

The Elements of Worship
(Educate congregants on the importance of this service and its various components by explaining its historical background and the symbolic significance. In your remarks of instruction you may want to use some of the material found above.)

The Call to Confession
Leader: Let this cup pass me by is an easy prayer—based on what we want—based on what we think we need.

People: Nevertheless, we are aware of how much you offer that lies beyond us—how limited our perspective actually is. . . . Nevertheless, in our doing and our being, O God, we believe in you. We believe that you will keep us, and we believe that ultimately you will render us whole.

Leader: Thy will be done is often the least of our prayers, for we know that to pray this is to relinquish some measure of control.

People: Nevertheless, with you, O God, all is turned around: to die is to live, to lose is to gain, to relinquish is to recover. May it be so.

(JB)

The Prayer of Confession
Forgiving, Calling God: We have entered this sacred place singing your praise and seeking your face. We have come just as we are, believing that you accept us and love us without condition. We trust you, and so we can be bold in our truth with you.

We come first asking for your presence in the lives of those we love whose physical, emotional, and spiritual needs are great. We ask your strength, your courage, and your healing for these. Hear those petitions we whisper in our hearts, we pray.

We confess, O God, that we have often fallen short of the mark you have set for us. We ask your forgiveness and seek renewed resolve to walk in the ways you have designed. Give us courage, we pray, to face the choices we must make this week.

Our pride and self-centered lives often cause us to overlook those whose needs we could meet, or at least assist. Forgive us for not helping. . . .

Our own desires often cause us to devalue other people and fail to develop healthy, kind relationships. Forgive us, and show us how to heal our relationship with. . . .

We are a stubborn and headstrong people, O God. We choose often to go our own way and not take the actions we could to shape our community to become more like your design. Forgive us, and cause us to respond to. . . .

Create in us a clean heart, O God, and renew our spirits that we may willingly, joyously, and courageously bear the sign of your love and your cross, and shed this gospel light in ways that will more nearly bring this world to become your Kingdom.

Through Jesus Christ, Our Lord . . . Amen.

(SE)

The Response   ST. MARGARET
O Love That Wilt Not Let Me Go

The Assurance of Forgiveness
"God shows love for us in that while we were yet sinners Christ died for us" (Rom 5:3). "The wages of sin is death, but the free gift of God is eternal life in Christ Jesus our Lord" (Rom 6:29).

The Imposition of Ashes
    Leader: The symbolic use of ashes upon the forehead is an Old Testament tradition conveying a sign of penitence, grief, and mourning. It is a reminder to us,: "Remember O people, thou art dust, and unto dust thou shalt return." As New Testament Christians, let the ashes be for us a visual reminder that "As in Adam all die, so in Christ shall all be made alive." So let us mark with the sign of Christ, a cross, on each other's forehead and convey to the world our sincere desire to take up our cross and follow the Son of God.

(CWG)

(Worshipers can come forward to receive the sign of the cross made on their foreheads by a minister. Or, the ashes can be divided and distributed so that worshipers can impose the sign of the cross on each other. For some people, the imposition of ashes is too much of a departure from their tradition. In order not to miss the meaning of this important day for that reason, these people may choose to receive a black ribbon to wear on their clothing rather than an imposition of ashes to be worn on their foreheads.)

The Sermon

"A Touch of Ashes"

(This service can be done without a sermon. If a sermon is included, however, this an appropriate place in the service for it.)

The Commission

Leader: Go now as marked people—people claimed by Christ, people committed to the God who brings healing from suffering and life from death.

(CWG)

The Recessional Hymn ELLESDIE

Jesus, I My Cross Have Taken

(Worship leaders recess during the singing of the hymn. At the conclusion of the hymn, worshipers depart in silence.)

THE WORSHIP OF GOD
First Sunday in Lent

The somber season of Lent is like no other season in the Christian year. The music, liturgy, visual environment, and mood of Lenten worship reflect serious worshipers' penitential preparation for retracing Jesus' journey to the cross. The following service communicates both in substance and spirit that this is no time for "alleluias."

The Prelude David Ashley White
Kum-Ba-Yah

The Prayer of Praise
No matter what we are doing here this morning, O God, open us all to a revival of your Spirit that finds expression in praise. Amen.
(CWG)

The Hymn of Praise NETTLETON
Come, Thou Fount of Every Blessing

The Old Testament Lesson Psalm 51:1-12

The Meditation J. Brahms
Create in Me a Clean Heart

The Prayer of Confession
Merciful Lord, you have called us to look at our crosses, to look into our hearts, to know ourselves. But often we are afraid of what we will find inside. We fear what we will discover about our sinfulness. Forgive us. Help us find our own "sense of sin," and when we do, help us not to despair, not to give up on ourselves. Help us pass through these days of silenced Alleluias* and make it to the joy of new life. Give us strength, courage, and comfort on this journey. Amen.
(KMF)

*Note: The basis for this reference is the custom of many churches to sing or speak no Alleluias during the Sundays of Lent. In contrast, Easter brings exclamations of joy and, once again, the church shouts and sings: "Alleluia! He is risen! He is risen indeed!"

Lent

The Words of Assurance
> If we claim to be without sin, we deceive ourselves, and the truth is not in us. If we confess our sins, he is faithful and just to forgive us our sins and purify us from all unrighteousness.

The New Testament Lesson   1 John 1:8-9

The Hymn   ST. MARGARET
O Love That Wilt Not Let Me Go

The Lesson

The Words of Grace   Psalm 103:1-18
"What Happened to the Alleluias?"

The Meditation   Walter Pelz
Show Me Thy Ways, O Lord

The Words of Commitment
> Leader: God, we come to You as trees withered by heat—weakened by drought;
> **People: for power comes forth from God—power to heal, refresh, to set people free!**
> Leader: God, we come to You as trees healthy and strong—from our fears and sins released;
> **People: for power comes forth from God—power to heal, refresh, to set people free!**
> Leader: We come to You, our God, to be cured of the expected—
> **People: to be released into freedom—the response ability—of change and growth, freely chosen.**
> Leader: Take our situation, bless our choices,
> **People: fill full every heart with joy, that we might laugh, be filled, and bear the good fruits of Your Kingdom.**
>
>   (JB)

The Hymn of Response   LEOMINSTER
Not What My Hands Have Done

The Postlude   Marcel Dupré
Kyrie, God the Everlasting Father

THE WORSHIP OF GOD
A Sunday in Lent

Even a mention of the word "Lent" conjures up thoughts of sacrifice. For many people, observing Lent is synonymous with giving up something. The following service examines that popular assumption and offers a biblical perspective on the subject of sacrifice. The results are emphases in and acts of worship that are far more positive than negative.

(Prior to the service, fill the altar with various sizes, shapes, and textures of temple jars—urns or vessels traditionally used as or associated with incense holders. The containers, randomly placed at different heights, should create the impression that they once held offerings deposited in the temple and that they could hold offerings made to God in this sanctuary. Place incense in several of these containers. Cover the communion table with black fabric.)

The Meditation of Preparation
"The world breaks everyone, and afterward, many are strong at the broken places."
(Ernest Hemingway)

The Prelude   R. Vaughn-Williams
Rhodymedre
(During the prelude, add more containers to the collection already in place and light the incense that has been placed in selected containers.)

The Prologue   D. Hurd
How Lovely Is Thy Dwelling

The Call to Worship
    Leader: The Eternal God calls us to this house of worship. Enter to offer praise and serve the Holy One. God's invitation is not to make a sacrifice but to become a sacrifice, regardless of cost.
    People: We have offered all that is required. We have obediently fulfilled our vows.

Lent

> Leader: Then your life should be filled with peace, abounding in eternity's joy.
>
> **People: Our lives are not complete. We have given halfheartedly and withheld our best. We have undergone few risks for our faith. Joy is nominal in our pilgrimage.**
>
> Leader: Come, not in fear or with anxious thoughts but with open intentions of beginning again. All that is required this day is to walk humbly and offer yourself in service to God.
>
> **All: Let us enter before the Holy One with worthy offerings and shouts of praise.**

(DWN)

The Introit   A. Pote

In This House of Worship

The Unison Prayer of Praise and Adoration

> Eternal God, we give thanks for the beauty of this place and for all the good things of life that you provide. Every need is supplied by your abundant love. In return, you deserve our best as we worship and serve you with our lives. In these moments of renewal, expose to us ways in which we can more effectively become your children. Show us meaningful ways to offer sacrifices for your kingdom's work. Humble our lives so that our offerings of praise and adoration might be exalted in your sight. You are the covenant-keeper. You are our God. To you alone we offer our worship and our lives. Amen.

(DWN)

The Hymn of Praise   KREMSER

We Praise You, O God

The Hebrew Lesson   Exodus 3:13-20

The Meditation   A. Lovelace

What Shall I Render to My God?

The Sermon

                      "What's This about Sacrifice?"

The Hymn of Response   HOLY MANNA
        Take My Gifts

The Call to Confession
    We have not lived faithfully in relation to the covenant made with God and promises vowed to God. We have denied ourselves in meager ways. Come to the One who takes no delight in burnt sacrifices but openly receives the prayers and confessions of a penitent heart. Let us say our prayers and confess our halfhearted commitment to our faith.
                                                (DWN)

The Silent Prayers of Confession

The Meditation   R. Thompson
        The Best of Rooms

The Words of Assurance
    God's sacrifice of love offers forgiveness and cleansing to all who repent. God does not repay us according to the gifts we offer but according to the grace and mercy of steadfast love. Rejoice and be glad. Receive today the gift of God.
                                                (DWN)

The Gospel Lesson   Matthew 13:44-52

The Commission
    Go forth from this place instructed about the kingdom of heaven. Live faithfully to the covenant you have vowed. Remember that God's generous love surrounds you as you face the journey of this week. May the sacrifices you are called to offer in the week ahead bring everlasting joy and eternal peace.
                                                (DWN)

The Recessional Hymn   AUSTRIAN HYMN
        God, Whose Giving Knows No Ending

The Benediction   D. Douglas
        Simple Gifts

The Postlude   J. Lemmens
        Fanfare

THE WORSHIP OF GOD
Preparation for Holy Week

Lent draws to a close. Holy Week is near. Preparations for retracing Christ's journey to the cross and beyond intensify. At this critical juncture of special times of worship, the following service facilitates a focus on Holy Week intended to enhance the meaning of worshipers' engagement with the life-altering truths that fill the days immediately ahead. This worship experience can be scheduled for the Sunday prior to Holy Week or, as we did the service originally, on the Wednesday evening immediately prior to Palm Sunday.

(Worshipers move to the sanctuary through a narthex filled with various vessels—bowls, pots, and vases of all shapes, sizes, textures, and hues of color. A careful study of these vessels helps prepare worshipers for the challenge of this service.)

The Call to Worship
- Leader: We gather in this sanctuary,
- **People: gratefully making our way through another draining week—stepping out, however briefly, of this wearying world with all of its cares.**
- Leader: We gather in this sanctuary,
- **People: a sense of peace—of rest—of acceptance and love, and we pray for enough to help us through the rest of this week and that special holy week— if we are careful.**
- Leader: God of restoration and transformation, keep us in your path,
- **People: and give us eyes to see your presence with us through our days, making holy every place, creating sanctuary at every time.**
- Leader: Give us ears to hear your voice saying,
- **People: not, be careful, but take good care.**

(JB)

The Processional Hymn   BEACH SPRING
  Come, All Christians, Be Committed

The Evening Prayer

O God, we come before you first in confession, because we need forgiveness. We confess our sins silently, because to speak them out loud is to take too big a risk. Silence is best because we know that if others really knew the truth about us, they might not understand. They might think less of us. We might let them down. So hear our sins, Lord, spoken silently—only to you. And grace us with the forgiveness we need.

And Lord, we need direction. The path is not very clear. As your church in this time and place, we are struggling to know our future. We need your guidance and vision. We need faith to press on. We need strength for the task and the courage to be labeled different. We need you to show us the way, Lord. Perhaps we are a congregation of dreamers. It's okay to dream, but now time has come to begin to see our dreams become reality. We need just a glimpse, Lord, just enough of a vision to go on—or we will give up. Lord, we need your guidance, your hand upon us. Give us the wisdom to envision how to build this church.

And we need healing, Lord—healing of our physical bodies that don't feel quite like they used to, bodies that don't work exactly like they used to work, bodies that are weak, bodies in pain. We need physical healing, Lord.

We need healing of our emotions—those inexplicable places of hurt deep inside, places we usually can't get to ourselves, places that don't get better with aspirin or Tylenol, places that don't even get better when we try to dull the pain with drugs or alcohol, places of our disappointment and rejection and self-recrimination. Heal our emotions, Lord. We can't get to them. We need the touch of your healing hand.

And we need spiritual healing, God. Sometimes we don't feel close to you. We wonder if you're still near. Our spiritual resources are depleted. Our faith is small. Our hope is wavering. We need a healing of our spirits, a cleaning of that deep-down place where you live. We need spiritual renewal and refreshing and re-creation.

And we need, O God, a healing of our memories, remembrances of losses that still cause us anguish. We are powerless to ease our own pain when memories of loss overwhelm us. We've all lost so much.

Most of all, O Lord, we need you—every day, every hour. And we can never seem to find the words to tell you. As best we can, we tell you now. We need you, Lord. Amen.

(KMF)

The Distribution of Clay
(During the meditation, a clump of soft, malleable clay is passed to each member of the congregation. Worshipers unwrap the clay and hold the clay in their hands until a moment in worship when the clay can be used to express personal sentiments and to shape an offering to God.)

The Contemporary Lesson
Worship this day is a dream of dancing a dance akin to flight. In the dream a master choreographer chooses you to demonstrate his new steps. Despite the pedestrian heaviness of the body that sleeps in the bed, in the dream you are as light, as flowing, as airy as the white chiffon fabric that trails behind you in the long, spare room, a room of mirrors alive with the amazing reflection of your perfect following. Every pore absorbs the movements of your partner's mind, every muscle is taut with his tuning, every nerve vibrant with his will. He bends you deep, shaping with his deft touch the arch of your back, the angles of your limbs, the curve of your neck, the point of your feet on the wooden floor worn from other feet. He looks you always full in the face. He loves you because you are supple as clay mixed with his spit, malleable as hot metal.

(RC)

The Hymn   I WANT TO BE A CHRISTIAN
Lord, I Want to Be a Christian

The Homily
"The Potter's House"

The Hymn of Response　　　　　　　　　　　　　　　　ADELAIDE
Have Thine Own Way, Lord!
(verse 1)

The Meditation of Transformation
(During this extended period of silence, as worshipers reflect on the assurances of God's forgiveness, the challenge of following Jesus, and the meaning of the week ahead, each worshiper shapes the held piece of clay into a form having personal significance for that worshiper.)

The Psalm of Assurance　　　　　　　　　　　　　　　　Psalm 91

The Hymn of Rejoicing　　　　　　　　　　　　　　　　KINGSFOLD
When Sorrow Floods the Troubled Heart

When sorrow floods the troubled heart and clouds the mind with fears,
Affliction presses from the soul the bitter flow of tears.
God's weeping children raise the prayer:
"Almighty God, how long till tears shall cease
and silence break and grief be turned to song?"

The voice is stilled, no words express the pain that lingers on;
Our prayer becomes a silent sign; all mortal speech is gone.
Then Holy Spirit groans in us with intercession strong;
When tears have ceased and silence breaks the Spirit stirs a song.

The sting of death cannot forbid the child of God to sing.
The scars we bear may long remain, but resurrection brings the healing of the broken heart,
The righting of the wrong. Our tears shall cease, our silence break in Christ, the living Song.

(Rebecca Turner Lawson/Paul Duke)

Holy Week

THE WORSHIP OF GOD
Palm Sunday

The moods of a Palm Sunday worship experience swing wildly from the elation of a jubilant procession and a warm welcome to the depression induced by harsh sounds of rejection and screams supportive of a mean crucifixion. A clown is a metaphorical figure both strong enough and flexible enough to bear the full weight of profound gladness and heavy sadness. The following service involves the unexpected appearance of a clown who dramatizes a discovery of the meaning of Christianity. The clown encounters compassion in front of a communion table set with symbols of God's great love.

(In preparation for this service, place on each side of the communion table large floor urns containing massive bouquets of purple balloons filled with helium.)

The Handbell Prelude   H. Hopson
Antiphonal Fanfare
from *Litany for Bells*

The Opening Voluntary   J. S. Bach
All Glory Laud and Honor

The Prologue   J. S. Bach, arr. Hopson
Lift Up Your Heads

The Call to Worship
> Leader: Behold, my servant.
> **People: The Spirit of the Lord God is upon me, because God has anointed me to bring good tidings to the afflicted.**
> Leader: Behold, my chosen one.
> **People: God has sent me to bind up the brokenhearted, to proclaim liberty to the captives and the opening of the prison to those who are bound.**
> Leader: This is the one in whom my soul delights.
> **People: God has anointed me to proclaim the year of God's favor, and also the day of God's vengeance.**

Leader: I have put my spirit upon my servant.
People: God has sent me to comfort all who mourn, to give them a garland instead of ashes, the oil of gladness instead of sorrow.
Leader: My servant will bring forth justice to the nations.
People: They shall have the mantle of praise instead of a faint spirit; they shall build up the ancient ruins; they shall repair the ruined cities, the devastation of many generations.
Leader: Behold, my servant.
People: Let earth receive her king.

(LKC)

The Introit   D. Music

Hosanna in the Highest

The Silent Prayer of Praise and Adoration

The Morning Prayer

At times, God, this wilderness journey we call life becomes long and hard. There are stones in the road and mountains to climb and paths that seem to go on forever, leading nowhere. And then there is the baggage we carry with us . . . heavy, cumbersome, oppressive, more burdens than we can possibly haul around. How will we make this journey? Where will we find the strength to walk such rough roads and climb such steep pathways?

God of our journey, where will we find streams of life-giving water in the desert? When will we make peace with the past and open our spirits to healing grace? When will we pick ourselves up from the dusty roadside and walk on to better days? When will our mourning turn to music?

Walk beside us when we must travel rough patches, God. Lead us, in sunshine and in shadow. When our aloneness disheartens us, give us companions and friends. Fill our souls with hope's music and give us the heart to sing. Amen.

(SS)

Holy Week

The Processional Hymn   ST. THEODULPH
    All Glory, Laud, and Honor

The Gospel Lesson   Mark 11:1-11
    Leader: This is the Holy Gospel of Christ.
    People: Praise be to Thee, O Christ.

The Meditation   K. Norris
    Ride On, Ride On in Majesty

The Litany
    Leader: He comes to you on a colt never ridden, and his face is set before you like flint.
    People: O God, you are our help! Who is this carpenter-kind whom we hail? What is this day that has swept us away?
    Leader: Do you not recognize the Bethlehem baby, who arrived to the singing of anthems and slept in the silence of awe?
    People: The baby who inspired the joy of the angels and kindled the hope of the peoples? Glory to you in the highest, and peace to all on earth!
    Leader: Do you not recognize the temple youth, who questioned the answers of sages and answered the questions of teachers?
    People: The youth who amazed the minds of the elders and astonished the hearts of his parents? Glory to you in the highest, and peace to all on earth!
    Leader: And do you not recognize the Nazareth prophet, who proclaimed release to the captives and demanded relief for the poor?
    People: The prophet who preached salvation for our foes and was thrown out of our city? Who is he to be glorified? How can he be the Chosen One?
    Leader: And do you not recognize the Jewish messiah, who was anointed king by a woman's hand, who established the kingdom for servants and sinners?

People: **The Messiah who sleeps in the house of outcasts and feasts at the table of fools? Who is he to be glorified? How can he be the Chosen One? O God, tell us: How can we hail this carpenter-king or honor this day that has swept us away?**
Leader: He comes to you on a colt that none has ever ridden. Tell me: How soon will you take him to the tomb where none has ever lain?

(Everett Tilson and Phyllis Cole[1])

The Anthem   William Mathias
Lift Up Your Heads, O Ye Gates!

The Sermon
"Festive Tragedy"

The Offering of our Lives and Labors unto God

The Offertory Meditation   Barber/Strickland
Adagio for Strings

(During the instrumental meditation a clown enters the sanctuary and haltingly saunters down the center aisle. The unfamiliar and surprising character, his face covered with a mask of clown-white makeup, wears tattered clothing and worn-out shoes. He carries in one hand a broom and in the other hand a tray holding the bread to be used for communion. As, with great reticence, the clown approaches the communion table on the chancel, a minister steps toward him to receive the bread. In the nervousness of the exchange, the clown lets the tray of bread slip and fall to the floor. Immediately, with obvious fear in his demeanor, the clown drops to the floor to pick up the bread. Simultaneously, the minister, with an equally obvious demeanor of compassion, gets on his knees with the clown and assists in picking up the tray of bread. As each gets to his feet, their eyes stay locked in a gaze of grace. In an apologetic manner the clown extends the tray of bread to the minister once again, eager to pass the tray along and leave. To everyone's surprise, however, the minister extends the bread toward the clown and gestures for him to share in the holy meal. After the minister serves the clown, he indicates his own desire to be served. Finally, with silent encouragement, the clown apprehensively offers bread to the minister. As the minister turns to fulfill his responsibility of preparing to offer communion to the whole congregation, the clown, seeing that all appears to be well, gently sweeps around the communion table before quietly walking away. Walking out the center aisle, he repeatedly looks back at the minister and the communion table with wonder and amazement.)

The Service of Communion
(After the clown departs, other ministers move to the communion table to assist in sharing the meal of reconciliation.)

The Invitation
(As communion concludes, the clown reenters the worship center and moves again to the communion table where he sweeps the floor once more. Setting the broom against the communion table, the clown turns to the vessels on each side of it and takes into his hands the two voluminous bouquets of balloons. With obvious joy and great dignity, the clown walks out of the worship center. When the clown is gone, the minister says with a smile:)

Leader: We're all clowns in one way or another. And this whole matter of worship is a party. Sometimes it goes well, but at other times we drop the bread—or worse, crucify the Savior of the world. We keep coming to this party week in and week out, hoping every time that everything will be better in the days ahead but staring honestly into the face of reality. For that reason, we dare not travel alone. We need each other in the messes of life. And we need the one who joins us wherever we are—whether riding into the Holy City of Jerusalem on a donkey or coming to us where we live, work, worship, and play.

(CWG)

The Meditation   H. Hopson
Meditation
from *Litany for Bells*

The Recessional Hymn   LANCASHIRE
Lead On, O King Eternal

The Benediction
> O God, your benediction is upon us in the form of your presence with us. Stay close as we move with our elder brother through this unholy week that for reasons beyond our comprehension we can continue to call "holy." Good God, great God, we travel with you in trust. Amen.
>
> (CWG)

The Response   B. Dennard
Great Day

The Closing Voluntary   Seger
Fugue in D

The Pealing

THE WORSHIP OF GOD
Maundy Thursday

Certain events in the life of Jesus and the truths that they convey for our lives evoke a hush among all who see, hear, and understand. Such a reaction occurs when gazing at the meal Jesus shared with his disciples on the evening prior to his crucifixion. The following service respects, provides, and protects that silence. Worshipers are guided by a printed order of worship that enables their silent participation. They can enter quietly and depart at will, moving at their own pace. Ministers sit or stand at the communion table to offer worshipers the bread and the cup. All of the materials in this service can be incorporated into a worship experience in which words are spoken and hymns are sung rather than read in meditative silence. If the liturgy of the service is presented audibly, a sermon can be included between "The Lesson" and "The Invitation."

(Use Leonardo Da Vinci's painting of *The Last Supper* as a model by which to create an environment for this service. On the chancel place fruits, breads, and a table setting for twelve. The worship center is dimly lighted except for the chancel, which is illuminated with brilliant lights focusing on the table. Throughout the service a robed attendant will care for the banquet table and replenish the stations at which congregants receive communion. If only one table is used for communion, ministers should rotate their services.)

The Prelude
(Outside the worship center, a recorder and a small drum provide a haunting musical prelude as worshipers prepare to enter the service.)

The Call to Worship
Amid all good things competing for our attention, where shall we go to find bread? Among all the activities we can choose, where shall we invest our time and efforts? The church invites our discipleship, calling us into the body of Christ. Among all who claim our loyalty, who encompasses the whole of life and truth? God in Christ offers us wholeness, bringing all the pieces of our lives together.

(CWG)

The Prayer of Invocation
   Redeeming God, this is a tough day. Maundy Thursday brings to mind the "Judas principle" in our lives. Still today love is betrayed, loyalties fail, courage weakens, promises are broken. The killing has not ceased. We continue to have a Golgotha or a Gulf of Sidra or a Kosovo or some other place where we can play havoc with the highest order of your creation.
   This is a tough day, God. We seek a Gethsemane of sorts. We desire to pray. Forgive us, God, for our failures, for our evil strategies, for our slumber in the face of tragedy, for our parts in the mass production of death.
   Now comes the toughest part of all, God. We seek to emulate the prayer of our elder brother and ask not for our wills to prevail, but for your will to be done. Not knowing precisely in what direction you may guide us or through what kind of revelation you may speak to us, we tremble before you as we talk to you. But for better or worse, we do mean it—let not our wills but your will be done. Cause your will be done in us even as it is done in heaven.
   Enable us to stay here to pray and worship for a while and then to be going—whether to a cross or to a tomb. Amen.
   (CWG)

The Hymn   text by Albert Schweitzer
         from *The Quest for the Historical Jesus*
   (For the passage to be read, see Jane Marshall's "He Comes to Us.")

The Reflection
   In the quietness of the moment reflect on your journey with the Christ of this world. Examine your commitment, repent of your weaknesses, and discover new possibilities for a closer relationship with your God. This is a night for laying aside our fears, hatreds, and alienations so that God's love may reign.
   (CWG)

The Collect for the Word
   I want, more than anything else, to hear the voice of one who loves, calling me home.
   (JB)

The Lesson   Luke 22:7-20

The Invitation

Our Savior invites those who trust him to share the feast he has prepared. The privilege is ours to accept his call to sup with him, ours to share his food, his presence, his breaking heart; ours to know his dream, his plans, his goal; ours to bear his load, his task, his cross; ours to eat, to drink, to carry on his work even to the uttermost parts of the earth.

(JWC)

The Call to Confession

We are welcome to come to Christ's banquet because of our own need. But we also are challenged to broaden our concern to include others—to identify with them in their difficulties, to feel with them the problems they face, to care about what happens to them, to be actively helpful. Unless our own needs are placed in this larger context, we cannot experience fully the forgiving love of God that Christ came to share with us. Let us come to God, recognizing how unworthy we are to approach the One who embraces the universe, yet believing that we are known and welcomed in this Awesome Presence. Let us confess our sin.

(CWG)

The Prayer of Confession

God, we are here, because you have called us to follow you, and we know that could mean following you to places we have never seen before. We pause here in this holy place to draw breath into our souls, to look around . . . to look within . . . to look up. We need your grace, because we want to hold on to what has been. We need your mercy, because we can't undo what we have done. We need your Spirit, because our flames burn low. We need your voice, because our faith is small and we are afraid. We need to hear your voice, so that we may not merely journey, but truly follow you. Amen.

(KMF)

(Print in the order of worship: "Following the Prayer of Confession you are invited to come to the front of the nave. A minister will share words of assurance and offer the elements of remembrance. After participation in communion, please return to your seat for reflection and meditation.")

The Reflection

I came not because I was worthy, not for any righteousness of mine. For I had sinned and fallen short of what, by God's help, I might have been. But I came because Christ bade me come. It is his table, and he invited me. I came because it is a memorial to him, as oft as it is done in remembrance of him. And when I remembered him, his life, his sufferings and death, I found myself being humble in his presence and bowing in worship. I came because here was portrayed Christian self-denial, and I was taught very forcibly the virtue of sacrifice on behalf of another that has salvation in it. I came because here I had opportunity to acknowledge my unworthiness and to make a new start. I came because here I found comfort and peace. I came because here I found hope. I came because I hoped to rise from this place with new strength, courage, and power to live for him who died for me.

(JWC)

The Commission

You have prayed and broken bread. You have been forgiven and fed. You have been cleansed. You have communed. You are new creatures in Christ Jesus. Christ sends you from this table into the world. You are a disciple on whom Jesus depends. Take with you the mandate we have from Christ: "Love one another, as I have loved you." Even in the face of rejection and suffering you can this night rejoice with Jesus the Christ. You are free to make your witness to God's love without fear of the consequences. You are the body of Christ and individually members of it; go forth to serve in Christ's name.

(CWG)

The Silent Recessional

The Tolling

THE WORSHIP OF GOD
Good Friday

The following service, planned for one of the most solemn and penitential days on the Christian calendar, is an adaptation of the ancient Tenebrae services. Tenebrae, a Latin word meaning "shadows" or "darkness," refers to the practice of a gradual extinction of candles. The service consists of seven scenes surrounding the crucifixion of Christ. The sanctuary is gradually darkened as a candle is extinguished following each reading of the scriptures. When the light of the final candle has vanished, the room remains in total darkness, symbolizing the death and burial of Christ. After a time for silent meditation, dim lighting is provided for worshipers exiting the room. All depart in a spirit of meditation, grief, and silence.

(To prepare for this service, use the time traditionally associated with the crucifixion—12:00 PM to 3:00 PM—to drape the main outside entrance to the church building in yards of black fabric and inside to place seven large candles within the confines of the chancel. These candles should be burning as worshipers enter the dimly lit room. Prepare also for the stripping of the altar at the end of this service when all seasonal banners, table coverings, and symbols should be replaced or veiled under black fabric.)

The Prelude   P. Manz
O Welt, ich muss dich lassen

The Tolling of the Hour

The Silent Processional
(During the processional, worship leaders enter the sanctuary wearing all black liturgical garments.)

The Prologue   H. Hughes
Te Deum

The Call to Worship
Honestly, I wonder why we are here—why we choose to attend this service held in memory of the day on which Jesus

died. Almost everything we don't like comes together in the focus of this hour—rejected love, betrayed friendship, innocent suffering, sick religion, law without justice, a loss of courage, a world gone mad.

We know enough Good-Friday-like days not to have to come here and remember that one. We have experienced power plays, manipulation, cowardice, compromise, selfishness, intolerance, and malicious words and deeds all justified as righteousness and paraded as signs of religious devotion.

But we are here. We have come to worship. We realize the worth of a love so strong that not even the threat of death can cause a denial of it and not even death itself can kill it.

With gratitude to God for extending such love to us and for inviting us to live in that love, by that love, and with that love, let us now worship God.

(CWG)

The Introit   Palestrina
Adoramus Te

The Evening Prayer
- Leader: In the stillness of the night, O God, we come to you.
- **People: Be ever near us through this night.**
- Leader: Teach us your way, O God.
- **People: In our coming in and going out,**
- Leader: In our lying down and in our rising up.
- **People: For you alone are God. You alone can keep us safe.**

(LKC)

Shadow of Betrayal

The Reading of Holy Scriptures   Matthew 26:30-32

The Meditation   P. Brandvik
Shall I Mother?

The Hymn   PASSION CHORALE
O Sacred Head, Now Wounded

Holy Week

Shadow of Desertion

The Meditation	G. Martin
What Wondrous Love Is This?	
The Reading of Holy Scriptures	Matthew 26:33-35
The Anthem	J. Rutter
Be Thou My Vision	

Shadow of Unshared Vigil

The Hymn	REDHEAD
Go to Dark Gethsemane	
The Reading of Holy Scriptures	Luke 22:39-42
The Meditation	Durufle
The Lord's Prayer	
The Lesson Continued	Luke 22:45-46
The Meditation	D. Wagner
When Jesus Wept	

Shadow of Accusation

The Hymn	OLIVE'S BROW
'Tis Midnight and on Olive's Brow	
The Reading of Holy Scriptures	Mark 14:43-65
The Anthem	D. Wagner
And No Bird Sang	

Shadow of Crucifixion

The Reading of Holy Scriptures	Matthew 27:27-31
The Anthem	Brandvorski
Calvary	
The Hymn	AVON
Alas and Did My Savior Bleed	
The Lesson Continued	Matthew 27:32-38

The Anthem   R. Christiansen
Lamb of God

The Homily
"My God, My God, Why Have You Forsaken Me?"

Shadow of the Tomb

The Reading of Holy Scriptures   John 19:38-40

The Desolation
(Print in the order of worship or state orally: "During the stripping of the altar—The Desolation—you are invited to participate in the removal of the symbols and paraments from the sanctuary. Then, please return to your seats for the closing hymn.")

(The stripping of the altar consists of completely removing from the worship center candles, candlesticks, banners, linens, pulpit and lectern hangings, and table coverings. Any permanent metallic objects that must remain in place should be draped with sheer black fabric. After the altar has been stripped, you may want to hang a long piece of black fabric above the chancel. When all of the stripping activity has ceased and worshipers have taken their seats, a simple introduction is given for the closing hymn.)

The Meditation   J. Travener
Song for Athene

The Hymn   WERE YOU THERE

Were You There When They Crucified My Lord?
(verse 1, congregation with organ accompaniment)
(verse 2, congregation a cappella)
(verse 3, solo from the back of the darkened sanctuary)

The Silent Meditation

The Tolling
(Print in the order of worship: "During the tolling we request worshippers to leave quietly and in the mood of reverence. As you live the remaining hours of this week, may your thoughts be upon the suffering and death of our Savior.")

NOTES

[1]Everett Tilson and Phyllis Cole, *Litanies and Other Prayers for the Common Lectionary,* Year B (Nashville: Abingdon Press, 1990) 18.

Maundy Thursday—Gathering at the table

Maundy Thursday—A vessel for cleansing

Easter

THE WORSHIP OF GOD
Easter Sunday

Christians know no day for rejoicing that exceeds Easter Sunday. Therefore, we plan two different but related services of corporate worship—a Service of New Fire held at daybreak and a traditional Easter Sunday service. The late morning service builds on the earlier service, though worshipers can find meaning in either one independent of the other. Because of the unusually high number of visitors attending the late morning service on Easter, we choose to serve communion at the early service, which is attended mostly by faithful members of Christian congregations. The order of worship that follows is for the late morning service.

(Outside the worship center, white linen fabric, replacing the black fabric of mourning, drapes every entrance to the building. Inside the sanctuary, massive white floral arrangements embrace the communion table. These arrangements exude the festivity and celebration befitting the highest holy day in Christendom. White banners made of linen or gauze hang throughout the room as reminders of the forsaken shroud. Towering standards of white flowers outline the main aisle directing a focus to the chancel. Enlist a brass quintet to join other instrumentalists creating the festive music for this service.)

The Prelude   J. Bender
Piece for Easter: "Christ ist estanden"

The Prologue   A. Zabel
Proclamation

The Call to Worship
    Leader: Christ has risen.
    People: Christ has risen indeed.
    Leader: God is alive . . .
    People: New birth is given . . .
    Leader: Hope is alive . . .
    People: A new age is dawning . . .

The Interlude   J. Sanborn
Christ Is Risen! Alleluia!

The Response
    Leader: Joy is alive . . .
    People: **Redemption is here.**
    Leader: Love is alive . . .
    People: **Death cannot harm us.**
    Leader: We are alive . . .
    People: **New life is within us.**
    Leader: The church is alive . . .
    People: **God's spirit is within us.**
    All: **God of life, we worship you. God of creation, we praise you. God of revelation, we learn from you. God of resurrection, we are here to celebrate you.**

                                                                   (DHC)

The Introit   T. Cousins
Glorious Everlasting

The Response
    Leader: From a world that leaves the just to the mercy of the strong,
    People: **we come to worship the God who turns crosses into crowns.**
    Leader: With hearts that long for the victory of life but fear the triumph of death,
    People: **we come to worship the God who turns the vanquished into victors.**
    Leader: The right hand of the Lord is exalted!
    All: **Thanks be to God, who gives us the victory through our Savior, Jesus Christ.**

                                                                     (DHC)

The Fanfare   R. Slater
Fanfare for Easter Day

The Processional Hymn   EASTER HYMN
Christ the Lord Is Risen Today
(During the processional hymn, banner carriers intersperse between members of the liturgical procession. The banners consist of long

white ribbons on "t" polls. Each also bears a bell. At the end of the procession the banners are placed in the extremities of the chancel.)

The Prayer of Praise and Adoration
Our souls bow before you in wonder and reverence as well as in praise and adoration, O God. You have demonstrated your sovereignty over death and life. You have left us with no doubt regarding the ultimate triumph of justice and mercy. All praise to you, God of heaven and earth. Amen.

(CWG)

The Assurance   J. Rutter
I Am the Resurrection
from *The Requiem*

The Lesson from the Hebrew Scriptures   Psalm 118:14-24
    Leader: This is the Word of God.
    People: Thanks be to God.

The Response   K. Lee Scott
Hilariter

The Gospel Lesson   John 20:1-18
    Leader: This is the Holy Gospel of our Lord Jesus Christ.
    People: Praise be to thee, O Christ.

The Response   R. Vaughan Williams
Let All the World in Every Corner Sing

The Hymn   HYMN TO JOY
Alleluia! Alleluia! Hearts to Heaven

The Litany
    Leader: Alleluia, Christ is risen.
    People: Christ is risen indeed. Alleluia.
    Leader: For the glorious resurrection of your son Jesus Christ our Lord,
    People: we rejoice and give thanks.
    Leader: For the Lamb of God who was sacrificed for the sins of the world,
    People: we offer glory and honor to our Eternal God.

Leader: By Christ's death he has destroyed death, and by his rising to life again he has won for us everlasting life.

People: Thanks be to God for the victory that is ours through Jesus Christ our Lord.

Leader: Join with those who through history confess—

All: Jesus Christ is risen today. Alleluia!

(DWN[1])

The Anthem   R. Vaughan Williams
Festival Te Deum

The Sermon
"The Last Place on Earth"

The Response   K. Lee Scott
Christ Is Now Arisen

The Recessional Hymn   LANCASHIRE
The Day of Resurrection
(During this hymn, banner carriers reclaim the banners and join the recessional, stopping past the main exit from the sanctuary to form a gateway through which all worshipers move back into the world.)

The Commission

Go now into a Christ-graced, God-inhabited world. Go claiming the promise of abundant life. Go not fearing death. Go to meet the risen Christ in unexpected places. Go to experience the living God in all places.

(CWG)

The Benediction

Caring God, we go now as blessed people. You have touched our lives with the power of your love. You have given meaning to all of our days with the promise of your grace. You have strengthened our faith with the gift of hope. We go assured that you go with us and eager to experience the fullness of your presence always and in all ways. Amen.

(CWG)

The Postlude   E. Beals
Fugue on "Unser Herrscher"

THE WORSHIP OF GOD
First Sunday after Easter

Some liturgical traditions refer to the Sunday following Easter Sunday as Low Sunday, recognizing a dramatic difference between the number of people involved in worship on Easter Sunday and the number of worshipers present on the next Sunday. The purpose of the following service is to continue the celebration that began the previous Sunday at a level that shows no diminishment in preparations, expectations, and festivities in response to the resurrection of Christ. Easter continues.

(The flowers of Easter remain in the sanctuary. The top flowers have been replenished so that it appears new life is coming from the top.)

The Prelude S. Rogers
Christ the Lord Is Risen Today
"Gwalchmat"

The Prologue A. Zabel
Easter Proclamation

The Call to Worship
- Leader: The whole world is filled with the news of resurrection. Christ is alive. Let us rejoice and sing.
- **People: We have come to this place to discover the news for ourselves. Tell us your story of victory; sing us your song of triumph.**
- Leader: God, the author of love and the Creator of life, has provided a way for our salvation. Join with us as we continue to celebrate God's goodness.
- **People: How can we experience such a joy? Our eyes have not seen nor have our hands touched this one who has risen. How can we who were not present at the sunrise accept your words as truth?**
- Leader: Trust and believe. Believe that with the Eternal God all things are possible.
- **People: Let us seek the truth and good news of this day.**

(DWN)

The Meditation   J. Sanborn
                        Christ Is Risen

The Processional Hymn   SINE NOMINE
                        All Praise to Thee

The Old Testament Lesson   Psalm 16:5-11
   Leader: This is the Word of God.
   People: Thanks be to God.

The Meditation   B. Marcello
                        I Will Forever Sing

The Pastoral Prayer
   O God, that music! That music sends our minds racing and sets our spirits soaring. We want to shout praise and offer thanks. Your very nature evokes adoration—your intimate distance, your humble sovereignty, your compassionate judgment, your forgiving holiness, your revelatory mystery. Great God. Good God.
   But we can't always hear the music. Sometimes our souls are not lifted up. We can't seem to hear you or see you. Our minds are fixed on the angry chants of people who are denied justice, the soft sobs of an elderly man who thinks everyone has forgotten him, the shrill sirens that signal danger or maybe tragedy, the moans that follow the bombs in Bosnia and the hunger pangs in Rhwanda, the loud debates between politicians who have elevated partisan platforms over needy persons, the empty ring of a congregational hymn sung by a fellowship not open to everyone, the loud cries of an abused child, the stinging questions of an unemployed woman, the bitter resentment of a man who kept his principles and lost his friends.
   O God, sometimes our hearts are not lifted up and we can't sing. Activate our memory, God, and sharpen our sensitivity that when we are most in need and when the heavens are most silent we can hear within our souls and see within our imagination the day that we heard the music—the music about you that transformed us. And, even if we can't yet sing

again, accept our quiet whispers as expressions of faith and stirrings of hope.

We pray in the name of the one who loves always and in all ways. Amen.

(CWG)

The New Testament Lesson   Mark 16:9-18
    Leader: This is the Word of God.
    People: Thanks be to God.

The Hymn   MARION
                    Rejoice, Ye Pure in Heart

The Offering of our Lives and Labors unto God
    (During this time of quiet meditation, members of the flower guild move to the chancel and begin removing the old, dying flowers from the once majestic arrangements. After all the decay is removed, guild members leave the sanctuary carrying the dead flowers.)

The Contemporary Lesson
    It is Easter again, and once more I will have to scrutinize this implausible story about a corpse rising. Every year is a test for me. Too many hot summer nights in a shanty perched on the edge of Ticfaw swamp hearing panthers' shrill wails that sounded like a terrified woman's screams; too many black nights when fear clung closer than the stifling air, closer than a damp, musty shroud, made me fearful of the imminent arrival of zombies . . . the living dead! They come out of shallow graves in the swamp. They come out of those old, above-the-ground tombs in St. Francisville.

    If Grandpa Lonnie, a kind soul who wore a fine Panama straw hat and a freshly starched khaki suit every day of his life, were to return from his resting place in that old family cemetery where the huge magnolias grew shinier leaves, and healthier branches, and larger blooms as place and waxy as a corpse's face because of their bountiful, frightful fertilizer, it would distress the entire family. Since we expected him to stay there until the final trump sounded, I, for one, would not be glad to see him! I would scream and run headlong into the night down the lane, across the road to Miz Needham's house, and my hair would be snow white, and I would have a perpetual twitch.

But every Easter we celebrate the risen Lord. I listen to Scripture give accounts so rich in wonder that I weep for the mystery and for gratitude for the brave women who did not run in terror; for sweet sister Magdalene who stumbled through shimmering curtains of tears running into the dawn having seen hope reborn, faith's assurance, with courage to tell the incredible truth that I never have to be afraid again. And every Easter I believe a bit more, sing a bit louder, pray a bit deeper, and meet with as many people as I can in order to sing with all the faith I can muster, "Christ the Lord is risen today, A-A-Allelujah!"

(RC)

The Anthem John Rutter
Christ the Lord Is Risen Again

The Sermon
"For Those Who Missed Easter"

The Meditation HALLELUJAH, WHAT A SAVIOR!
"Man of Sorrows," What a Name
(During the singing of the meditation, flower guild members pass through the congregation with large garden baskets filled with individual stems of white flowers. Each congregant is encouraged to take a flower from the basket.)

The Invitation
(A minister invites members of the congregation to come forward with their individual flower stems and place the new flowers into the exposed mechanics, symbolically recommitting their lives to keeping the resurrection story alive. The new is constantly replacing and keeping fresh the old story.)

The Commission
    Leader: The Risen Christ goes with us as we walk the ways of our journey.

People: **We go from this place confident of God's truth and love. We are enriched by the new words of grace and empowered to be people of the risen Lord.**

Leader: Sing and rejoice. Take into the world the spirit of celebration. May each day be filled with the joy of resurrection song.

People: **That is the news we go to proclaim. That is the life we celebrate.**

Leader: Though the journey may be steep and the nights become long, the spirit of this day will be the courage, the faith, the way for your journey home. Amen.

People: **Amen.**

(DWN)

The Recessional Hymn   AUSTRIAN HYMN
We Are Called to Be God's People

The Benediction
Perpetually loving, always surprising God: Continue to bless us as we bless others with the love and joy instilled and empowered by the risen Christ who assures the sovereignty of grace forever and ever. Amen.

(CWG)

The Closing Voluntary   J. Lemmens
Fanfare

THE WORSHIP OF GOD
A Sunday in Easter

As the joy of Easter continues, thoughts of the resurrected Christ lead to a consideration of how local communities of faith—each bearing the designation "the body of Christ"—reflect the character, grace, and glory of the Risen One. Inevitably the imperfections and weaknesses of a fellowship of faith emerge when it is viewed alongside the Lord of the church. Hope, not despair, follows, however, as believers discover once again that the power of God that made possible the resurrection of Jesus is able to accomplish incredible good using imperfect instruments. The following service of worship acknowledges flaws in followers of Christ and celebrates God's power to continue the work of Christ through the ministry of flawed people.

(Well in advance of this service, invite congregants to bring to the space outside the worship center vessels that are symbolic of their lives, that are valued treasures, or that hold special meaning for them. These vessels, displayed on pedestals or bases, will serve as visual illustrations of the vessels described in today's readings from the epistles. Also prior to the service, display in various locations inside the worship center common objects that symbolize imperfect instruments that God has employed in the divine work of creation and redemption—for example, a bowl of dirt, a wooden stick, a rock, a plate filled with mud, a loaf of bread, a crude cross.)

The Prelude   H. Friedell
Draw Us in the Spirit's Tether

The Prologue
>   Leader: Look around you. Prominent in this sanctuary are common objects—a stick that is not straight, a common rock, the kind of dirt we wipe from our shoes, mud that we try to avoid, a loaf of bread that we may take for granted, a rough cross that we associate with the horrors of injustice and death. Now think. Think how God used these kinds of objects

to accomplish incredible acts of goodness, healing, and love. God used a stick to teach Moses obedience. God brought water from a rock to quench the thirst of wandering pilgrims. God breathed life into a mass of dust and brought forth the highest order of creation. Jesus transformed a mass of mud into a healing balm that brought sight to a blind man. God transformed a crucifixion into an act of redemption so that a symbol of death became a symbol of life. Imagine. Imagine what God can do with us!

(CWG)

The Call to Worship
- Leader: Come saints, to worship God.
- **People: We offer ourselves for service to God.**
- Leader: Come sinners, to worship God.
- **People: We acknowledge our sins against God.**
- **All: We gather as saints who know that we are sinners and as sinners eager to realize our potential as saints. We gather to worship God.**

(CWG)

The Introit   C. Hubert Parry
I Was Glad When They Said unto Me

The Call to Praise
- One: O come let us sing unto the Lord.
- **All: Let us make a joyful noise to the rock of our salvation.**

The Processional Hymn   ABBOT'S LEIGH
God Is Here! As We Your People Meet

The Prayer of Praise and Adoration
- One: God of Eternity, you alone are our Creator, you alone deserve our praise, and to you alone we offer honor and worship. Your love has led us in the past and promises to uphold and fulfill the days of our

future. We call upon your name to be present among us as we gather in this place. Alert our senses to receive your truth revealed in this hour. Enlighten our beings to the fullness of your love.

All: Let the words of our mouths and the meditations of our hearts be acceptable in your sight, O God, our Rock and Redeemer.

(DWN)

The Biblical Confession of Who We Are　　　　Psalm 51:1-5
   Leader:　This is the Word of God.
   People: Thanks be to God.

The Response　　　　　　　　　　　　　　　　M. Bedord
O Sing a New Song to the Lord

The Biblical Assurance of Who We Can Be　　　1 Peter 2:9-10
   Leader:　This, too, is the Word of God.
   People: Thanks be to God.

The Response　　　　　　　　　　　　　R. Vaughn-Williams
The Old Hundredth

The Prayers of the People
(This time of prayer consists of several prayers composed and voiced by different members of the congregation. Focused on concerns and celebrations in the life of the church, the prayers include: prayers of thanksgiving, prayers for the vision and mission of the church, prayers for the guidance and leadership of the clergy, prayers for responsibility and calling within other churches, prayers for social concerns, prayers for specific personal needs, prayers for individuals who suffer, and prayers for the unification and celebration of the children of God.)

The Biblical Promise　　　　　　　　　1 Corinthians 12:14-27
　　　　　　　　　　　　　　　　　　　　2 Corinthians 4:1-7

   Leader:　This is what the Spirit is saying to the churches.
   People: Praise be to God.

The Hymn　　　　　　　　　　　　　　　WESTMINSTER ABBEY
Christ Is Made the Sure Foundation

The Offering of Our Lives and Labors unto God

The Offertory Meditation   A. Pote
Many Gifts

The Sermon
    "Hitting a Home Run with a Broken Bat"

The Dedication   A. Parker
How Can I Keep from Singing!

The Recessional Hymn   AUSTRIAN HYMN
We Are Called to Be God's People

The Commission
Go from this place to be the church in the world. Remember the faith in which you stand. Share with people the grace that shapes your life. Press on as children of God—vessels entrusted with the Word of God—toward the high calling that is ours. Go to do the work of the One we recognize as the cornerstone of our faith.

(DWN)

The Benediction   P. Langston
God of Grace and God of Glory

The Postlude   Gigout
Toccata

THE WORSHIP OF GOD
Ascension Sunday

Mystery wrapped in wonder, physical imagery in the service of theological reality, and a biblical narrative of comfort and assurance point to the central truth of Christ's ascension. The following service, planned for the Sunday closest to Ascension Day, which comes forty days after Easter, honors the imagery of the ascension, bows before its mystery, and introduces worshipers to the important practical truth inherent in this ethereal event.

The Prelude   J. S. Bach
    Prelude and Fugue in G Major

The Silent Gathering
    Love is most nearly itself
    When here and now cease to matter.
                                  (T. S. Eliot)

The Prologue   Acts 1:6-10
    Let Thy Holy Presence   Tschesnokoff
                                      Acts 1:11

The Response   R. Vaughan Williams
    O Clap Your Hands

The Call to Worship
    Leader: The God of mystery and wonder calls us to this place. The immortal, invisible God of holiness is with us.
    People: We have come to worship the Eternal One and catch a glimpse of God's truth and way.
    Leader: The ways of God are not always within our understanding. We cannot always recognize the Almighty Presence in predictable form. Moments of vision are sometimes revealed in the circumstances of life and in the daily routines of living.

People: God has promised never to leave or forsake us. The absence of His "here and now" creates fear and anxiety as we face the realities of life.
Leader: Love is only complete when it is no longer dependent on time and place. God is eternal. "Eternity is an existence that is entirely love."
People: To experience God's physical absence is to know God's spiritual presence completely. God's going away really means that God is with us.
All: Thanks be to God for the new form of life that surrounds and sustains our days. Let us worship the God of grace and our God of glory.

(Gregory Wolfe[2])

The Hymn of Praise   GWALCHMAI
  Hail the Day That Sees Christ Rise

The Silent Prayers of Praise and Adoration

The Hebrew Lesson   Psalm 93
  Reader: The Word of God.
  People: Thanks be to God.

The Response   E. Titcomb
  God Is Gone Up

The Gospel Lesson   John 14:6, 25-29
  Reader: The gospel of Christ.
  People: Praise to you, O Christ.

The Hymn   BRYN CALFARIA
  Christ, Enthroned in Heavenly Splendor

The Gospel Lesson   John 16:5-11
  Reader: The promise of Christ.
  People: Thanks be to God.

The Prayer for Enlightenment
  Revealing God, today we once again bump up against mystery, not knowing exactly how best to respond to the jolt. The Scriptures tell us that Jesus thought it best that he go away

from us. We could protest that decision, you know. The fact is that we need the divine presence dramatically obvious in our lives every step of every day. How could it be best that he go away? Do you really expect us to believe that distance can nurture intimacy? Well, of course, you do. You are the mystery whom we encounter.

Teach us, God. Teach us to avoid assigning holiness to that which is transient. Stop us from giving ultimate importance to institutions, projects, and professional goals lest we spend our lives in pursuit of purposes that have no lasting value and clutching things that do not give us life. Sensitize us to the presence of the holy that can be found in a friendship based on unconditional love, in a love that will never settle for less than a good friendship but will constantly reach for much more, in a word of grace, and in a work of mercy. Open our eyes that we may see the profile of the Jesus who told us that we would find him in the laughter of a child, in the brokenness of a person who has been abused, in the hunger of a person deprived of food and care, and in all the people who need housing, clothing, and compassion. Enable us to know that the one who went away is still here.

Guide us, God. Guide us in thoughts, words, and actions so that even when we are away from each other, we convey care for each other. Instruct us in the ways to nurture intimacy through absence even as you show us how to convey love through presence.

O God, we pray to you amid the mystery of this day, longing for a time when there is never a thought of absence and never a moment of separation but always a joyous celebration of presence and a profound communion of love that make us whole. Amen.

(CWG)

The Anthem   E. Titcomb
         I Will Not Leave You Comfortless

The Sermon
                "Creative, Redemptive, Absence"

The Response   J. Rutter
I Will Sing with the Spirit

The Commission
> Go now assured of the comfort, counsel, and encouragement of God's Spirit. Go now in the power of God's Spirit to live as Christ's presence in the world. Go to live transparent lives in order that others may see in us the grace, courage, forgiveness, compassion, and inclusive love that we see in Christ. Go in peace.
>
> (CWG)

The Retiring Procession   HYFRYDOL
Alleluia! Gracious Jesus!

The Benediction
> Every moment of our lives, we need you, O God. But our sensitivity to that need increases inestimably as we move from a sanctuary of worship into the rough-and-tumble life of the world. Your blessing is the benediction for which we pray—the blessing of your presence with us even to the end of the age. We welcome your presence. We exult in your presence. We find strength in your presence. Even as we understand the necessity of your going away from us, we give thanks that you keep coming to us. Come, Lord Jesus! Amen.
>
> (CWG)

The Postlude   Mendelssohn
Allegro
from *Sonata No. 1*

NOTES

[1]Adapted from *The Book of Common Prayer* (The Church Hymnal Corporation and The Seabury Press, 1977) 285.

[2]Gregory Wolfe, based on "Ascension," in *Stories for the Christian Year* (New York: Macmillan, 1992) pp. 143-151.

Easter—Glorious Resurrection

Pentecost

THE WORSHIP OF GOD
Pentecost Sunday

The following service dramatizes as well as declares the New Testament story of the eruption of God's Spirit among first-century Christians living in Jerusalem. The significance of the event called "Pentecost" stems as much from its promise for today as from its consequences in an earlier day.

The Preludes   Stearns
        Veni Sancti Spiritus
        Veni Creator Spiritus
        Down Ampney

The Prologue I   Acts 2:1
(A minister walks to the middle of the main aisle in the worship center, followed by choir members and other worship leaders carrying baskets filled with fruits that bring to mind the harvest celebrated in the ancient Jewish festival of Pentecost. No sooner has the minister read the biblical words about "gathering" in Acts 2:1 than the other worship leaders set down their baskets and rush to gather in groups in the four corners of the room. Once there, they immediately sing an a cappella setting of the call to worship.)

The Call to Worship   Tschnesnikoff
        Let Thy Holy Presence

The Prologue II   Acts 2:2-4
(At the conclusion of the singing, the minister reads the scripture. While this text is being read, four dancers enter the sanctuary carrying four torches that appear as one. When the dancers reach the location of the reading minister, the flames divide, each moving to a separate corner of the room. As each flame approaches a gathered group, a distinctive language is heard emanating from that group. All four groups are speaking at once in languages that represent the "four corners" of the earth. As the sound of the languages reaches a crescendo, the organ voluntary begins.)

The Opening Voluntary   D.H. Clark
        Improvisation on *Veni Creator Spiritus*

(During the organ voluntary, the four groups take their respective places in the chancel. Sounds of four distinctive languages are maintained until the individuals reach the chancel steps at which point all begin to speak in unison the English words of the Gloria Patri. The four flames are reunited behind the communion table and left burning as one flame for the remainder of the service.)

The Introit   B. Red
Listen to the Rustle of the Mighty Wind

The Hymn of Praise   SINE NOMINE
All Praise to Thee, O Christ

The Invocation
God of the Spirit, calming and consuming, come as fire to energize and enlighten. Kindle our hearts, but govern our actions. Ignite our minds, but curb our tongues. As you give us passion, so also grant us gentleness, that our living may disclose your love as well as your law, your grace as well as your grandeur. We pray in the name of Jesus, the powerful word of creation and the light of the world. Amen.

(PR)

The Old Testament Lesson   Ezekiel 37:1-14
  Leader: The Word of God.
  People: Thanks be to God.

The Meditation   Hal Hopson
Send Your Holy Spirit

The Pastoral Prayer
At Pentecost we pray "spirit come," and we await transformation. But God's spirit is here, and we are transformed when we work for transformation. We are about the business of turning the world upside down when our values—our business dealings, our personal relationships—when our day in and day out the body of Christ takes shape in our world. So together we pray for our sick, and we visit them. Together we work to feed the hungry and clothe the naked. Together we work for freedom from all forms of oppression and struggle with those

areas of our lives in which we participate in oppression. Together we stand against the deification of profit and power, expediency and efficiency. Together we say no to Madison Avenue. We say no to it our way every day and yes to have it your way, God. Every day is Pentecost. Amen.

(JB)

The New Testament Lesson   Acts 2:5-21
    Leader: The Word of the Lord.
    People: **Thanks be to God.**

The Hymn   SLANE
Be Thou My Vision

The Litany
    Leader: We come to our place of worship to mourn, to rest, to seek guidance.
    People: **While we are here, we see the holy; we feel it all around us.**
    Leader: We hear God's word and respond.
    People: **We want to serve; we want to make a difference; we want to work for peace.**
    Leader: Then we get caught up in dailiness, and the deadlines and assignments become our gods.
    People: **We no longer see the holy;**
    Leader: we only see the immediate.
    People: **We no longer hear God's word for us;**
    Leader: we only hear the clock and the noise outside our window.
    People: **We must learn to see through the clutter of our schedules and grasp the eternal.**
    Leader: We must learn to filter out the noise and hear the essential voice.
    People: **Let us see, hear, and feel our God.**
    All: **To relight the flame of commitment and peace in our hearts.**

(LKC)

The Anthem   D. Church
    Holy Spirit, Revive Your Church

The Sermon
    "The Promise of Pentecost"

The Response   M. Hayes
    And the Father Will Dance
(As the music of the response begins, children move to the baskets of fruit and discover among the fruit long pieces of ribbon with colors corresponding to those of the fruits. As the children move with the streamers, their dancing becomes an interpretation of the musical text. The four torch bearers move to the center of the base of the chancel and reunite the four flames into one flame around which the children conclude their dance.)

The Commission
    Leader: Our hearts are the kindling of the Refiner's fire.
    People: Let the flames from that kindling of the Refiner's fire, let the flames from the Holy Spirit's fire, rise from the ashes to offer warmth and light to our brothers and sisters in the world.
    Leader: We rejoice in our connection to the Spirit.
    People: Let us go celebrating the miracle of that connectedness, in the name of Jesus, the embodiment of your Spirit, who teaches us how to embody your Spirit.
                                             (adapted from JWC)

The Recessional Hymn   HYFRYDOL
    Christ Has Called Us to New Visions

(The children with streamers and the flame made from four torches lead the recessional out of the worship center.)

The Benediction
>Go with the sure and certain awareness of God's presence. Take with you the metaphors of the Holy Spirit—the wind and flame and dove—and by the Spirit's guidance and grace become living signs of God's presence in this world.
>
>(PR)

The Closing Voluntary   J. S. Bach
>*Come Holy Ghost, Creator*

THE WORSHIP OF GOD
Trinity Sunday

Pentecost, with its emphasis on the presence and power of God's Spirit, prompts questions about the nature of God: How are we to think about and speak about the oneness of God and the divinity of Jesus along with the Holy Spirit? Can we explore a mystery using specific words and concrete images? The following service encourages a festive affirmation of the Sovereign God and honest reflection on the meaning of the revelation of God as Creator, Redeemer, and Comforter.

(Using the simplistic imagery of three forms of water, create a visual interpretation of the sermon text for today and the subject of the trinity. On a table in the narthex, or just outside the entrance to the worship center, display a large basin of water, representing God the Creator, and place beside the basin a printed sign that reads "Love." Also on the table display a block of ice, representing the Incarnate God, and place beside the ice a sign that reads "Grace." Finally, on the same table display steam [using either a burner or vaporizer], representing God's Spirit, and place beside the steam a sign that reads "Communion." Worshipers will more fully appreciate the depth of meaning in this visual after the closing lines of the sermon.)

The Prelude   D. Clark
    Creator, Christ, Constant Companion

The Prologue   J. Martin
    Who Knows Where the Wind Blows?

The Call to Worship
    Reader 1: Genesis 1:1-27
    Reader 2: John 1:1-14
    Reader 3: Acts 2:1-4, 14-21

    Leader: Throughout time, Yahweh has searched for ways to reveal eternal love.
    People: Like those before us, we have gathered to know more fully the greatness of our God.
    Leader: The Eternal One is far beyond the measure of time or reality.

People: **Yet the very heart of divinity has been demonstrated and brought to us through the life of Jesus Christ.**

Leader: Yet for centuries the presence of Christ has dwelt with the Eternal. Why would you on this day search for God's presence?

People: **The spirit of God can be as new to us now as it was then. God's spirit reaches to give us power and courage, even today.**

Leader: Come, let us celebrate the mystery of our faith. Let us search for the depth of God, and let us experience anew the love of our creator.

(DWN)

The Response　　　　　　　　　　　　　Palestrina/Lundquist
Praise Be to Thee

The Prayer of Confession:

O God of all things, big and small:

There are times when we feel so very small inside, times when we are afraid, when we feel lonely and isolated, when we are disappointed in ourselves, when we wish we could be and do more than we have done with our lives. Give us a new vision of ourselves, of what and whose we are. Forgive us when we do not remember our worth and our value because we have forgotten for a moment that you created us in your own image—all of us, every one of us—and you said: "It is good! Very good! What I have created is good. Each one of you."

And God, as church, so many things can be said of us. So many words can be used to describe us: different, open, innovative, new, gutsy, ecumenical, inclusive, courageous, liturgical . . . so many words. . . . And yet, what we focus on to describe ourselves as a church is that same word: small.

Forgive us for not accepting who we are, what you have made us. Forgive us for trying to be something we are not, for wanting to be like every other church because we are afraid of being different.

Help us to be what you want us to be. Help us to seek your will and your direction and to have the courage to walk through the door you have opened to us.

Give us a renewed dream and a renewed dedication to describe ourselves with the names you gave us: "a chosen people, a royal priesthood, a holy nation, a people belonging to God."

Come, Eternal God. Come, Creator. Come, Lover. Come, Divine Presence. Come close, O God. Show us what it means to be your children. Holy God, what a thought! Amen.

(KMF)

The Words of Assurance
God the Creator gives you life. God the Christ gives meaning to your life. God the Comforter gives direction for your life. Come and celebrate the good news of our Eternal God.

(PR)

The Processional Hymn — LAUDA ANIMA
Praise with Joy the World's Creator

The Psalm — Psalm 33

The Response of Assurance — R. Vaughan Williams
Let All the World in Every Corner Sing

The New Testament Lesson — Romans 5:1-5

The Hymn — BEACH SPRING
Womb of Life, and Source of Being

The Silent Prayers of the People

The Epistle Lesson — 1 Corinthians 12:4-6
2 Corinthians 13:5-14

The Anthem — Mark Hayes
To Love Our God

The Sermon
"Speaking Honestly about the Trinity"

The Ancient Response of Thanksgiving J. Rutter
Te Deum

The Commission
> Leader: The Eternal God sends us into the world to be the children of light.
> **People: We will go from this place back into our daily routines, taking with us the presence of the Almighty.**
> Leader: Reveal to all that can see the Light, the source and the goodness of your God.
> **People: We will commit our lives to the revelation of the heart of the Divinity.**
> Leader: As you go, may the grace of Jesus Christ and the love of God and the communion of the Holy Spirit be with each of you this day and forevermore. Amen.

(DWN)

The Recessional Hymn Spanish Hymn
We Believe in One True God

The Benediction Healey Willan
Apostolic Benediction

The Postlude T. Canning
Nicae

THE WORSHIP OF GOD
A Sunday after Pentecost

Superstition and religion are often difficult to distinguish from each other—at least on the surface—especially when acts or references related to the Holy Spirit are involved. Persons unfamiliar with the nature of God's work in the world and with the substance of faith can confuse providence and luck, offering a prayer and repeating a magical formula, and spiritual transformation and a skillful slight-of-hand trick. Centered around a post-Pentecost story in Acts, the following service challenges misunderstandings of spiritual power and stresses the importance of living by faith.

The Meditation of Preparation
"Christianity without living Christ is inevitably Christianity without discipleship, and Christianity without discipleship is always Christianity without Christ."
(Dietrich Bonhoeffer)

The Prologue R. Vaughn-Williams
O Taste and See

The Call to Worship Psalm 84, *The Message*[1]

The Introit C. Beaudrot
O Be Joyful

The Call to Praise
Leader: Give thanks to the Lord. Sing praise to God's holy name.
People: With glad hearts we will enter into the presence of the Almighty. With thanksgiving we will celebrate God's steadfast love and faithfulness.
Leader: Come, let us seek the spirit of One who gives us life.
(DWN)

The Hymn of Praise LEONI
The God of Abraham Praise

The Hebrew Lesson	Psalm 12
The Meditation	J. Martin

Trust in the Lord

The Morning Prayer

O God, sometimes talking about the gift of your spirit reminds us of someone screaming, "Fire!" in a public gathering as a joke. Our hearts pound against our chests, anxiety rises, and expectation searches to sight the realization of that which has been announced. Admittedly, relief washes over our emotions as we discover the absence of fire in the public gathering. But despondency weighs down our spirits when we see no evidence of God's Spirit in the world. This is no joking matter. How can we live without fire? How can we love without breath? How can we move without strength? How can we hope without counsel?

Of course, we understand that the problem may reside in what we do rather than in what you have left undone, God. You instruct us to build community, but we undercut each other. You call on us to encourage each other, but we talk about each other critically rather than talk with each other helpfully. You show us the value of diversity, but we view differences disparagingly. You commission us to share the gospel, but we look to a few to carry out that commission for all of the rest. The problem well may be with us, God. Not recognizing the presence of your spirit in the world may be a consequence of our thoughts, talk, and actions. If so, it is time for that to stop.

Today, as we continue to meditate on the meaning of the gracious gift of your spirit, sensitize us to the counsel, comfort, strength, and encouragement of your spirit. At the same time, sensitize us to the way in which our lives must conform to the leadership of your spirit. We fear that what we do, in contradiction to the work of your spirit, may make it difficult, if not impossible, to see what you have done and are doing.

> O God, come to us as fire, breath, comfort, and power. But give us the good sense as well as the grace to be warmed, to be comforted, to be strengthened, and to breathe. Amen.
>
> (CWG)

The Anthem   K. Matthews
If Not by the Spirit

The Sermon

"Where's the Magic?"

The Response   P. Manz
E'en So Lord Jesus

The Commission

    Leader: God, send us from this place to share the stories of our faith.

    People: **We go from this time of renewal committed and strengthened to fulfill our task.**

    Leader: The presence of God's spirit goes with each of you as you search for ways to express your faith.

    People: **May we authentically live the message of grace this week. As we journey, let us be assured that a redemptive spirit guides us and empowers a recommitted faith.**

    Leader: You have experienced the source of belief. You have committed your lives in obedience.

    All: **Let us go forth trusting the spirit of the Eternal One.**

    Leader: Amen.

    People: **Amen.**

(DWN)

The Postlude   J. Rheinberger
Trio in E-flat Major

THE WORSHIP OF GOD
A SUNDAY AFTER PENTECOST

The Sundays after Pentecost run on and on—an endless season, it sometimes seems. In the past, liturgists often referred to this stretch of time as "Ordinary Time." The following service takes form around fundamental questions that honest people often raise as they examine the nature of their faith amid mundane circumstances on ordinary days—What is it with God? What does God want from us? Is God for us or against us? Responses to these inquiries come from basic biblical truths that prompt reflection, prayer, thought, action, and the corporate worship of God.

The Prelude   F. Peters
Love Divine All Loves Excelling

The Prologue   H. Hopson
The Gift of Love

The Call to Worship
- Leader: The God of love calls us to this time of renewal and celebration.
- **People: We say with our mouths, "God is love," but can we believe in our hearts such astounding reports?**
- Leader: What then can we say? It is God who gave love for the sake of your soul. It is the lover of all creation who will not let you go.
- **People: Love so amazing must require some response, some offering. What then can we say?**
- Leader: Rejoice and give thanks. Nothing in this life can separate us from the compassion and grace of the Almighty. Sing and celebrate, for God's love endures forever.

(DWN)

The Introit   D. Peterson
Antiphonal Praise

The Hymn of Praise   HYMN TO JOY
Joyful, Joyful, We Adore You

The Hebrew Lesson   Nehemiah 9:16-20

The Response   St. Margaret
O Love That Wilt Not Let Me Go

The Attestations of Love
    (Congregants selected well in advance of the service give testimonies of how God's unconditional love is reflected and shared through others. Two or three individuals relate contemporary experiences of unbounded love alive and powerful in today's world.)

The Reflection   J. Brel
If We Only Have Love
from *Jacque Brel Is Well and Alive*

The Silent Prayer of Thanksgiving

The Hymn   JEFFERSON
God Our Author and Creator

The Lesson   Max Lucado[2]
You Are Special
(A worship leader reads the entirety of this children's book.)

The Anthem   M. Hayes
To Love Our God

The Sermon
                           "The Integrity of God"

The Response   A. James
The Love of God

The Silent Prayers of Commitment and Dedication

The Commission
  It is not enough to know of God's unlimited love. We are challenged to be responsible with that good news. We are to go from this place and share what we have received. Nothing can separate us from the love of God! In every step of this new

week, be assured that the Eternal One walks with you. Go now to fulfill your calling. Be at peace, find courage, and rest in the knowledge of God's love.

(DWN)

The Recessional Hymn　　　　　　　　　　　　　　Beecher
Called as Partners in Christ's Service

The Benediction　　　　　　　　　　　　　　　　　H. Willan
The Apostolic Benediction

The Postlude　　　　　　　　　　　　　　　　　　Dunstable
The Agincourt Hymn

THE WORSHIP OF GOD
A Sunday after Pentecost

Celebrating Pentecost leads to a personal commitment to living as a child of God empowered by the Spirit of God and conformed to the Son of God. The following service is intended to bring worshipers into a confrontation with God that results in a recognition of the complex challenges to be faced by commitment as well as an awareness of the divine call to commitment to be accepted by every person of faith.

(Prior to the service, create a visual interpretation of the theme of commitment. Place at the front of the sanctuary a large iron gate that is partially open. Floral arrangements on each side of the gate disguise the mechanics that allow the gate to stand. Behind the gate, place a large cross. At the base of the cross, position a scroll that unfurls through the gate and falls across the chancel. The text on the scroll raises the question, "Dare You?" On the side of the gate closest to the congregation, place shoes of every size and description.)

The Prelude   G. Faure
Siciliene

The Prologue   Jeremiah 31:31-36

The Meditation   Mendelssohn
Cast Thy Burdens

The Call to Worship
    Leader: Deep calls unto deep in the roar of the waterfalls.
    People: Out of the depths I cry unto the Lord.
    Leader: Schedules and deadlines roar over my head, voices clamor around me, and old tapes keep running in my mind.
    People: I cry out to my God for a moment of peace, a season of silence, a glimpse of the holy.
    Leader: Pain comes crawling down upon me like angry waters, and despair wells up from deep within.
    People: I cry out to you, God, for healing; I cry out to you for hope.

Leader:	Just when I feel that I cannot stand the chaos,
People:	**You whisper, softly, and my world is remade.**
Leader:	Just when I feel that I cannot stand the pain,
People:	**You come to me with healing in your wings.**
Leader:	I wait for your touch. I hope in your word.
People:	**More than those who watch for the morning, I wait for your touch.**
All:	**More than those who watch for the morning, I hope in your word.**

(LKC)

The Hymn of Praise   LAUDES DOMINI
When Morning Guilds the Sky

The Invocation

Lord, this is the time in our service that we usually ask you to join us, to let your presence be felt among us. We really don't think much about what we are asking for; Annie Dillard says it is madness to invoke your presence without first handing out crash helmets and lashing ourselves to the pews.

There is a part in each of us that hopes you will not come —a part that just wants to sleep or be left alone for an hour. There is a part in each of us that knows your presence is sometimes uncomfortable and even scary. There is also a part in each of us that wants to know you better, even if it is uncomfortable and scary. There is within us a God-shaped void that we long to open and let you fill.

We ask that you would listen to that part of us that aches and hungers for your presence. Come and be among us. This time we really mean it. In Christ's name. Amen.

(LKC)

The Meditation   Zingarelli
Go Not Far from Me, O Lord

The Old Testament Lesson   Jeremiah 15:15-21

The Response   Parry
Thou Wilt Keep Him in Perfect Peace

The Prayer of Confession

O God of ages past: You are our fortress and our refuge, a sanctuary of strength and reassurance. You are the God of our adoration, the God eternal and everlasting.

You ask us to follow you and to forsake our worldly goods, but we confess our attachments to comfort and habits. Be patient, Lord, and teach us your ways.

You ask us to trust you, Lord, to live in courage even unto death, and yet at times our faith weakens. Fortify us, Lord, and embolden our hearts.

You ask us to stand firm in your love even when crusades of evil rage against us. Send determination, O God, for though we may tremble, our souls will seek your truth, and it shall triumph through us.

Forgive us, Lord. We are exposed, overwhelmed, vulnerable; without you we are but a sign on the winds of time. Be with us; do not forsake us. Let your favor fall upon us and prosper the work of our hands. Let your power be made manifest to the world. We will praise you above all else—magnificent, infinite, majestic—the God eternal and everlasting.

(ET)

The Hymn of Assurance　　　　　　　　　　　　　　FOUNDATION
　　　　How Firm a Foundation

The New Testament Lesson　　　　　　　　　　　Matthew 16:24-28

The Anthem　　　　　　　　　　　　　　　　　　　　M. Hayes
　　　　Here's One

The Sermon
　　　　"Commitment on the Run"

The Response of Dedication
　　Leader:　I want it, and I want it now.
　　People:　Whip out the credit card, pay for overnight express; if it's worth it, we should get it quickly.
　　Leader:　The diet fad, the how-to shortcuts—I'm in too much of a hurry to reach my goal step by step, to grow my dream.

People: **Why even work at it? Shouldn't someone else do the work? We'll just reap the benefits. And why pray? The results are not guaranteed.**
Leader: But you know, somehow this doesn't sound right; somehow this sounds wrong.
People: **Short-term gratification diminishes us over the long haul. Slow us down, God.**
Leader: Teach us to linger over our living.
People: **Teach us to wait. Teach us to pray.**

(JB)

The Silent Prayers of Dedication

The Anthem of Renewal   R. Thompson
    Best of Rooms
(During the singing of the anthem, congregants are invited to take the dare and move to the gate at the front of the worship center and place their names on the scroll as a symbol of a first commitment or a renewed commitment to Christ.)

The Hymn of Response   MORE LOVE TO THEE
    More Love to Thee

The Benediction
God of the flaming spirit, give us the light and warmth we need. When our hearts are cool, rekindle them, that we may be passionate for justice and mission. When our minds are dim, reignite them, that we may be enlightened to learn and lead. When other fires rage within us, purify our motives by your own spirit, that we may feel and think and act according to your will. We pray in the saving name of Jesus Christ our Lord. Amen.

(PR)

The Response   J. Rutter
    The Lord Bless Thee and Keep Thee

The Closing Voluntary   G. F. Handel
    Fantasy in C

THE WORSHIP OF GOD
A Sunday after Pentecost

The apostle Paul observed that Christians have no faith apart from the resurrection of Jesus. Not surprisingly, then, Christian worship can never occur in isolation from the resurrection—focusing on it, exploring its meaning, and celebrating its reality. During the long stretch of Sundays in the season after Pentecost (formerly known as "Ordinary Time"), paying close attention to the resurrection keeps us in touch with the nature of our faith and fills us with the power of Jesus' living presence. The following service is planned to facilitate attention focused on the resurrection and inspiration derived from the resurrection as worshipers give glory to the God of life and death and resurrection.

The Prelude　　　　　　　　　　　　　　　　　　　　J. S. Bach
Arioso

The Prologue　　　　　　　　　　　　　　　　　N. Coke-Jephcott
Surely the Lord Is in This Place

The Call to Worship
    Leader: It is the year that King Uzziah died—the year someone we love died, the year we had many changes in our lives.
    People: **We go to our place of worship to mourn, to rest, to seek guidance.**
    Leader: While we are there, we see the holy; we feel it all around us.
    People: **We hear God's word and respond.**
    Leader: We want to serve; we want to make a difference.
    People: **Then we get caught up in dailiness, and the deadlines and assignments become our gods.**
    Leader: We no longer see the holy;
    People: **we only see the immediate.**
    Leader: We no longer hear God's word for us;

People: **we only hear the clock and the noise outside our window.**
Leader: We must learn to see through the clutter of our schedules and grasp the eternal.
People: **We must learn to filter out the noise and hear the essential voice.**
Leader: Let us return to the temple, to see and hear our God,
People: **to relight the flame of commitment and celebration in our hearts.**

(LKC)

The Processional   R. Johnson
Praise the Lord

The Hebrew Lesson   Psalm 66:8-20

The Response   R. Nelson
Hear O Israel

The Affirmation of Faith

You, O God, are supreme and holy. You create our world and give us life. Your purpose overreaches everything we do. You have always been with us. You are God. You, O God, are infinitely generous, good beyond all measure. You came to us before we came to you. You have revealed and proved your love for us in Jesus Christ, who lived and died and rose again. You are with us now. You are God. You, O God, are Holy Spirit. You empower us to be your gospel in the world. You reconcile and heal; you overcome death. You are our God. We worship you.

(*A New Zealand Prayer Book*³)

The Hymn of Praise and History   CONSTANTINE
God of Abraham and Sarah

The New Testament Lesson   Acts 17:22-33

The Anthem   J. Marshall
My Eternal King

The Sermon
                      "Everyone Laughed"

The Reflection   D. Church
                            Sanctus

The Call to Awareness
    Leader: It is easy to say words—spout phrases. The old, old story is so familiar. Yes, it is easy to speak.
    People: **For my words are not made flesh. My words can float, all too easily—abstracted from living—unrelated even to who I am.**
    Leader: Make it hard, O God, to speak. Braid together my speaking and my being, and should I choose to speak with you,
    People: **let your Word be near. Let your Word assume my flesh such that my living and your way of life fit my words and reflect your Word, that I might honor you and worship you.**
                                                                                           (JB)

The Hymn of Response   St. Denio
    Immortal, Invisible, God Only Wise

The Benediction
    The holy peace of God, which passes all understanding, keep your hearts and minds in the love of God and of the Son, Jesus Christ, our Savior, and may the blessing of God your Creator, Redeemer, and Holy Comforter be among you and remain with you always. Amen.
                                                                                            (DHC)

The Postlude   J. S. Bach
                         Fugue on a Theme by Corelli

THE WORSHIP OF GOD
A Sunday after Pentecost

Pentecost introduces a season of growth—a time for spiritual maturation as Christians learn of the work of the Spirit, the nature and ministry of the church, and the ways of discipleship. Movement toward spiritual maturity involves the mind as well as the heart, development in beliefs as well as in behavior. The following service helps participants focus on fundamental theological questions, the answers to which either impede or enhance significant spiritual growth.

The Prelude   Widor
Adagio
from *Symphony No. 5*

The Prologue   J. Rutter
Kyrie
from *Requiem*

The Questions Asked
(Prior to the service, enlist several persons to read the following questions. Position the readers in different locations in the worship center. The final "Why" should be spoken in unison by all readers.)

Leader: If all things work together for good,
A Voice: Why do bad things happen to those who love God?
A Voice: Why does God allow children to go to bed hungry?
A Voice: Why do the young die with visions in their souls?
A Voice: Why does God permit us to create arms that enable us to destroy each other?
A Voice: Why did God make people with different colors of skin and fail to make all of us color blind?
A Voice   Why does God not intervene when people seek ways to undermine and ridicule those whom they should call "sister" and "brother?"
A Voice: Why does God seem to love all people yet allow those known as "the children of God" to proclaim who is "in" and who is "out?"

A Voice: Why does God allow people to suffer?
A Voice: Why does God select some people to live with abundance while others have to scratch out a meager existence day by day?
A Voice: Why does God allow some people to have life and others to be taken from life?
A Voice: Why?
A Voice: Why, God?
A Voice: Why?
All: Why?

(CWG/DWN)

The Reflection   Rich/Gazeley/Malamet
Lesson Learned
(Either play Barbara Streisand's solo recording of "Lesson Learned" from the CD *Higher Ground*, or have a worship leader present this piece of music as a solo.)

The Call to Worship
Leader: Come all who search for truth. The Sovereign God invites each of us to bring our questions and concerns to this hour of liberation.
People: We gather as complacent followers, having chosen to ignore the difficult issues of life. We have lived a shallow existence content to place all circumstances within the will of God.
Leader: The nature of the Almighty is good. God is a lover of all creation and the revealer of all truth. God values freedom and respects the choices people make. In turn, God calls each of us to maturity and expects us to be responsible in our decision-making.
People: Open our eyes, O God. In this hour, reveal to us the mysteries of life. Teach us your ways and show us the good in life.
Leader: Rejoice and be glad. Come with joy and celebration. The God of grace is the one we have gathered to worship. The God of goodness is the one we adore.

(DWN)

Pentecost

The Processional Hymn   HANOVER
O God, Whom We Praise

The Contemporary Lesson   Douglas Wood/Khee Chee[4]
Old Turtle
(A worship leader reads the entirety of this children's book.)

The Meditation   J. Rutter
All Things Bright and Beautiful

The New Testament Lesson   Galatians 6:7-10

The Hymn   HOLY MANNA
God, Whose Purpose Is to Kindle

The Sermon
"God Is No Jezebel"

The Reflection   J. Roff
Prayer from Outer Space
(After the presentation of this piece of music, a worship leader reads the text of the prayer offered by Colonel Frank Boreman on Christmas Eve 1968 while orbiting the earth in Apollo 8.)

Give us, O God, the vision that can see thy love in the world in spite of human failure. Give us the faith, the trust, the goodness in spite of our ignorance and weakness. Give us the knowledge that we may continue to pray with understanding hearts, and show us what each one of us can do to set forth the coming of the day of universal peace. Amen.

The Retiring Procession   Lancanshire
Lead On Eternal Sovereign

The Benediction   J. Martin
A Festive Call to Praise

The Postlude   Mendelssohn
Allegro from Sonata No. 1
handbells

NOTES

[1] Eugene Peterson, *The Message* (Colorado Springs CO: Navpress Publishing Group, 1996) 200.

[2] Max Lucado, *You Are Special* (Wheaton IL: Crossway Books, 1997).

[3] *A New Zealand Prayer Book*, cited in *The New Century Hymnal* (Cleveland: The Pilgrim Press, 1995), No. 886.

[4] Douglas Wood and Khee Chee, *Old Turtle* (West Michigan: Pfeifer-Hamilton Publisher, 1993).

Pentecost—Empowered by the Spirit

The Greens of Pentecost

Civil Holidays

THE WORSHIP OF GOD
New Year's Day

Whether or not New Years Day falls on a Sunday, the first day of a new year is an appropriate time for public worship. The following service sets before worshipers basic spiritual priorities for a new segment of time.

The Prelude   A. Fedak
Now Greet the Swiftly Changing Year
(Prominently, display timepieces that are special to members of the congregation. For example, display a grandfather's mantel clock, a father's retirement pocketwatch, or a mother's wedding-gift wristwatch. These treasures from various individuals call attention to the importance of time generally and to the focus on time in this service specifically.)

The Prologue   J. Marshall
We Would Offer Thee This Day

The Call to Worship
> Leader: We stand on the threshold of the new—grateful for what has brought us here.
> **People: We look back with thanksgiving, but we press on with anticipation.**
> Leader: We have the rest of our lives with which to accomplish much—in which to become more.
> **People: The process of being church will challenge us all the days of our lives.**
> Leader: We begin anew—day by smile by tear by day.
> **People: God is at work in and through us, and what will be, will be wonderful.**
>
>   (JB)

The Introit   J. S. Bach
Break Forth, O Beauteous Heavenly Light

The Processional Hymn   HYMN TO JOY
Joyful, Joyful, We Adore Thee

The Invocation
>   Almighty God. . . Our help in ages past . . . Our highest hope for the days to come: Your grace has brought us safely to this moment in our history. In our hearts we hold memories from our journey . . . some good memories, and some not so good. Help us, Lord, to make peace with the past.
>
>   O God of new beginnings, today feels a little like beginning again . . . starting over once more . . . dreaming a fresh dream and getting a glimpse of a new vision. Some of us need a healing of memories. Some have experienced a time of mourning, a time of exile. Some of us have shed more than a few tears over our losses, broken relationships with persons who have been so much a part of our pilgrimage of faith.
>
>   Heal us, O God, and forgive us if success became our idol . . . if we glorified our efficient structure and brilliant organization. Help us to be willing to let go of all that we called "success," and to embrace a greater glory. And God, help us to know in the depths of our being that greater glory doesn't necessarily mean bigger or better or more successful.
>
>   Remind us, O God, that the hour of Jesus' glory was the hour of his cross. And so give us courage to take up the cross of our Lord Jesus Christ, to follow him into a wounded world, and to be found in the ghettos of racism, poverty, oppression, and injustice.
>
>   Pour out your spirit again and again and again on us all, O God, liberating us to dream a new dream and to embrace a vision for the future. Anoint us—your daughters and your sons—to proclaim the gospel good news and to throw open the doors of your kingdom so that all people might find a home. Amen.
>
>   (KMF)

The Lesson from the Hebrew Scriptures   Exodus 20:1-3
>   Leader: This is the Word of God.
>   **People: Thanks be to God.**

The Meditation   Mendlessohn
    The Lord is God
    from *Elijah*

The New Testament Lesson   1 Corinthians 10:14-17
    Leader: This is the Word of God.
    People: Thanks be to God.

The Hymn   BONHOEFFER
    By Gracious Powers

The Morning Prayer
    Where do we go from here, God? What's next? We raise these questions because we prize honesty. But we don't necessarily want to hear their answers because of our discomfort in struggling with anxiety. Perhaps we would do best to focus on what we know rather than to spend time pondering what we don't know. But you understand our tendency to want to know everything.

    Speak to us, God, about that which will enable us to live with confidence and joy in the days ahead. We are concerned about surgeries to resolve medical difficulties, worried about a fragmented nation enduring additional divisions, troubled by destructive conditions in the lives of those we love, intensely interested in the health of our church, and bothered by innumerable other dimensions of our lives. We don't have to receive what we want in every outcome. But we do want assurance that you are in the outcomes or that you will help us cope with whatever developments come our way.

    In this very hour, God, speak to us or move among us in such a way that we embark upon this new year with confidence that you are with us and that you hold us with a love that will never let us go. Amen.

                                                                (CWG)

The Silent Prayers of the People
    By gracious powers so wonderfully sheltered and confidently waiting, come what may, we know that God is with us night and morning and never fails to greet each new day.

Yet is this heart by its old foe tormented, still evil days bring burdens hard to bear; O give our frightened souls the sure salvation for which, O God, you taught us to prepare.

And when this cup you give is filled to brimming with bitter sorrow, hard to understand, we take it thankfully and without trembling, out of so good and so beloved a hand.

Yet when again in this same world you give us the joy we had, the brightness of your sun, we shall remember all the days we lived through, and our whole life shall then be yours alone.

(Dietrich Bonhoeffer, 1944)

The Response   D. Schwoebel
Speak, Lord in the Silence

The Contemporary Lesson

How to measure the immeasurable, how to chart the universe, how to see back to the beginning when so little is observed by the human eye?

God has scattered secrets in the vastness of the stars, noting time and space intertwined like spiraling bubbles emanating from twice-fermented wine.

God is watching from what vantage point? Thinking with such a creative, powerful mind that it has thought all that was, is, and shall be into being; while tending fragile life on this small orb and caring about my experience during an existence that flickers a nanosecond juxtaposed against the twelve billion years some poor scientist has conceived as the age of the universe; by examining feeble formulae that express information little more concisely than a shaman does poking among chicken viscera. Yet, I believe: God has seen fit to let me be, and see, and partake in this reverie.

(RC)

The Anthem   D. Bridges
O Splendor of God's Glory Bright

The Sermon
                        "First Things First"

The Offering of Our Lives and Labors unto God

The Commission of Expectations
- Leader: Surprising God, keep us expectant, open, sensitive, alive.
- **People: When we expect heat, give us a cool rain.**
- Leader: When we expect noise, give us silence.
- **People: When we expect "enough," give us abundance.**
- Leader: When we expect strangers, give us friends.
- **People: When we expect exhaustion, give us rest.**
- Leader: When we expect to receive, give us hands that give.
- **People: When we expect curses, give us blessings.**
- Leader: When we expect things rightside-up, give us upside-down.
- **People: When we expect rewards, give us humility.**
- Leader: When we expect a crowd, give us community.
- **People: When we expect a meal, give us a feast.**
- Leader: When we expect "shoulds," give us grace.
- **People: When we expect walls, give us windows.**
- Leader: When we expect religion, give us a spirited church.
- **People: When we expect fairness, give us lavish love.**
- Leader: When we expect enemies, give us children of God.

(SS)

The Recessional Hymn　　　　　　　　　　REGENT SQUARE
Great Creator God

The Postlude　　　　　　　　　　　　　　Marcel Dupre
The Old Year Is Passed Away

THE WORSHIP OF GOD
Martin Luther King, Jr.'s Birthday/Black History

The observance of the birthday of Martin Luther King, Jr. presents an opportunity for Christian worship built upon and vibrant with themes of the Christian gospel. A worship service related to this occasion can focus on understanding and reconciliation that reach across lines of racial division or any other socially damaging rift in relationships between various members of humankind. Viewed from the convergence of the gospel's message about freedom through Christ and Dr. King's historically-renowned exclamation, "Free at last, free at last," this day begs for worship pulsating with the Christian message of freedom. The service that follows explores, elaborates, and celebrates all of these important themes.

The Prelude   Max Reger
    Prelude and Fugue on "America"

The Prologue   Freedom Song
    Freedom Bound
(The singing of the prologue occurs against the backdrop of actual news film footage of the civil rights movement.)

The Call to Worship
Notice the images and symbols amid which we gather for worship. We live within the tension between that which frees us and that which binds us. The God who said to Pharaoh, "Let my people go," says to us, "Be free and be freeing." Let us worship the God of freedom.

(CWG)

(Display black and white photographs of all races of people struggling for freedom. In close proximity to each photograph, set on display-pedestals various symbols of oppression and bondage—for example: ropes, yokes, chains, bridles, and leather whips.)

The Introit   Freedom Song
    Hallelujah, We Sing Your Praises
(The choir sings from the back of the sanctuary.)

The Processional Hymn LOBE DEN HERREN
Praise to the Lord, the Almighty
(During the singing of the final verse of this hymn, a worship leader walks down the center aisle carrying a simple banner [a large piece of frayed white fabric tied to a rough-hewn pole] and places the banner on the steps to the chancel. Once the banner is placed on the steps, four persons, preferably of different nationalities, carry small massed arrangements of red flowers and place them on different steps alongside the banner, symbolizing persons who have suffered or died as a result of a freedom struggle.)

The Call to Prayer
   Leader: My heart needs a resting place; it is heavily ladened.
   People: We come to this place with our aching hearts to find an easy yoke and a light burden, and discover a shared burden—
   Leader: a yoke across the shoulders of the body of Christ. And amidst the cares of the world,
   Leader: within the pain, with our sisters and brothers in Christ, our hearts find their haven.

(JB)

The Invocation
Gracious God, comfort of the comfortless and hope of the hopeless, grant us hope as we look for a brighter dawn. Give us visions of the City of God, which has no unsightly ghettos or exclusive suburbs. Enable us to dream of the City of God that embraces every race and clan, every nation and land. Give us glimpses of the painful past as we remember the life of Martin Luther King, Jr., and give us glimpses of a brighter future as we pray for our nation this day. Most of all, God, fashion us into makers of peace and prophets of justice. Amen.

(KMF)

The Old Testament Lesson Exodus 6:2-10
   Leader: This is the Word of God.
   People: Thanks be to God.

The Meditation William Dawson
   Soon-ah We'll Be Done

The Contemporary Lesson
> His face drooped, hardened like a frozen mask of tragedy. Inside he wanted to scream, lash out, hurt someone. But who was there to hurt that would lessen his pain? Only himself.
>
> So he took sharp shards of shattered dreams, brittle, broken hopes, and sliced away at the little red demon that had secured itself to his soul. Sharp teeth attached to the tender flesh of his heart causes pain, causes death, causes him to catch his breath, causes him to long for the time before his countenance wilted like a heavy sunflower bowed under the burden of ripeness.
>
> No one knew that behind that contorted face was a wounded heart longing to smile and express the inexpressible longing to melt and open his ego to the world, longing to be noble and lovely, longing to scatter ideas about beauty and truth. But the little red demon chokes him. Beauty and truth do not save him. His heart splinters, and his face bows down to the ground and tears like sunflower seeds fall to the earth and die. Can his tears water the seeds and bring forth something other than his sad, broken, salty story?
>
> (RC)

The Response   WE SHALL OVERCOME
We Shall Overcome

The New Testament Lesson   Galatians 3:23-28
   Leader: This is the Word of the Lord.
   People: Thanks be to God.

The Remembrance
   Leader: When in the streets of America our people were suffering the indignities of injustice and segregation, how beautiful in the streets of Montgomery was this prophet's cry for justice. Yet the shadowed fist of hatred stilled the music of his voice. And now the world awaits to hear the voices of those who, like himself, can sing of peace.
   People: Who dares to lift the song of justice in unjust and dangerous times?

Leader:	When in Birmingham Christian leaders were protesting the agitation of outsiders who cried out for social change, how beautiful from that Birmingham jail was the prophet's call for the radiant stars of love.
Reader:	"Let us hope that the dark clouds of racial prejudice will soon pass away and the radiant stars of love and brotherhood will shine over our great nation."
People:	**But who dares to lift the song of justice in these times?**
Leader:	Those of us who have heard God's voice calling us to be prophets of peace and proclaimers of the gospel of love. And so we respond, "Speak, Lord, for your servant is listening." We take our stand with our oppressed brothers and sisters, and declare the song of liberation. We lift our voices, and our rejoicing rises to the heavens, for our faith has envisioned the rising sun of a new day filled with hope.

(JB)

Hymn   LIFT EVERY VOICE
Lift Every Voice and Sing

Reader:	"Even though we face the difficulties of today and tomorrow, I still have a dream . . . I dream . . . of that day when all of God's children, black and white, Jews and Gentiles, Protestants and Catholics, will be able to join hands and sing . . . 'Free at last! Thank God Almighty, we are free at last!'"
Leader:	Once one person has stood without fear before injustice and felt the focused aim of death, and yet gone on . . . Once the bells of freedom have rung out and broken forth upon the land . . . Once justice has begun to roll down like waters . . . then can love become sovereign and rule gently from sea to shining sea. Brothers and sisters, we have been to the mountain heights; we have seen the promised land. Lift up songs of peace. We shall build anew the cities of our God and reap the harvest of God's

joy among the valleys of grace. We shall be keepers of every previous child of God. The dawn will come at last. The pealing of the freedom bells will cascade from the hills and roll like mighty rivers into the desert of the past.

(KMF)

The Sermon

"You Are God's Children"

The Anthem R. Ringwald
Precious Lord, Take My Hand
(from a speech by Martin Luther King, Jr.)

The Offering of Our Lives and Labors unto God

The Commission
- Leader: I have this dream
- Women: In which pieces
- Men: And in which parts
- **All: Are all brought together—it's a dream of wholeness, a dream of community—**
- Leader: And God says:
- **All: "I will put breath in you, and you will come to life"—a dream made flesh, making its dwelling among us.**
- Leader: Whether rich or poor, male or female, black or white,
- **All: The hand of the Lord is upon us; we are called to prophesy: we have a dream—a dream that can live and breathe in the name of God. Amen.**

(JB)

The Recessional Hymn WESTMINSTER ABBY
For the Healing of the Nations

The Benediction K. Christopher
We Shall Be Free

The Closing Voluntary Henry Purcell
Rondeau

THE WORSHIP OF GOD
Memorial Day

Although Memorial Day began as a civil occasion for recognizing and honoring men and women who lost their lives while serving in the nation's military forces and defending freedom, the day has become an opportunity for recalling the lives of deceased members of a church or a family. Fully aware of both the importance and the pain of remembering loved ones now gone, this service provides opportunities for offering thanksgiving, expressing grief and, most importantly, embracing the challenge to live by a faith that moves us beyond grief.

(Prior to the beginning of worship, in a space outside the worship center, post the names of people in the congregation who have died during the past twelve months. All who gather for worship should be able to see these names as they enter the sanctuary.)

The Prelude   T. G. Albinoni
Adagio in G Minor
(During the Prelude, worship leaders distribute roses—one to each person—memorializing the life of a deceased friend or family member. Attach to each rose a written statement instructing the worshiper to remove the petals from the flower head during the opening of the service and to hold the petals until the offertory during which the separated petals should be placed on the communion table, symbolizing an honest recognition of the reality of death and a faithful committal of the deceased person to the Eternal God.)

The Tolling of the Hour

The Processional
(As the ministers and choir members silently process toward the chancel, readers spaced throughout the processional lines in the various aisles of the worship center read the following verses, creating an antiphonal presentation of fundamental truths.)

Reader 1: I am the resurrection and the life, saith the Lord. He that believeth in me, though he were dead, yet shall he live; and whosoever liveth and believeth in me shall never die.

Reader 2: I know that my Redeemer liveth, and that he shall stand at the latter day upon the earth; and though this body be destroyed, yet shall I see God; whom I shall see for myself and mine eyes shall behold, and not as a stranger.

Reader 3: For none of us liveth to himself, and no man dieth to himself. For if we live, we live unto the Lord; and if we die, we die unto the Lord. Whether we live, therefore, or die, we are the Lord's.

Reader 4: Blessed are the dead who die in the Lord; even so saith the Spirit, for they rest from their labors.

The Book of Common Prayer

The Silent Prayers of Praise and Adoration

The Hymn   St. Anne
O God, Our Help in Ages Past

The Contemporary Lesson   "712" by Emily Dickinson

Because I could not stop for Death—
He kindly stopped for me—
The Carriage held but just Ourselves—
And Immortality.

We slowly drove—He knew no haste
And I had put away
My labor and my leisure, too,
For His Civility—

We passed the school; where children strove
At Recess-in the Ring-
We passed the Fields of Gazing Grain—
We passed the Setting Sun—

Or rather—He passed Us—
The Dews drew quivering and chill—
For only Gossamer, my Gown—
My Tippet—only Tulle—

> We paused before a House that seemed
> A Swelling of the Ground—
> The Roof was scarcely visible—
> The Cornice—in the Ground.
>
> Since then—'tis centuries—and yet
> Feels shorter than the Day
> I first surmised the Horses' Heads
> Were toward Eternity.

The Meditation   D. McCullough
We Remember Them

The Sermon
"Living Beyond Grief"

The Commendation   *Requiem* by David Huff

Introit
Kyrie
Sanctus
Benedictus
Offertory

(During the singing of the offertory, invite the congregants to bring their rose petals to the chancel and place them on the altar as a memorial to the lives of the persons remembered.)

Pie Jesu
Agnus Dei
Communion

The Call to Confession   Matthew 11:28
Come to me, all you who are weary and burdened, and I will give you rest.

The Silent Prayers of Confession

The Words of Assurance   Romans 8:26-39

The Silent Communion

The Retiring Procession   Psalms 90; 121

(As the ministers and choir members silently move toward the exit of the worship center, once again readers spaced throughout the processional lines in the various aisles of the worship center read antiphonally, this time using the texts of the two psalms.)

The Commission   P. Leddington Wright
Fight the Good Fight

The Postlude   C. Saint-Saens
Maestroso
from Symphony No. 3

THE WORSHIP OF GOD
Independence Day

Giving thanks to God for freedom is an act of worship as ancient as the children of Israel offering praises to God on their way out of slavery in Egypt headed toward the freedom of the promised land. On Independence Day, worship leaders must exercise great caution lest a service of Christian worship degenerate into a celebration of nationalism or a glorification of exclusivistic patriotism. The Fourth of July is a good time for focusing on the meaning of freedom, distinguishing between political freedom and spiritual freedom, and celebrating the freedom we enjoy as Christians and as Americans.

The Prelude   J. W. Kerr
Festival Fanfare and Prelude on God of Our Fathers
(As congregants enter the worship center, designated individuals wrap strips of white gauze, 15-18 inches long, around their wrists and present to them a printed order of worship marked with a ribbon tied to a small bell on each end.)

The Prologue   Psalm 44:1-8

The Prayer of Invocation
> O Lord, in you our souls find rest. You, Eternal One, set our spirits free to soar. But, O God, how often do we find ourselves shackled with the chains of our passions? How can we freely fly when our souls are heavy with the yokes we choose to wear? Have mercy, O God. Reach out your hand once again. Forgive us for the bondage we have accepted. Forgive us for the bonds we have created for others. Free our lives. Make your light to shine through our darkness so that we can find that way. Free us to climb to the heights you imagined. Loosen the things in our lives that hold us back from being the creation you intended. Shelter us in the shadow of your wings. Call us louder, O God. Call out so that the noise and wars of our lives will not distract us, but that we will clearly hear your voice, so still, so small. Call us to this new day and free us to bind closer to you for the rest of the journey. Amen.
>
> (DWN)

The Processional Hymn   NETTLETON
                    Once a People Came Together
(On verse 2, two people move down the center aisle, with their arms extended above their heads. They pull a piece of red fabric, 8-10 yards long, up the chancel steps, across the chancel, and move out of sight on the right side of the chancel. On verse 3, two other people move down the center aisle, with their arms extended above their heads, pulling a similar piece of blue fabric up the chancel steps and across the chancel, exiting out of sight on the left side. Neither fabric should touch the tables at the front of the worship center. On verse 4, two more people move down the center aisle, with their arms extended above their heads, pulling a similar piece of white fabric. The fabric flows across a table that sits at the base of the chancel steps with the front edge of the fabric ascending the chancel steps and resting across another table positioned in the center of the chancel. The white fabric has become the tablecloths for the two tables that, later in the service, will be used as communion tables.)

The Call to Worship
    Leader: Come, let us declare our Jubilee and proclaim liberty to the captives . . .
    Reader: Let us stand in the shadow of bondage and sing a song of anger!
    People: But our song is a gentle song. We must not sing a song of anger.
    Leader: **Come, let us declare Jubilee and proclaim freedom to those who are bound in huge and heavy chains.**
    Reader: Let us stand in the darkness of slavery and sing a song of anger!
    People: **But our song is a quiet song. We must not sing a song of anger.**
    Leader: Come, let us declare the year of Jubilee and proclaim new hope to those who are oppressed.
    Reader: Let us stand in the gloom of injustice and sing a song of anger!
    People: **But our song is a pleasant song. We must not sing a song of anger.**

Leader: Come, let us declare glorious Jubilee and proclaim release to all who are enslaved.
Reader: May our songs of anger transform us . . . shattering our prisons of the spirit . . . breaking the bars that hold us.
All: As liberated children of a liberating God, let us stand in the freedom Christ has given us until that day when our songs of anger become songs of lively hope . . . until the spirit of God's Jubilee descends upon us.

(KMF)

The Meditation   African American Spiritual
Let My People Go

The Silent Prayers of the People

The Gospel Lesson   John 8:31-38
    Leader: The holy gospel of our Lord and Savior Jesus Christ.
    People: Praise be to you, O Christ.

The Epistle Lesson   Galatians 5:1, 13a
    Leader: This is what the Spirit is saying to the churches.
    People: Thanks be to God.

The Hymn   AZMON
O for a World

The Attestations of Liberty
    Leader 1: Magistrates are not by virtue of their office to meddle with religion or matters of conscience, to force or compel people to this or that form of religion. (John Symth, 1612)
    People: We rejoice in our freedom and accept the charge to live faithfully within it.
    Leader 2: No king or bishop can or is able to command faith that is the gift of God. To constrain princes and peoples to receive the one true religion of the gospel is wholly against the mind and merciful law of Christ. (Leonard Busher, 1614)

People: **We rejoice in our freedom and accept the charge to live faithfully within it.**

Leader 1: Every person ought to be left free with respect to matters of religion. The Holy Author of our religion needs no compulsive measures for the promotion of God's cause. (General Committee of Baptists in Virginia, 1785)

People: **We rejoice in our freedom and accept the charge to live faithfully within it.**

Leader 2: Everyone must give a personal account to God, and therefore all people ought to be at liberty to serve God in a way that each can best reconcile to [their] own conscience. (John Leland, 1719)

People: **We rejoice in our freedom and accept the charge to live faithfully within it.**

Leader 1: Religion must be forever voluntary and uncoerced. It is not the prerogative of any power to compel people to conform to any religious creed or form of worship, or to worship, or to pay taxes for the support of a creed they do not believe. God wants free worshipers and no other kind. (George W. Truett, 1920)

People: **We rejoice in our freedom and accept the charge to live faithfully within it.**

(Reid Trulson[1])

The Hymn   CWM RHONDDA
God of Grace and God of Glory

The Sermon
"The Price of Freedom"

The Anthem   Roy Ringwald
The Battle Hymn of the Republic

The Prayer of Dedication
Almighty God, you are the author of all that is worthy and just. We are drawn close to you. In your boundless compassion you have awarded us an immeasurable gift. You have

given us freedom to follow and to worship you in this land. Lord, you are merciful; you care for us in the midst of our struggles. And you have sent a son so filled with love that his life and death and life again shattered the bond of oppression.

Our souls yearn to bring forth your kingdom on earth, to continue the inheritance of freedom, to stand against injustice wherever it may be found. Lord, we pray for strength to resist tyranny that blights, distorts, and maims. We know that through Christ's resurrection the chains of captivity can be broken; we know that the promise of liberty is in your Truth. We thank you for this precious gift and for your vision of loving equality. Help us and guide us, O Lord, as we seek to fulfill your mission on earth. Amen.

(ET)

The Invitation

Now it is time for us to unbind our neighbors and ourselves and to experience freedom. As strange as it sounds, we unbind ourselves to bind ourselves. We put off bondage in order to take on liberty. Please turn to the person beside you and untie the symbol of bondage on that individual's wrist.

(CWG)

The Hymn of Commitment   ST. ANNE
   We Bind Ourselves in Freedom's Chains
(During the singing of this hymn, worshipers are invited to bring their broken symbols of bondage to the altar and leave them there.)

The Sign of Freedom

Now, free and freeing people, let freedom ring. Let freedom ring in this worship center. Let freedom ring throughout this land. O, people of God, let freedom ring. Let freedom ring!

(CWG)

(Worshipers lift the bells from the printed order of worship and begin to ring them as an act of renewed commitment to living as children of God. Worshipers continue ringing the bells as they exit the sanctuary.)

The Postlude   Flor Peeters
   God of Our Fathers

THE WORSHIP OF GOD
Labor Day

Work and worship are integrally related in a Christian's life. Worship is a form of work—liturgy is the "work of the people"—and work properly done is a form of worship. The following service explores this important relationship and recognizes the spiritual meaning of our daily labor.

The Preludes
Prelude on Gibbons Song 46 — Leo Sowerby
Prelude on Tallis' Canon — Richard Purvis
Partita on O God Our Help in Ages Past — Jan Bender

(As congregants gather for worship, they encounter people dressed in clothing appropriate to their respective daily jobs—e.g., doctors in scrubs, construction workers in hard hats, dancers in leotards and dance shoes, nurses in uniforms. These individuals represent using their daily skills to help persons in need. For example, an interior designer may be making draperies for a homeless shelter, a dentist may be working in a makeshift office in a community center, and a teacher may be instructing immigrants in the English language.)

The Welcome

The Prologue — J. Rutter
All Things Bright and Beautiful

The Call to Worship
Leader: When my rights become more important than the right thing,
All: Create in me a clean heart, O God.
Leader: When his job well done causes me to become undone,
All: Renew a right spirit in me.
Leader: When I can't celebrate her contribution because of my own ambition,
All: Sustain in me a willing spirit.
Leader: When my labor lacks your love,
All: Create in me a clean heart, O God.

(SE)

Civil Holidays

The Introit   MORNING SONG
Awake, Awake to Love and Work
(Prior to the service, set assorted alarm clocks in the chancel area—on tables, pedestals, the floor. Set each clock to alarm at the time of the introit. As the alarms sound, the people whom worshipers encountered prior to the service performing their jobs in unlikely places go to the clocks, turn off the alarms, and then take seats in the congregation. The congregation consists of different people with a variety of gifts that can be used for others and the glory of God.)

The Prayer of Invocation
God, we confess that we are weary, because we have allowed our lives to be taken over by the mundane. We no longer expect surprises from you. We no longer greet each day with joy. We think we've seen it all, and we're bored with most of it. We don't want to face our pain or each other's pain. We want to sit in numbness and let platitudes wash over us like some kind of harmless balm. We ask that you would wake us up to the eternal, the joyful, the delightful.

    Give us strength to withstand the afflictions that go with our earthen natures. Give us energy to cope with the changes happening around us. But most of all, we ask that you would not allow us to sleepwalk through our journey with you. We ask that you would come among us and make your presence known in such a way that we cannot remain numb, in such a way that we will say, with new energy and delight, "Here we are. Tell us what to do." In Christ's name, we pray. Amen.

                                                                                               (LKC)

The Processional Hymn   HYMN TO JOY
God, Creation's Great Designer

The Psalm   Psalm 90:1-2, 16-17
    Leader: The Word of God.
    People: Thanks be to God.

A Litany of Awareness
    Leader: Moses was keeping the flock of his father-in-law. Meg Cullar was working with Habitat. Gayland Sims was in the operating room at Hillcrest.

People:	**We are busy with our daily schedules—juggling family, and work, and leisure, and church.**
Leader:	Linda McManness is teaching in Spain. Alan House is doing a social work internship in Virginia.
People:	**We are spread out—affirming the unique calling each of us has to be and to do.**
Leader:	It is in the ordinariness of our living that we look for our God; it is in the ordinariness of our living that our God is at work:
People:	**In the building of homes for those without—in the healing of the sick—in the excitement of learning—in serving others—**
Leader:	In as many ways as there are people here, God works to redeem creation.
People:	**We are a community of believers affirming that it is here, and now, that our God speaks to us—our God calls us—our God leads us—into worship, and into the way we are to be.**

(JB)

The Meditation   D. Schwoebel
A Reflection of Christ

The New Testament Lesson   Ephesians 4:11-16
    Leader: The Word of God.
    People: Thanks be to God.

The Hymn   BEACH SPRING
Take My Gifts and Let Me Love You

The Litany
Leader:	For the tacks, splinters, and bare floors.
All:	**God, in everything we give you thanks.**
Leader:	For the landings and the corners.
All:	**God, in everything we give you thanks.**
Leader:	For the darkness.
All:	**God, in everything we give you thanks.**
Leader:	For the work of our hands and the labors of our love.
All:	**God, in everything we give you thanks.**

> Leader: For the hope and faith, for the crystal stair.
> **All: God, in everything we give you thanks.**
>
> (SE)

The Anthem   Allen Pote
> *Many Gifts, One Spirit*

The Sermon
> "What Is Your Work?"

The Offering of Our Lives and Labors unto God

The Meditation   Bob Burroughs
> *Jesus, My Lord, My Life, My All*

The Invitation

The Commission
> Leader: Alright. We've been given a job. We are not as we were created to be, and neither is our world.
> **People: God has trusted us with the work of redemption. We are the body of Christ,**
> Leader: And the same mind that was in Christ Jesus is ours for the asking.
> **People: God, incarnate in us, is working to transform all that is, and the choices of our day-to-day will help—or hinder.**
> Leader: How unsearchable are God's judgments; how inscrutable are God's ways.
> **People: We believe that we shall see the goodness of the Lord in the land of the living.**
> **All: Be strong—let our hearts take courage. We work for what is good and acceptable and perfect.**
>
> (JB)

The Recessional Hymn   AUSTRIA
> *We Are Called to Be God's People*

The Closing Voluntary   D. Wood
> *Guide Me Ever, Great Redeemer*

THE WORSHIP OF GOD
Thanksgiving Day

The following service is planned for mid-morning on Thanksgiving Day to provide worshipers an opportunity to express thanks to God in the context of a community of faith. The service is simple in structure and eucharistic in spirit. Its central focus is the collection of individual prayers brought together as "the great thanksgiving."

(On the Sunday prior to Thanksgiving Day, request members of the congregation to compose one or two sentences that express their most basic reasons for gratitude and collect these statements at the conclusion of the morning worship service. Categorize the various contributions by topic or theme—e.g., daily needs, treasures of the church, companions on the journey—and combine these categories, with natural progression, to form "The Great Thanksgiving," which is a prayer of the people. Display various expressions of bounty throughout the entrance to the worship center—offerings of grain; offerings of the sea; offerings of flowers, vegetation, and fruit. Each offering, bound in small clusters or containers, can easily be carried into the sanctuary by an individual. Worshipers respectively choose an offering of importance to their lives because of its power to reveal the presence of holiness. Using these offerings, upon entering the worship center, every worshiper is encouraged to present an expression of thanksgiving to a worship leader standing at the chancel. As the various items of offering are collected, a worship leader assembles them on a table as a visible sign of thanksgiving.)

The Carillon Prelude   Wilbur Held
    Come Ye, Thankful People, Come

The Call to Worship   Psalm 95 from *Psalms Now*

The Bidding
    Leader: God, you surround us with invitations to abundant living:
    People: **The beauty of creation, the wonder of relationships, and, above all, the mystery of your presence.**

Leader:	You created us with eyes to see and do not expect us to live as though blind.
People:	**We choose to see . . . or not. We choose to live . . . or not.**
Leader:	Bring wisdom to our choices, O God,
People:	**That our lives might be abundant, bringing honor and glory to you.**

(JB)

The Prayer of Praise and Adoration

God of Brother Sun and Sister Moon, Sister Water and Brother Fire, we thank you together for the gifts that are all about us: for the majesty and variety of your creation and for the fact that you seem to want us to enjoy these gifts—the colors in the sunset, in a field of flowers, in each other's faces—and that you seem to want us to delight in the size of the oceans and the orchid seed and to wonder at the tiny light of Brother Firefly.

But we have grown too weary, too hectic, and too wise to take delight in your gifts anymore. We thirst for beauty, but we have forgotten how to see it. This is our confession.

We ask you this morning to come and dwell with us. We ask you to restore our sense of wonder and awe, to restore our joy in knowing you and exulting in the simple surprises you have placed all around us. Heal our weariness, our busyness, our self-importance, and our cynicism. May we never fail to see what you want us to see: the world in need or the random beauty.

(LKC)

The Processional Hymn — LAAST UNS ERFREUEN
To You, O God, All Creatures Sing

The Hebrew Lesson — Deuteronomy 8:7-18

The Response — OLD HUNDREDTH
All People That on Earth Do Dwell

The New Testament Lesson — Ephesians 5:24

The Sermon
  "Give Thanks for Everything?"

The Organ Meditation   Alice Jordan
  Dialogue for Thanksgiving

The Great Thanksgiving
  (Four worship leaders offer this congregationally-constructed prayer with each standing at one corner of the communion table facing into the table.)

The Offering of Our Lives and Labors unto God

The Silent Thanksgiving

The Recessional Hymn   DIADEMATA
  Praise to the Living God

The Postlude   G. F. Kaufman
  Nun Danket Alle Gott

NOTE

[1]Reid Trulson, *For the Living of These Days: Resources for Enriching Worship*, ed. Michael Hawn (Macon GA: Smyth & Helwys, 1995) 36.

Thanksgiving Gathering (above)
"Many Gifts, One Spirit" (right)

Special Services

THE WORSHIP OF GOD
WORLD COMMUNION SUNDAY

Seldom does a congregation have the privilege of acting in unison with other Christian congregations throughout the world. An observance of World Communion Sunday allows worshipers to identify with Christians everywhere and experience the joy of sharing communion with seen and unseen members of the community of faith. The following service draws each participant into the life and ministry of the whole family of God.

(Prior to the service, place an auxiliary table at each corner of the communion table. Drape each table with a fabric that distinctly represents a specific area of the world—ex: Asia, Africa, South America, and Europe. Carefully select fabrics with different textures and colors.)

The Carillon Prelude   Peal on Te Deum

The Opening Voluntary   Cook
  Fanfare

The Prologue   K. Lee Scott
  Holy God, We Praise Your Name

The Call to Worship   Psalm 105:1
  (Repeat this verse in as many different languages as possible—Spanish, German, French, Italian, Russian, and Hebrew as well as English. Position readers in each of the four corners of the worship center to symbolize readings from the four corners of the earth.)

The Introit   G. Young
  From All That Dwell Below the Skies

The Prayer of Praise
  Dear God, we thank you for this band of pilgrims gathered here today, for the glad reunion we experience when we see each other's faces, and for the communion we have with those we lift in prayer. Remind us that in your Spirit we are one pilgrim band with all who travel toward you. Remind us of that

crazy paradox: that even as we travel toward your city, we also live there. So, do not let us grow weary in sharing our stories, in helping each other along the way, in inviting others to join us. Thank you for sending us Jesus to be our guide. Amen.

(JWC)

The Processional Hymn   LASST UNS ERFREUEN
To You, O God, All Creatures Sing
(Position four people among the choir processional, each carrying a banner that represents a region of the world. Behind each banner bearer, position two people, one carrying a loaf of bread typical of that region and the other carrying a cup representing that area of the world. One banner should be placed behind each of the auxiliary tables as the bread and cup from that region are set on the table.)

The Call to Community
    Leader: Our paths converge. Who will I be to you? I choose:
    People: **To extend my hand—open; or to withdraw my hand—closed.**
    Leader: Will I show you me, or some carefully constructed façade?
    People: **Do you matter to me, or could I care less? Are you enjoyed, or endured?**
    Leader: I could learn from you:
    People: **In laughter shared . . . and tears; telling you my dreams . . . and fears.**
    Leader: Our paths converge. Who will I be to you? I choose:
    People: **. . . in so many small ways . . .**
    Leader: I choose . . .
    People: **. . . in all my ways.**
    Leader: Our paths converge. Who will I be? I choose,
    People: **. . . and that will make all the difference.**

(JB)

The Reflection   R. Thompson
The Road Not Taken

The Prayer of the People
O God, our creator, whose love sustains us with every breath we take, we offer ourselves in worship to you.

As we listen to the silence that surrounds us in these moments of prayer, we confess that often we have no space in our lives for the working of your Spirit.

So many desires and concerns drown out the quiet voice of your presence within our hearts.

Forgive us for our cluttered lives, for our inattention to your voice.

We confess, O God, that often not only do we not love our enemies—those who do us wrong—but we also do not acknowledge our common humanity.

We fail to remember that you gave yourself freely to be reconciled with them as well as with us. Empower us, Lord, with mercy and compassion towards all those who have caused us grief and pain. Suffer with them as you suffer with us.

And as we gather today in communion with believers all over this world, we pray for them even as we pray for ourselves.

Dear Lord, comfort those who are grieving, whose loved ones are in danger or who face death. Give wisdom to those who are in confusion about which direction to take. Send your deep peace to those whose hearts are so wracked with anger and hatred that they are unable to recognize your face in the faces of those around them.

Let the good news of your redeeming love be made known to all people on this earth who do not know you, and strengthen those who minister in your name.

Incline our hearts to you, O God, as we worship you and commune with one another this day,

In the name of Christ, who is himself our peace, Amen.

(JRS)

The Gospel Lesson   Matthew 12:46-50; 26:26-29
    Reader: This is the holy gospel of our Lord and Savior Jesus Christ.
    People: **Praise be to you, O Christ.**

The Hymn   NETTLETON
        Christian Hearts, in Love United

The Revelation to John   Revelation 7:9-17

The Anthem   John Weaver
    The Joyful Feast

The Sermon
    "All in the Family"

The Doxology   OLD HUNDREDTH
  Praise God from whom all blessings flow,
  Praise Christ all creatures here below.
  Alleluia! Alleluia!
  Praise Holy Spirit, Comforter,
  One God, triune, Whom we adore.
  Alleluia! Alleluia!
  Alleluia! Alleluia!
  Alleluia! Amen.

                                                                                                (DHC)

The Service of Communion

The Communion Meditation
    The world is spiritually hungry, so we throw out stale religious crumbs to tempt sparrow-souls into prim, proper, Protestant prisons of ornate orthodoxy. Trapped behind black iron bars of dogma and doctrine, these fragile creatures are forced to consume exact ideas of a deity who performs only after a litany of flattery.

    Such religion is a pitifully diluted nourishment giving to nurturing sustenance. Having consumed such a sour, scant meal, their spirits starve. In desperate hunger they then turn to any offered spirituality, drinking more and more thin milk when they need bread and wine for life.

    God, the bountiful provider, is outside their prison. Bigger than their lamentable, clinical systematic theologies, the sparrow-souls seem too weak to soar across expansive vistas, through azure others where freedom waits hidden behind the purple pencil line of the horizon.

                                                                                                (RC)

The Communion Prayer
> God of body—God of blood, Word made flesh in our midst: speak to us. God of body—God of blood: speak through us words of transformation, words of healing, and love words for each one here, words for our community, words for our world, words made flesh in our ministry and in our love as we grow in our faith.
>
> God of body—broken for all, God of blood—shed for all: prepare us for our breaking, that of our bodies and of our blood your word might anoint all your children to proclaim the time of God's favor, to proclaim freedom and justice for all, and we might once again hear the sound of God walking in our midst and joyfully and thankfully choose to walk humbly with our God. Amen.
>
> (JB)

The Distribution of the Elements

The Meditation   E. Copley
> *Surely He Hath Borne Our Griefs*

The Invitation

The Recessional Hymn   WESTMINSTER ABBEY
> *Christ Is Made the Sure Foundation*

The Benediction
> O God, make of us a fellowship of people who share in common the taste of bread and wine in our mouths and an impassioned love for each other in our hearts. O God, bless us, sustain us, and keep on strengthening us as the body of Christ. Amen.
>
> (CWG)

The Closing Voluntary   Soler
> *The Emperor's Concerto*

THE WORSHIP OF GOD
World Hunger Sunday

The specter of hunger in our homeland and around the world challenges the spirit of compassion and the commitment to mission that throb at the heart of a Christian fellowship. Many denominations now recommend an annual observance of a world hunger emphasis. The following service contains elements to inform, educate, and motivate Christians to address the critical problem by means of prayer, financial support, and social action.

(Set up a community information desk at the entrance to the worship center. Enlist representatives of various social service organizations to share literature on their work and offer suggestions as to how the church can become involved in their missions—e.g., food banks, food pantries, shelters, soup kitchens.)

The Carillon Prelude　　　　　　Paraphrase on *Mit Freuden Zart*

The Opening Voluntary　　　　　　　　　　　　Buxtehude
　　Prelude, Fugue, and Chaconne

The Prologue　　　　　　　　　　　　　　　　J. Rutter
　　Open Thou Mine Eyes

The Call to Worship
　　Leader:　God is great.
　　People:　God is good.
　　Leader:　Let us thank God
　　People:　for our food.
　　Leader:　More than 34 million Americans are threatened by hunger; 11 million actually go hungry each year.
　　People:　God is great.
　　Leader:　Well over one billion people—nearly 6% of the world's inhabitants—survive on less than $1 a day.
　　People:　God is good.
　　Leader:　In developing countries 34% of children under the age of 5 are undernourished.
　　People:　Let us thank God?

Leader:	Numbers are connected to names, and names to real people in real poverty. Figures and facts translate into tragedy and pain. We can change the facts.
People:	**Open our eyes to these, your children. Help us be your goodness. Allow us to reveal your greatness.**
All:	**Let us thank God.**

(JB)

The Introit   K. Lee Scott
Open Your Eyes

The Prayer of Praise

Our God, there is much we don't understand, much that we as human beings do to each other that shouldn't even be possible.

And we tend to want to find answers; we tend to want to find reasons so that we can understand, so that we can explain, and we don't know what to do when we can't find any.

May we be reminded that it is not in answers and reasons that we find you, but that within the reality of our experiences, we find you, find your grief, find your tears.

Within the reality of our experience, we meet you to be comforted—not by answers but by presence, not by explanations but by love.

We gather here today, a group of people with diverse experiences, and we pray for each other, that within all our experience, we might find you—alive, real, overwhelming.

May we then make your presence real through our experience with others.

We do this with your grace. We do this through your Spirit. We do this in hope.

We pray this in the name of Jesus Christ, our Lord. Amen.

(JB)

The Call to Praise   Jane Marshall
We Would Offer Thee This Day

The Processional Hymn   LYONS
We Worship You, God

The Old Testament Lesson   Deuteronomy 15:11
   Leader: This is the Word of God.
   People: Thanks be to God.

The Meditation   Roy Ringwald
           The Crowded Ways

The New Testament Lesson   1 Corinthians 11:20-29
   Leader: This is what the Spirit is saying to the churches.
   People: Thanks be to God.

The Hymn   SEMINARY
           Because I Have Been Given Much

The Gospel Lesson   Matthew 25:31-46
   Leader: The holy gospel of our Lord and Savior Jesus Christ.
   People: Praise be to you, O Christ.

The Anthem   K. Medema
                  I Was Hungry
               from *The Gathering*

The Sermon
        "A View of Hunger from the Communion Table"

The Offering of Our Lives and Labors unto God
   (Invite congregants to gather at the conclusion of worship to assemble food baskets. Form numerous small groups that will depart from the church and immediately distribute this food where homeless people congregate throughout the community or in other obvious place of need. Local police officers can help identify the places where needs are the greatest. These officers will gladly accompany the various groups of worshipers on their missions of mercy.)

The Meditation   Menken/Schwartz
              God Help the Outcast

The Service of Communion

The Call to Communion
   Leader: God of compassion, we stand before you with heads
              that are full of confusion and hearts that are heavy,

for there is pain all around us and throughout the world. We know that you never intended this pain, and we grieve.

People: **As you once healed the sick and the blind, the lame and infirmed in Palestine, we ask you to heal again. We ask for healing of inner hurts and outer infirmities.**

Leader: Our sisters and brothers, God, in faraway lands and in nearby cities, are suffering from poverty and dying from hunger. We watch in mounting desperation, for we know not what to do; we know not how to stop the pain.

People: **As you once increased the loaves and fishes, the lunch offering of a small boy, we ask you to increase our humble gifts and use them to feed the hungry multitudes.**

Leader: We want to be good stewards of your gifts. We search for ways to pour ourselves out for the needs of the world, but we do not always know the right way. Sometimes we stumble, and sometimes we grope.

People: **Maker of light, illumine our ways. Guide our faltering steps. Show us the way to walk and the way to give. Show us the need on our doorstep. Help us to see your face in the faces of our brothers and sisters in need.**

All: **Grant that you might never say to any of us, "I was hungry, and you turned me away."**

(LKC)

The Prayer Before Communion
Leader: God of the poor and the oppressed, God of the downtrodden, God of all of us: We are wealthy Christians in a world of hunger and poverty. We have wept for hungry and suffering children in the Third World. We have wept for people in our nation who live in want. And now, O Lord, we are

weeping because they seek food on the streets—our city, in the shadow of our state capitol, in the porticos of our buildings, and on the steps of our churches—Baptist, Methodist, Catholic, Episcopal—wherever they might find help. They wander aimlessly on our streets—Louisiana, Main, Chester, University. Now, O Lord, they have come to our own doorstep seeking to be filled from our overflow. And we are weeping now for those nearby, not far away. We see them up close now, and it is not so easy for us to turn away.

Unison: **Lord, who executes justice for the oppressed; who gives food to the hungry; who lifts up those who are bowed down; give us strength to cease our weeping, and give us the heart to share our possessions with the poor—those who are nearby and those who are far away, those who meet us at our doorstep and those who are in distant places. And forgive us, O Lord, for our excesses, for our lifestyles of wasting rather than sharing. Help us to avoid laying up treasures and possessions. Help us to know prosperity and poverty with equal grace. Through Jesus Christ our Helper, who knew weeping and sharing. Amen.**

(*Use street names in your city, with the last one being the street on which your church is located.)

(KMF)

The Invitation to the Table

Ordinarily we come to the communion table to eat. Today, however, we come to the communion table to give. Regularly, from this table we have received the gifts of God to satisfy our hunger. Today we lay on this table our gifts to satisfy the hunger of others.

(DWN)

(Worshipers move to the communion table and place on it their gifts to help feed other people—staple food items or money that after the service will be delivered to places where people are hungry.)

The Invitation   S. Curry
    If Not Us, Then Who?

The Recessional Hymn   HYFRYDOL
    Christ Has Called Us to New Visions

The Benediction
    God of compassion, we want to be good stewards of your gifts. We search for ways to pour ourselves out for the needs of the world, but we do not always know the right way. Sometimes we stumble, and sometimes we grope.
    Maker of light, illumine our ways. Guide our faltering steps. Show us the way to walk and the way to give. Show us the need on our very doorstep. Help us to see your face in the faces of our brothers and sisters in need.
    Grant that you might never say to any of us, "I was hungry, and you turned me away." Amen.

                                                              (LKC)

The Closing Voluntary   Beatrice Miller
    A Balm in Gilead

THE WORSHIP OF GOD
Reformation Sunday

Though Reformation Sunday is sometimes associated exclusively with congregations in the Lutheran tradition of Christianity, observances of this special Sunday hold the potential for meaningful worship in a wide variety of Christian churches. The following service draws from the Reformation of the sixteenth century the inspiration and courage to take a hard look at fundamental convictions of importance to the maintenance of integrity in the life and ministry of the contemporary church.

(In preparation for this service, hand print—in calligraphy or in some other special lettering—your church's covenant on 8-10 yards of white canvas. Hang this canvas as a canopy over the chancel area of the worship center so that it forms a backdrop for the pulpit. Also place large wooden boards or constructed frames against the walls of the worship center. These pieces should contain the heads of nails already driven into them. Make available numerous hammers in various places throughout the worship center. Place in each printed order of worship a blank sheet of paper.)

The Prelude   Jan Bender
   Ein feste Burg ist unser Gott
   "A Mighty Fortress Is Our God"

The Opening Voluntary   Dietrich Buxtehude
   Choral Prelude on Ein Feste Burg

The Opening Sentences
   Reformation Sunday directs attention to the distant past. In the sixteenth century, Martin Luther, inspired by Christian scriptures and motivated by an impassioned love for the Christian church, would not be silenced or stopped as he began a reform movement in the Roman Catholic Church. In Wittenburg, Germany, the courageous former monk posted propositions for debate intended to strengthen God's work in and through the church.

Reformation Sunday calls attention to the recent past. In the second half of the twentieth century, Pope John XXIII, committed to a meaningful communication of the gospel and concerned with the church's relevance to those to whom it would minister, called the Roman Catholic Church to a period of *aggiornamento*—a time of updating and change. The gentle beloved pontiff opened the windows of the church and allowed the fresh winds of God's Spirit to stir changes within that enhanced the church's ministry to the world.

Reformation Sunday focuses attention on the present and the future. Though celebrated primarily by congregations in the Protestant tradition of Christianity, Reformation Sunday poses the question as to whether or not other communions can change as dramatically and as positively as has the Roman Catholic Church. What about this church, our church?

Reformation Sunday is a time to celebrate church reforms of the past and to open the church of the present to reforms needed to enhance its ministry now and in the future.

(CWG)

The Prologue   J. Van
Psalm 131

The Prayer of Praise and Adoration
> O God, we praise you as the source of our strength. We reach out to you for help in times of trouble. We rush to you when we seek refuge. We know you as a bulwark never failing. O God, we adore you as the source of our salvation. We meet you in the Christ. We sense your power even within the smallest word you speak. We discover that your saving reign is ever. O God, hear our praise and accept our adoration. Amen.

(CWG)

The Call to Worshyp
> Leader: This is the day of our Sovereign God. We gather to affirm our faith.
> **People: Eternal God is our refuge and strength.**
> Leader: We have come to worship the God of our mothers and fathers.

People: **The Lord Almighty is with us; the God of Jacob is our fortress.**
Leader: We open our hearts and our lives to our Sovereign and consider the greatness of the Eternal One.
People: **We place our trust in the Almighty. Our God is from everlasting to everlasting.**

(DWN)

The Introit   J. Ness Beck
Psalm 46

The Processional Hymn   HYFRYDOL
God of History, Recent, Ancient

The Epistle   Romans 1:8-17
  Leader: The Word of the Lord.
  People: **Thanks be to God.**

The Response   LANDAS
My Faith Has Found a Resting Place

The Lesson   C. Welton Gaddy[1]

God does a surprising amount of good with very bad situations. This truth has been readily apparent since the divinely orchestrated exodus of Israel from Egypt. Nowhere was it ever clearer than in God's ability to transform a hideous crucifixion in the Middle East into an event of cosmic redemption. Now, God is at it again.

Out of the denominational turmoil of recent years, the conflicts that have arisen in local congregations, and the sense of spiritual homelessness that has shrouded so many individuals, God is shaping new families of faith and creating novel structures for faith development. New visions are generating influential missions. Fellowships dedicated to inclusiveness are developing. The gospel is being proclaimed apart from the prejudices and traditions of certain mindsets and particular cultures.

Involvement in new initiatives can be scary at first. Friends do not understand the impatience with old ways and eagerness to try something better. Criticism abounds. Enemies proliferate. "The establishment" plasters the new venturers with labels aimed at raising suspicion about them and nurturing a fear of them. In the midst of suspicion and hurt, however, certainty develops: "God is in this; we are doing right."

The Anthem   M. Hayes
A Mighty Fortress

The Sermon
"96 Theses"
(At the conclusion of each section of the sermon, the preacher moves to the communion table and places there his or her theses for consideration and discussion by members of the congregation.)

Theses on Liberty

The Hymn   EIN FESTE BURG
Behold what wondrous deeds of peace
God does for our salvation;
God knows our wars and makes them cease
In ev'ry land and nation.
The warrior's spear and lance
Are splintered by God's glance:
The guns and nuclear might
Stand withered in God's sight;
The Lord of hosts is with us.

Theses on Theology

The Hymn   EIN FESTE BURG
God's Word forever shall abide,
No thanks to foes, who fear it;
For God on high fights by our side
With weapons of the Spirit.
Though they may take our house,
Goods, fame, or child, or spouse,
Or wretch our life away,
They cannot win the day.
God's realm is ours forever!

Theses on Polity

The Hymn   EIN FESTE BURG

> Though hordes of devils fill the land
> All threat'ning to devour us,
> We tremble not, unmoved we stand;
> They cannot overpow'r us.
> This worldly prince may rage,
> In fiercest war engage.
> His plan is doomed to fail;
> God's judgment must prevail!
> One little word subdues him.

Theses on Worship

The Hymn   EIN FESTE BURG

> No strength of ours can match God's might!
> We should be lost, rejected.
> But now a champion comes to fight,
> Whom God alone elected.
> Ask ye who tis may be:
> Lord Jesus Christ is he!
> The Great Atoning One,
> God's own Redeemer, Son.
> He holds the field victorious.

Theses on Ministry

The Hymn   EIN FESTE BURG

> A mighty fortress is our God,
> A bulwark never failing:
> Protecting us with staff and rod.
> And power all-prevailing.
> What I the nations rage
> And surging seas rampage;
> What though the mountains fall,
> The Lord is God of all;
> The Lord of hosts is with us.

Special Services

The Invitation
Do people still hold convictions with the passion evidenced in Martin Luther? What about you? For what, if anything, are you willing to sacrifice for your faith—position, reputation, monetary gain, relationships, freedom, or perhaps even life?

In your printed order of worship, you will find a blank piece of paper. Use it as a canvas on which to record the nonnegotiable of your faith.

Around the room you see hammers and boards intended to serve as your Wittenberg Church Door. Please move to the space of your choice and nail to one of the boards your statement of the most important convictions of your faith. Then, return to your seat in the worship center.

(DWN)

The Response   P. Langston
God of Grace and God of Glory
(As the worshipers' hammering of their statements of faith reaches a crescendo, the instrumentalists pick up the rhythm of the hammers and begin the introduction to the choral response, "God of Grace and God of Glory," which the choir then sings.)

The Commission
Leader: The heavens declare the glory of God,
People: And we will choose in the course of the days whether or not we'll accompany the heavens.
Leader: May God bring wisdom to our daily choices,
People: That each of our days might participate in the mighty chorus of celebration.
All: We want to join the song of creation worshiping the Creator, and we rejoice in awe with our songs of thanksgiving.

(JB)

The Recessional Hymn   NUN DANKET
Now Thank We All Our God

The Closing Voluntary   Charles Ore
Ein Feste Burg

THE WORSHIP OF GOD
Minister Ordination

The first Sunday of Advent was the setting for this service in which our church ordained a young woman staff member as a minister of the gospel. On this Sunday of hope, the courageous initiative of the church exemplified in recognizing, affirming, and encouraging the gifts of Anna Catherine Lowe Nixon, called by God to minister, both celebrated hope and perpetuated hope. Note the convergence of traditional and nontraditional elements of ordination with traditional seasonal emphases and special ecclesiastical concerns.

The Prelude   J. S. Bach
Now Come Savior of the Nations

The Prologue
Today we begin a new pilgrimage and participate in an ancient tradition. As we start our journey toward Bethlehem to celebrate the birth of Christ once more, we join people of faith throughout the ages who have recognized and set aside for special ministry those in their midst whose lives have been touched by God's call. On this Advent Sunday of hope, our church's ordination of Cathe Nixon signals our affirmation of hope as a present reality. The blessing of this day is overwhelming; the challenge is exciting. Let us begin.

(CWG)

The Call to Worship
    Leader: Let us rejoice on this good day. Under heaven's blessed gaze, come we now to sing God's praise! For now we affirm the light we see dancing in her because of God's mercy! Alleluia! Our thanks to God we say!
    People: Dance, dear sister, take our hands. Tell us how your steps began. Tiptoe lightly when bestowing grace. Stomp angrily on the injustice we face. Do

	not let Christ's music die. Dance, dance dear sister! Then the world will dance, because of you and me.
Leader:	Come one and all to give a blessing. Arch your arms to prepare the way. Remember when you first danced that day. Reach out your hands to offer caressing. Invite her life and yours to intertwine. Enter into new partnerships with the Divine!
People:	**Dance, dear sister, take our hands. Tell us how your steps began. Tiptoe lightly when bestowing grace. Stomp angrily on the injustice we face. Do not let Christ's music die. Dance, dance dear sister! Then the world will dance, because of you and me.**
Leader:	Very gently, Cathe, begin now. After all, you'd begun before our meeting! Let the Spirit set your heart to beating. Especially determined, begin e'en if you're not sure how. Never let another keep you from your moves. The path of the Spirit is the one you must choose. It's time! It's time! Hand clapping is allowed!
People:	**Dance, dear sister, take our hands. Tell us how your steps began. Tiptoe lightly when bestowing grace. Stomp angrily on the injustice we face. Do not let Christ's music die. Dance, dance dear sister! Then the world will dance, because of you and me.**

(DDW)

The Revelation   John Rutter

II. from *Gloria*
Liturgical Dance

The Symbol of Hope   Ryan-Wenger

In the Beginning

(Because this service occurs on the first Sunday of Advent, during this musical offering, an acolyte [or a family or another individual] carries into the room the illumination for the first candle in the

Advent wreath. The appearance of the light is placed at this particular moment in the service to enhance further a recognition of the presence and holiness of the Almighty created by the liturgical dancer.)

The Prayer of Praise and Thanksgiving
> How can we begin to thank you, O God? Your faithfulness is immeasurable. Your call persists beyond all barriers. Your insistence pursues us until we receive you. Your desires sing out to us over all other voices. You wait unabatedly for our "yes" to you.
>
> How can we begin to thank you, O God? Cathe's courage is immeasurable. She follows your call past barriers erected by your people. She insists that we receive the gospel you have given her. She listens to your love song over the noise of condemnation. She is unabashedly saying "yes" to you.
>
> We are deeply grateful for the irresistible power of your call. We are deeply grateful for Cathe's costly obedience!
>
> Hear our prayer, O Lord, for your church. Keep after us with your truth, tenacious teacher. Challenge us to hear your calling out to us. Don't let us rest until sons and daughters are prophesying from our pulpits and everyone is dreaming God-dreams. Encourage us with the example of this beloved sister whom we set apart today. Help us to say "yes" to you, too.
>
> How can we begin to thank you, O God? Amen.

(DDW)

The Processional Hymn LEONI
The God of Abraham Praise

The Old Testament Lesson Isaiah 40:1-11
 Leader: This is the Word of God
 People: Thanks be to God.

The Meditation Felix Mendelssohn
How Lovely Are the Messengers
from *St. Paul*

The Sermon
"A Wilderness, a Woman, and a Voice"

The Response   Gounod/Lyall
Lovely Appear
from *Klassics for Kids*
(A children's choir presents this musical offering to glorify God and to honor as their minister the person to be ordained.)

The Charge   Deuteronomy 6:4-12
(The charge is presented by the rabbi of a local temple who is a caring friend of the congregation. He reads the *Shema Israel* in both Hebrew and English.)

The Consecration
(The ordinand kneels at the front of the chancel steps. All worshipers are invited to come forward and share in the ancient tradition of blessing the new minister by laying hands on her. The "Laying on of Hands" symbolizes an individual's blessing of the candidate and participation in the consecration of this moment. Choral meditations are offered during the congregation's blessing of the minister.)

How Beautiful Are the Feet   G. F. Handel
Love's Blessing   P. Wright

The Prayer of Dedication

God of Creation, Author of Redemption, Prompter of Ordination: In this moment we dedicate Cathe Nixon to you as much as we can dedicate anyone or anything. Not trying to make a decision for her, we celebrate with you decisions Cathe already has made—to serve you, to speak your word, to extend your grace. Help Cathe to sense the intensity of our affirmation of the choices she has made and the sincerity of our encouragement as she translates decisions into actions.

God, deliver Cathe from crippling untruths—a sense that she must save the church, an idea that she represents all women, a perception that following her ordination she can achieve perfection. Set her free from ministry-stifling misperceptions—that she must be more a minister than a person, that the church is more her responsibility than her family, that she must please everybody, or anybody, other than you.

God, continue to call Cathe to ministry. Give her discretion. Enable her to know when to speak and when to be silent, when to lead and when to follow, when to comfort and when to be comforted. Prod her to keep growing in spirit as in intellect, in truth as in imagination, in creativity as in history. Grant her vision.

God, make Cathe a minister of grace more interested in helping people than judging them, committed to the transforming power of love, captivated by the yes of your promises. Keep Cathe conscious of the presence of the holy in the ordinary, aware of the possibilities of the sacred amid the secular. Surprise her with your goodness and mercy as a trip to a museum with young friends becomes a pilgrimage of faith, a crayon placed in the hands of preschoolers becomes an instrument of education about joy, a conversation with parents anxious about their children becomes a discussion of the meaning of the family of God.

God, we dedicate Cathe Nixon to you. Take care of her. Lead her. Strengthen her. Give her mercy. Speak through her. Use her talents for your glory. Nurture her faith. Embrace her with your love. Fill her with hope. Make her an instrument of your peace. And, God, give her reasons to laugh.

We pray in the name of the Christ who defines the ministry to which he summons all of us. Amen.

(CWG)

The Presentation of Symbols
(Representatives of the church present the newly ordained minister with equipping gifts—e.g., a Bible, a commentary, a robe, a hymnal.)

The Blessing
Leader: Cathe, you are joining the ranks of crazy dreamers. And because you believe that God has given you authority to lead your people, folks will be jealous of you. People will try to send you to a place where you will affect them no more.
People: But the Lord will be with you.
Leader: Cathe, if you are faithful in the small tasks, if you choose integrity over cheap thrills, people will seek your ruin. People will try to confine your spirit.

People: **But the Lord will be with you.**
Leader: Cathe, if you show compassion to those who suffer around you, if you trust that God speaks through you, people will at last remember you. People will realize they need you.
People: **And the Lord will be with you.**
Leader: Cathe, if you are as honest with the pharaoh as you are with the baker, if you tell it like it is every time, people will ask you what to do in times of crisis; people will follow your lead.
People: **And the Lord will be with you.**
Leader: Cathe, if you will forgive those who choose to leave you for dead rather than to cheer you on for life, if you will rejoice in the reunion of relationships once torn apart, people will be fed by your generosity. People will be healed by your ministry.
People: **Because the Lord will be with you.**
Leader: Your chosenness was not your idea; it was not your family's idea; it was God's idea. You will be powerful.
People: **Because the Lord will be with you.**
Leader: Gather around, and I will tell you about the days to come: Cathe is a fruitful bough by a spring; her branches run over the wall. The archers fiercely attacked her; they shot at her and pressed her hard. Yet her bow remained taut, and her arms were made agile by the hands of the Mighty One, by the name of the Shepherd, by the Rock of Israel, who will help her, by the Almighty who will bless her with the blessings of heaven above—blessings of the deep that lies beneath, blessing of the breast and the womb. These blessings are stranger than the blessings of the eternal mountains, the bounties of the everlasting hills; may they be on the head of Cathe, on the brow of she who was set apart from her brothers and sisters. Amen.

(DDW)

The Response of the Newly-Ordained Minister

As long as I live, I will remember you for your blessing to me on this day. As the apostle Paul expressed, "I will thank my God every time I remember you. In my prayers for all of you, I always pray with joy. It is right for me to feel this way about all of you, since I have you in my heart."

You, dear people of Northminster Church, will always be in my heart. You have encouraged me, affirmed me, and stirred up gifts within me.

The journey that leads to ordination is often long and filled with waiting—waiting for clarity of call from God, waiting for completion of education, waiting for a clear sense of direction in ministry. During waiting times of life, strength often wanes. As I waited for this day of ordination, I was reminded of the promise in Isaiah: "They that wait upon the Lord shall renew their strength, they shall mount up with wings as eagles; they shall run and not be weary; they shall walk and not faint."

I will always remember you. I will remember that during my waiting time, as I hoped that my strength would be renewed, I heard your voice of blessing. It was this church, this people, that God used to help restore my strength.

In the days and nights ahead, when I feel like fainting, I will remember you and continue to walk in faith. When running has wearied me, I will remember you and continue to run with hope. And on those glory days—those days of soaring—those days when I feel as if I might be able to mount up with the wings of an eagle, I will remember that it was you who gave me the wings to fly.

May God grace you all the days of your lives as you have graced me on this ordination day. And now, people of God, may your faith grow exceedingly, and may you have patience and courage in all persecutions and tribulations. May you stand firm in the liberty and freedom that Christ has granted, escaping the yokes of bondage that others would place upon you. And may God give you good hope, and establish you in every good word and work in this place. Amen.

(KMF)

The Offering of Our Lives and Labors unto God

The Celebration   J. Rutter
O Clap Your Hands

The Benediction

Our God, lay your hands over ours on this woman, and may she feel on those hands the scars the world gives to those who dedicate their hands to service and lives to love.

May she know the pain that is worth the suffering of it, and never sell herself short.

May she feel those scars and be strengthened in her innermost being by the grace of the abundant life, the abundant love, that shines in the outermost darkness. May she be strengthened by the assurance of this light that the darkness cannot comprehend. May she feel those scars and be strengthened to risk something big for something good.

May she feel your scars, God, and know your hands as beautiful. May her living be one of finding beauty and wonder in places and times and people the world passes by.

May she discover herself to be surrounded all the days of her life by the riches you so liberally scattered throughout experience. And in her the light will continue to shine in darkness, for the world is now too small for anything but truth and too dangerous for anything but love.

May your hands over our hands on her remind her always of those who have seen in her and affirmed in her the good work begun—the good work you will complete both in and through her.

So take her mind, God, and think through it. Take her lips and speak through them. And take her heart and set it on fire through Jesus Christ our Lord. Amen.

                                                                                                                  (JB)

The Recessional Hymn   CATHERINE
To Those Whom God Ordains

The Closing Voluntary   J. S. Bach
From Highest Heaven to Earth I Come

THE WORSHIP OF GOD
Holocaust Memorial

People of the Jewish faith annually remember the Holocaust in a service of worship. Christians, too, do well to remember this horrific, beyond-imagination tragedy. The following service allows Jews and Christians to worship together in a memorial service intended to produce the firm resolve—Never again!

(For each worshiper, prepare a small plastic bag containing two white rocks. Distribute these bags along with printed orders of service. The floral designs for this service consist of red geraniums, cabbages, and barbwire placed in urns that stand at each side of the communion table. A large white column candle is lighted and placed on the communion table in memory of Holocaust victims.)

The Prelude   J. S. Bach
> *Passacaglia* and *Fugue in C*

The Prologue
> (The choir encircles the worship center and chants antiphonally the names of victims of the Holocaust who were family members and friends of local Jewish congregants. These names can be secured from a local synagogue. The chant begins as a quiet remembrance and builds to a crescendo. The mounting volume of the chant moves choir members in procession toward the main aisle. Choir members remain lined up in the main aisle until the processional hymn.)

The Call   Brandt/Corita[3]
> Leader: With the living and eternal God as my goal and guide, fear and anxiety preempt no place in my life.
> **People: The evils of this world seek to destroy our security in the living God; their attempts are to destroy those within God's loving embrace.**
> Leader: The very legions of hell lay siege to our souls, only to be thwarted by a power far greater.
> **People: I have one primary and ultimate desire: to abide within the love and acceptance of the eternal God. Within that tender care I know I am safe.**

Special Services

> Leader: Stand tall, regardless of threatening enemies and the tyranny of evil. Counter the voices of temptation with exclamations of praise.
> **People: Our needs are not ignored. God does hear our cries, and to our desires God is not indifferent.**
> Leader: Then take courage and step out in faith. In an uncertain and tumultuous existence, it is possible to know and experience the love of God, to discover light even in the midst of darkness, and to encounter incomprehensible joy in the midst of our deepest sorrow.
> **People: Times of darkness will come, tempests will continue to rage, the faithful and the faithless both will suffer the uncertainties and insecurities of this life, but the child of God can always depend on the refuge of a loving parent, who feels and bears with them their pains and problems, who reaches out to help those whom we battered down with despair, who will keep them and watch over them no matter how dark the night.**
> **All: God is forever our sure refuge and strength. Our security is in the promise that God will be near to us always and in the knowledge that God will never let us go.**

The Prayer of Praise and Adoration   Psalm 132:1-5, 13-18
(A paraphrase of these verses provides an alternative prayer of praise and adoration.)

The Introit   G. Pitoni/N. Greyson
Cantate Domino
("O Sing Ye to the Lord")

The Processional Hymn   LEONI
The God of Abraham Praise
(based on Jewish Doxology)

The Response   H. Leck
Hallelujah, We Sing Your Praises

Torah Reading   Deuteronomy 6:4-9; Leviticus 19:17-18
   Leader: This is the Word of God.
   People: Thanks be to God.

The Remembrance   L. Lewandowski
   S'u Sh'orim
(A liturgical dancer, accompanied by a flutist, interprets the history of Israel and the significance of the Torah to God's people. During the dance, the scroll of the Torah is opened, and the manuscript is unfurled. The dancer reveals the struggles, the comfort, and the companionship that the Torah brings to the life of a pilgrim.)

The New Testament Lesson   John 13:34-35
   Leader: This is the Word of God.
   People: Thanks be to God.

The Commandment   J. Ryan-Wenger
   In the Beginning
(A second liturgical dancer visually conveys the meaning and importance of the new commandment voiced by Jesus. While the first dancer's movements were very traditional in style, the second dancer moves in a more modernistic manner.)

The Sermon
   "O Happy Guilt"

The Prayer of Penitence for Christians
   "Without doubt an abyss yawns between Christian supersessionism and Auschwitz. The Holocaust world sought the death of Jewish bodies and souls, whereas to Christian faith, human life—and hence Jewish life—is sacred. . . Even so, the terrible fact is that there is a thread which spans the abyss."
                                            (Emil Fackenheim)

"Jews are slayers of the Lord, murderers of the prophets, enemies of God, haters of God, adversaries of grace, enemies of their father's faith, advocates of the devil, brood of vipers, slanderers, scoffers, men of darkened minds, leaven of the Pharisees, congregation of demons, sinners, wicked men, stoners, and haters of goodness."
                                      (St. Gregory of Nyssa, 4th c.)

All: **Lord have mercy.**

"He who can never love Christ enough will never have done fighting against those who hate him. Flee then from their assemblies, flee their houses, and far from venerating the synagogue because of the books it contains, hold it in hatred and aversion for the same reason. I hate the synagogue precisely because it has the Law and the prophets. I hate the Jews because they outrage the Law. . . . Indeed they have surpassed the ferocity of the wild beasts, for they murder their offspring and immolate them to the devil."

(St. John Chrysostom, 4th c.)

All: **Christ have mercy.**

"The Jews held (Jesus); the Jews insulted him; the Jews bound him; they crowned him with thorns, dishonored him by spitting on him; they scourged him; they heaped abuses upon him; they hung him on a tree; they pierced him with a lance."

(St. Augustine, 5th c.)

All: **Lord have mercy.**

"We desire to combat the enemies of God in the East, but we have under our eyes the Jews, a race more inimical to God than all the others."

(A Crusader, 11th c.)

(In the First Crusade, ten thousand European Jews were killed after choosing between baptism or death.)

All: **Christ have mercy.**

"The Jews, against whom the blood of Jesus Christ calls out, although they ought not to be killed, . . . yet as wanderers they must remain upon the earth, until their countenance be filled with shame and they seek the name of Jesus Christ the Lord."

(Pope Innocent III, 12th c.)

(During Innocent's reign, Italian Jews were required to wear identifying badges.)

All: **Christ have mercy.**

"It would be licit, according to custom, to hold Jews, because of their crime, in perpetual servitude, and therefore, the princes may regard the possessions of the Jews as belonging to the State; however, they must use them with a certain moderation and not deprive Jews of things necessary to life."

(St. Thomas Aquinas, 13th c.)

All: **Lord have mercy.**

"If it is Christian to hate Jews, then we are all good Christians."

(Erasmus of Rotterdam, 15th c.)

All: **Christ have mercy.**

"Let me give you my honest advice. First, their synagogues or churches should be set on fire, and whatever does not burn up should be covered or spread over with dirt so that no one may be able to see a cinder or stone of it. And this ought to be done for the honor of God and of Christianity in order that God may see that we are Christians. . . Secondly, their homes likewise should be broken down and destroyed. For they perpetrate there the same things they do in their synagogues. . . Thirdly, they should be deprived of their prayerbooks and Talmuds in which such idolatry, lies, cursing, and blasphemy are taught. Fourthly, their rabbis must be forbidden under pain of death to teach anymore. . . . To sum up, dear princes and nobles who have Jews in your domains, if this advice of mine does not suit you, then find a better one so that you and we may be free of this insufferable, devilish burden—the Jews."

(Martin Luther, 1543)

All: **Lord have mercy.**

"Any Jew who intends to hang himself is requested to have the kindness to place a paper with his name thereon in his mouth so that we may know who he is."

(A Nazi loudspeaker announcement/
"Night of Terror," 10 Nov 1938)

All: Christ have mercy.

"Let us not weep, for weeping is too easy. Let us hear their six million tears flowing silently in our hearts."
(From a synagogue haShoah memorial)
(PC)

The Observance of Silence

The Response   Randall Thompson
Paper Reeds by the Brooks

The Mourner's Kaddish
Let the glory of God be extolled. Let His great name be hallowed, in the world whose creation He willed. May His kingdom soon prevail, in our own day, our own lives, and the life of all Israel, and let us say, Amen.

Let His great name be blessed for ever and ever. Let the name of the Holy One, blessed is He, be glorified, exalted, and honored, though He is beyond all the praises, songs, and adorations that we can utter, and let us say: Amen.

For us and for all Israel, may the blessing of peace and the promise of life come true, and let us say: Amen.

May He who causes peace to reign in the high heavens, let peace descend on us, on all Israel, and all the world, and let us say: Amen.[4]

(Suggested reader: a rabbi or cantor)

The Prayer   J. Van
Psalm 131

The Litany
Leader: We remember with sorrow those persons whose lives were taken from them in a senseless rage of evil so terrible that we know it as the Holocaust.
People: We call to mind those who "left a name behind them, whose remembrance is as honey in the mouth," and those who "left no memorial,

	whose names have vanished as though they had never been."
Choir:	Have mercy on us, O God, according to thy steadfast love. Wash us thoroughly from our iniquity and cleanse us from our sin.
Leader:	"What is precious is never to forget . . . those who in their lives fought for life, who wore at their hearts the fire's center. Your children who have perished through the cruelty of the oppressor, victims of demonic hate . . . driven in multitudes along the road of pain and pitiless death."
People:	"They lie in nameless graves, in far-off forests and lonely fields. And the substance of many was scattered by the winds to the earth's four corners."
Choir:	"Yet they shall not be forgotten."
All:	"We take them into our hearts and give them a place beside the cherished memories of our own loved ones. They now are ours."
Leader:	Thou desirest truth, God. Therefore, teach us wisdom.
People:	O God, help us. We dare not, we cannot ever let such dastardly evil visit this earth and destroy your people again.
Choir:	Deliver us from rampaging nationalism. Save us from uncritical patriotism. Eliminate our prejudices. Eradicate our penchant for violence. Give us a liking for justice. Fill us with a passion for mercy. Hinder us from all that cheapens life. Rush us toward the things that make for peace.
All:	Create in us a clean heart, O God, and put a new and right spirit within us.[5]

The Flame of Memory

Leader 1: O God, we come before you as sons and daughters of promise, remembering those who left a name behind them and those who left no memorial whose names have vanished as though they had never been.

Leader 2: May we never forget, God, those who were forced to fight for life itself . . . for liberation, for freedom, for their own humanity. May we remember them, God, your children who have perished through the cruelty of the oppressor and the taskmaster.

Leader 3: They lie in nameless graves, in southern swamplands, in far-off forests and lonely fields. And the substance of many was scattered by the winds to the earth's four corners.

People: Yet they shall not be forgotten. Let us hear again their silenced music. Let us take them into our hearts and give them a place in our memories.

(The two dancers move to the communion table. Each places her hands around the candle—the modern dancer following the traditional dancer. Together the dancers lift the candle and carry it to a floor candlestick placed at the base of the chancel. After securing the candle, each dancer positions herself at one side of the candle, as if the two were standing guard over the flame.)

The Moment for Remembrance and Resolution
I. Treblinke
II. Nursery Rhyme for Dead Children
III. Ne Csuggedj (Do Not Despair)[6]

Leader: This is a moment for remembrance and resolution. Using a Jewish ritual for honoring the dead, at least as old as the seventeenth century, come and, here by this flickering flame, place a stone to register your presence at this memorial. As we remember those who have died, let us also state our resolutions about living.

People: " 'Alas for those who cannot sing, but die with all their music in them.' Let us treasure the time we have, and resolve to use it well, counting each moment precious—a chance to apprehend some truth, to experience some beauty, to conquer some evil, to relieve some suffering, to love and

> **be loved . . . to fulfill the promise that is in each of us, and so to conduct ourselves that, generations hence, it will be true to say of us: The world is better because, for a brief space, they lived in it."**

Choir: Restore to us the joy of thy salvation and uphold us with a willing spirit.[7]

(At the conclusion of the reading and while the choir is singing, worshipers move forward and place one stone at the base of the candle. The other stone is kept as a memorial of this service and as a source of firm resolve: Never again!)

The Witness
(A survivor of the Holocaust speaks personally of appreciation for people today who are willing to remember the horrors of the past and to work for a future of reconciliation and peace.)

The Benediction   B. Dennard
Great Day

The Recessional Postlude   Albinoni
Adagio in G

THE WORSHIP OF GOD
Arts Festival/Honoring an Artist

The following service took place during a weekend filled with a sanctuary exhibit of Mrs. Clyde Connell's works of art—oil paintings, block prints, sculptures, mixed media collages, wall hangings, and altar pieces. The worship experience, built around this art and artist, purposes to inspire a responsible stewardship of each person's resources as well as to celebrate creativity and fidelity.

The Prelude   George Brandon
       Voluntary on Veni Creator Spiritus
(Worshipers enter a sanctuary filled with various works of art—large, free-standing pieces of sculpture as well as small paintings displayed on the walls. Seats in the worship center are rearranged around the various pieces of art.)

The Welcome

The Call to Worship

          The Opening Sentences
God calls us to worship knowing that it is in worship that we achieve our fullest potential as individuals. In a sense, worship is like creation itself. Creation is a gift from God that we accept with gratitude and then use for the betterment of other people and use ultimately for the glory of God; thus returning creation to God and allowing creation to reach its fullest potential. As we gather for worship today, surrounded by reminders of God's creation and of God's call to us to participate in creativity, we give thanks for the gift of God in worship, and we use this time of worship to return gifts to God—the gifts of creation, praise, song—the gifts of worship. Recognizing that we live with giftedness, please join me now as we focus on the worship of God.

                                                            (CWG)

The Silent Meditation
   Like a motherless child, I felt like a motherless child you had promised not to leave. So, I promised to believe. Yet, you were there; I was here.
   Like a motherless child, feeling abandonment and grief with no possibility of relief, only aching loneliness . . . Loneliness metamorphosed into a leathery-winged creature of horror that sank curved claws deep into my paralyzed brain. I could not, in my terror, hear you call my name. I could not hear past my weeping, see past my error.
   Then I took the bread you had to offer, symbol of your broken body. I was a doubter, no worse—a scoffer; but as it began to melt on my tongue, I bit that bit of crust, and it crumbled into galaxies, then cosmic dust inside my mouth. I swallowed. It then exploded like a super nova, consuming worlds of materiality; Corpus Christi once dead, alive in me.
   Oh, Jesus, you have been faithful, indeed; I, less than I intended. Next came the blood—red reminder of redemption, mine and yours mingled like blood brothers. (We both knew what it meant to suffer.) But my blood tasted like salty gall, yours like sweetest wine . . . as your death becomes mine, your cross mine, your life mine; as you continue to lead me toward the divine.

(RC)

The Dance Arr. Sand Lawn
Found Song
Sometimes I Feel Like a Motherless Child
(A modern liturgical dancer, accompanied by an organist and a soloist, brings new insights into traditional pieces of music much like Clyde Connell used old, traditional items as media for new works of art. Fresh expressions of creativity spring from the commonplace.)

The Revelation of God

The Hebrew Scriptures Isaiah 42:5-9b
   Leader: This is the Word of God.
   People: Thanks be to God.

Special Services   241

The Hymn   TERRA BEATA
In My Creator's World

The Gospel   John 1:1-18

The Response   Ralph Vaughan Williams
Ring Out, Ye Crystal Spheres
from *Hodie*

The Pastoral Prayer

    Great Creating God: We pray for artists not yet recognized and affirmed—a young girl whose scrawled sketches with crayons beam the promise of portraits in oils and pastorals in water colors; a teenage boy who feels musical notes dancing in his soul eager for a translation on paper that will inspire the majesty of a symphony; an elderly man for whom simple photography has become a medium of staggering beauty; a diseased woman who has found in her pain and sleeplessness the impulse for shaping clay into figures that evoke others' deepest emotions.

    Great Revealing God: Make of our church a community of encouragement and support for people with artistic interests and promise. Give us the wisdom to praise creativity and to prompt people to express their artistic abilities without fear of embarrassment, criticism, or rejection. Speak through us to invite the offering of all talents to you as media of worship.

    Great Inspiring God: Remember those of us who cannot carry a tune, draw an attractive line, match one color with another, or even fully appreciate the genius of great art. Fill us with the soul-nurturing wonder inspired by a warm spring rain splashing against the petals of deep-hued azaleas; a pastoral collage of colorful autumn foliage; a brilliant winter sunset filling the sky with streaks of rose red, orange, pink, and gold; or a summer moonrise that transforms the darkness into a canopy filled with millions of beautiful luminaries—your art. Then guide our richly enhanced lives that we may share with others what we see, hear, feel, taste, and smell for their good and for your glory. Amen.

    (CWG)

The Celebration of a Life

The Music of That Life   arr. Lawn
   Swing Low, Sweet Chariot

The Sermon
   "The Art of Prophecy"

The Dance of Response
   (The liturgical dancer interprets the sermon through movement.)

The Choral Response   arr. John Carter
   My Life Flows On in Endless Song

The Benediction
   You are light, God, and we are created in your image. You are light, God, in all circumstances, and we are created in your image. Remind us who we are—whose we are. Fill us with light and creativity against which darkness cannot prevail that we might go from here to illuminate the circumstances of our lives and our world. Amen.

                                                                              (adapted—JB)

The Closing Hymn and Doxology   Ralph Vaughan Williams
   All Creatures That On Earth Do Dwell

THE WORSHIP OF GOD
CHRISTIAN EDUCATION

The New Testament says far more about maturing as a Christian than about becoming a Christian. Of course, the two concerns cannot be separated except for purposes of emphasis and discussion. To follow Christ faithfully is to grow in Christ and with Christ consistently. The following service emphasizes the importance of Christian education in the organizational life of a Christian church and Christian formation in the personal life of an individual Christian.

(Items related to children cover the communion table and spill onto the chancel. Place a small Bible in the midst of this collection.)

The Prelude   Peter Stearns
    Prelude, Chorale, and Fugue on ORA LABORA
    ("Come Labor On")

The Opening Voluntary   Gordon Young
    Prelude in Classic Style
(Near the end of the voluntary, a child walks down the center aisle and approaches the collection of children's items on the chancel. The child moves to the communion table and sifts through the materials there, laying aside several books before finding the Bible.)

The Prologue   R. Clausen
    Set Me As a Seal
(As the prologue is sung, the child moves to the steps of the chancel with the Bible in hand, takes a seat, and begins to read. When the call to worship begins, the child takes a seat in the congregation.)

The Call to Worship
    Leader: As children of truth, we gather once again to seek new and refreshing means for understanding the message of God.
    People: Teach us your ways, O Lord; show us your truth.
    Leader: "These words which I command you this day shall be upon your heart, and you shall teach them diligently to your children."

People: **God's truth was given to deliver the people of God. Its purpose was to be shared with all, not enshrined or preserved for a few. The message of God is given to the children of God.**
Leader: Christ the revelation of truth came to teach and preach the good lessons of the kingdom of God.
People: **Teach us this day, O Christ. Reveal your word anew.**
Leader: Even today God raises up servants who continue to make known the story of redemptive love.
People: **Their gifts are essential to the life of the church. Their mission is our goal.**
Leader: Christ entered into the world to reveal the graceful mind of God.
People: **Let us as teacher and student enter into the experience of fully knowing the message of God for this new day.**
Leader: Come and look into the ways of God. Learn the lesson as if the whole story depended on your wisdom.
People: **Fill us with your truth O God. Challenge us to the practical exercise of learning by doing.**

(DWN)

The Prayer of Praise

Author of all truth, Giver of every good and perfect gift, we offer our thanks for the way in which wisdom and knowledge have been preserved and taught throughout the ages. For faithful people who have unselfishly given in order to reveal your story, we give you thanks. For those, even in this day, who diligently teach, inspire their insight and understanding. Grant them courage to use and search your word for the deepest revelation of truth. You alone are omniscient. Remind each of us that a quest for knowledge will draw us closer to you and strengthen our faith.

We thank you for unfolding the discoveries of each generation, for the possibilities yet to be opened and the unlimited generosities of grace, which are far beyond our thoughts. We pray through your Holy Spirit for you to instruct us in these moments of worship so that we might go forth from this time better equipped to divulge that which has been made known to us.

Breath of God, Wisdom of the ages, teach us your ways, show us your truths, fill us with your grace so that we can offer the best of life in worship to you. Let all that hath life and breath praise our God.

Through Jesus Christ our revelation of truth we pray. Amen.

(DWN)

The Call to Praise
> Leader: In the various circumstances of my living, there is one constant on which I rely.
> **People: For the One who has seen me through this far will see me through what's here; the One in whom I place my trust is worthy of my living; the God to whom I belong will ever be my present help.**
> Leader: We lift our voice in grateful praise
> **People: To you our God, this day and forevermore.**

(JB)

The Introit   Dale Peterson
Antiphonal Praise

The Processional Hymn   LAUDA ANIMA
Laud Thy God Who Reigns in Heaven

The Old Testament Lesson   Deuteronomy 6:4-9
> Leader: The Word of God.
> **People: Thanks be to God.**

The Meditation
If Ye Love Me, Keep My Commandments   T. Tallis
Show Me Thy Ways, O Lord   W. Peltz

The New Testament Lesson   Philippians 2:5-11

The Hymn   SINE NOMINE
All Praise to Thee

The Litany
> Leader: Prepare us, Lord. Prepare us to see
> **People: With your eyes, our God, to see clearly: the priorities our society inverts that distort relationships, compromise our integrity, and isolate you from our day-to-day experiences.**
> Leader: Prepare us, Lord. Prepare us to hear
> **People: With your ears, our God, to hear clearly: your voice, your truth, your way, and to understand how you would have us live.**
> Leader: Prepare us, Lord.
> **People: Prepare us for a service of worship through which we discipline ourselves to better see, better hear, and better live.**
>
> (JB)

The Anthem   Jane Marshal
He Comes to Us

The Sermon
> "The Challenge of Christian Formation"

The Offering of Our Lives and Labors unto God

The Prayer of Commitment
> Leader: Our God, let us be useful to you.
> **People: Let our minds be open so that we might know your will.**
> Leader: Our God, let us be useful to you.
> **People: Let our words be honest so that others might know the truth.**
> Leader: Our God, let us be useful to you.
> **People: Let our hearts be full of love so that we might live in peace.**
> Leader: O God, let us be useful to you.
> **People: Let our actions be honorable so that all of your creatures might experience the joyful life that you intended in your creation of us.**
> Leader: Our God, let us be useful to you.

All:	**Yours will be the glory, and our joy will be in knowing that we have pleased you. Amen.**

(JMG)

The Meditation A. Pote
Many Gifts, One Spirit

The Commission
(A minister invites to the foot of the chancel those church leaders involved in ministries of Christian formation. The following commission is a means of the congregation dedicating and affirming these leaders.)

Leader:	We are gathered to recognize your gifts of leadership to our family of faith.
People:	**Whoever would be great among you must be your servant.**
Leader:	Through your teaching may we gain wisdom and understanding.
People:	**Teach us the ways of the Great Shepherd who leads us all to grace, reconciliation, and forgiveness.**
Leader:	Through your teaching may we model the early church.
People:	**Continually devoting themselves to the instruction given by the apostles, to the fellowship, to the breaking of bread, to the prayers.**
Teachers:	May we have a servant's heart as we give direction to our church family.
People:	**O God grant these, your servants who are gifted to teach, your grace and wisdom.**

(TS)

The Prayer of Dedication
Our Father: We offer praise and thanksgiving that you are not only our Savior, but also our Teacher. As a family of faith, may we be a people who applies the great truths you have taught us through Scripture. Grant our leaders wisdom and understanding as they interpret your Word to our family. May we use your teachings to bring unity, justice, peace, and salvation to

your people. In all of your teaching may we remember the great lesson you taught us: to love our neighbors as we would love ourselves. We ask this in the name of the Great Teacher, Christ Jesus our Lord. Amen.

(TS)

The Recessional Hymn   HYFRYDOL
Called As Partners in Christ's Service

The Benediction   J. Rutter
God Be in My Head

The Closing Voluntary   D. Zipoli
Offertorio
Allegro Maestro from Sonata II.

THE WORSHIP OF GOD
Renewal/Revival

Because of another event, a large tent had been set up behind our worship center. Cognizant of the early roots of many Protestants in the Free Church tradition, we designed a service that would allow us to revisit the tent-revival heritage out of which we came. This service that looks back also has the power to be a source of renewal in the present.

The Prelude   Haan
Three Spirituals

The Prelude   Seth
Rock of Ages

The Prologue   S. Caracciolo
Adoro Te Devote
"Jesus, I Adore Thee"

(The choir sings the prologue from the back of the worship center. Worshipers sense no variation from the regular liturgical style of worship in this church.)

The Call to Worship
> Reader A: Tell me the story of Jesus. Tell it straight from your heart.
>
> **People: I will celebrate the story of my Savior, will relate it with excitement and joy, seeking to demonstrate the difference Christ can make for you.**
>
> Reader B: Now tell me the story of you. I can embrace that with all my heart.
>
> **People: For we offer to each other our love, our care, kinship, and hope. We commit ourselves to weep together, sing together, struggle together, grow together.**
>
> Reader A: And in your story we find our story,
>
> Reader B: And in our story together we find God's story—
>
> **All: That the whole world might see a miracle. Let it be.**

(JB)

The Prayer of Praise and Adoration
   Our God, you have been and are involved in history beyond anyone's capacity to know or understand, and for this we are grateful. You have been the foundation of our community of faith. You have worked in ways and through people long forgotten. You have been a part of stories untold. People have encountered you in this fellowship, worshiped you here, prayed to you here, worked in your name here, played in your spirit here, learned more about you here, and moved on changed. For the stories we know, we give you thanks. We celebrate our rich tradition of encompassing love. We pray that this church will continue to be a family of faith in which you move, in which people live in a manner that bears witness to you. Amen.

(JB)

The Introit   REVIVE US AGAIN
                    Revive Us Again

The Call to Praise
   Looking at the tent outside this building has prompted thoughts of where we have been and of how far we have come in our pilgrimage. My, what a distance we have traveled. How reviving it could be to go back and revisit aspects of those former days. Only a door separates us from that experience.
   Come, friends, let's go outside and into the tent to remember the past, to hear the gospel again in a sawdust setting, and to be both renewed and revived in our faith today.

(CWG)

The Processional Hymn   HOLY MANNA
             Brethren, We Have Met to Worship
(During the singing of this hymn, worshipers follow the worship leaders from the familiarity of the worship center, across the lawn, and into an open-air tent where the service continues. As the choir and other worship leaders exit the sanctuary, they leave behind their liturgical attire. The pipe organ continues to sound inside the sanctuary while a piano provides accompaniment for the singing with which worshipers enter the tent. Once inside the tent, a choir takes

form on risers behind a wooden platform on which a homemade lectern is set. All who want to join the choir come forward. Other worshipers sit in folding chairs on the grass. Large formal arrangements of mixed greenery remain in the sanctuary. The floral designs in the tent consist of wild flowers native to the area.)

The Old Testament Lesson   Psalm 51
    Leader: This is the Word of the Lord.
    People: Thanks be to God.

The Meditation   K. Kaiser
Tell It to Jesus

The Attestations of Faith
(Invite two people, preferably senior adults, to tell of their personal memories of tent revivals. Ask them to describe a typical service; reflect on their individual connections and responses to "old time" revivals; and recall specific ways in which these services impacted their lives, the life of the church, and the life of the community. Question them about what was so good about these times.)

The Response   arr. M. Hayes
Leaning on the Everlasting Arms

The Lessons   Psalm 85:4-7; Romans 3:21-34
    Leader: This is the Word of the Lord.
    People: Thanks be to God.

The Response   J. Coates
Amazing Grace

The Sermon
    "Remembering Revivals, Praying for Renewal"

The Offering of Our Lives and Labors unto God

The Meditation   M. McDonald
I Must Tell Jesus

The Service of Communion

The Call to Communion
>Leader: We are reminded, our God, of our rich heritage, and it is with thanksgiving that we hear the stories that have brought us to where and who we are.
>
>**People: It is with gratitude that we acknowledge our part in a larger whole: our debt to those who have gone before, our responsibility to those yet to come.**
>
>Leader: We are the people of God in this time and place,
>
>**People: And it is in the interaction of one with others that we learn more of who you are, our God.**
>
>Leader: We celebrate these words of God made flesh—in our midst and in our experience.
>
>**People: Thanks be to God.**
>
> (JB)

The Words of Institution   1 Corinthians 11:23-26

The Distribution of Elements
>(Though the congregation comes forward to the chancel to receive the bread and wine of communion in many churches, today worship leaders carry the bread and the cup to the worshipers.)

The Invitation

The Recessional Hymn   REVIVE US AGAIN
>*Revive Us Again*

The Hand of Fellowship   PROMISED LAND
>*On Jordan's Stormy Banks*
>
>(As the congregants shake hands with each other and leave the tent, each receives a cardboard fan reminiscent of revival days. Print on one side of this fan: "Remembering Revivals." Print on the other side of this fan: "Praying for Renewal" "Will you not revive us again?" [Psalm 85:6].)

THE WORSHIP OF GOD
Dedication of a Hymnal/Music

Next to the Bible, a hymnal is the most important book in the life of a church. A church's selection of a hymnal is a reason for celebration and dedication in an experience of corporate worship. The following service illustrates the resourcefulness of this particular hymnal to provide substance for every major element of worship in our tradition. The hymnal dedicated in this service is *The New Century Hymnal*.[8]

(For this service, arrange the seats in the sanctuary after the pattern of seating in cathedral choir stalls—all rows face to the center aisle. At the front and back of the center aisle, place large arrangements consisting of flowers and musical instruments associated with hymnody. For example, in these arrangements utilize organ pipes, a shofar, tambourines, drums, and brass instruments. Display a collection of photographs of angels on the walls for worshipers to view as they enter the sanctuary. Underneath the photographs, position pedestals holding collections of hymnals used through the ages.)

The Prelude   Clark
Improvisations on Hymn Tunes
from *The New Century Hymnal*

The Welcome

The Prologue   SAKURA
Praise to God

The Opening Sentences   (CWG)
"The Poetry of Spirituality"

The Introit   NICAEA
Holy, Holy, Holy

The Call to Worship   Hymn No. 822
from *Psalms 113 and 92*

The Hymn of Praise   ENGELBERG
When in Our Music God Is Glorified

The Invocation   from Hymn No. 847

Eternal One; Silence from whom my words come; Questioner from whom my questions arise; Lover of whom all my loves are hints; Disturber in whom alone I find my rest; Mystery in whose depths I find healing and myself: enfold me now in your presence; restore to me your peace; renew me through your power; and ground me in your grace. Amen.

The Silent Meditation

The Response   EBENEZER
    Come, O Spirit, Dwell Among Us

The Old Testament Lesson   Psalm 66
    Leader: The Word of the Lord.
    People: Thanks be to God.

The Hymns of Response
    From All That Dwell Below the Skies   LAAST UNS ERFREUEN
    Yigdal Elohim Chai   LEONI
    Sing Praise to God, Who Has Shaped   LOBE DEN HERREN
    Joyful, Joyful, We Adore You   HYMN TO JOY

The New Testament Lesson   Colossians 3:16
                                                           Ephesians 5:18b -20
                                                           1 Corinthians 14:15
                                                                    Acts 16:25

The Hymns of Response
    If You But Trust in God to Guide You   NEUMARK
    My Hope Is Built on Nothing Less   SOLID ROCK
    Great Is Your Faithfulness   FAITHFULNESS
    When Peace, Like a River   VILLE DU HAVRE
    Blessed Assurance   ASSURANCE

The Preparation for Confession   ORWIGSBURG
    I Must Tell Jesus

The Call to Confession
   The Word became flesh and dwelt among us, full of grace and truth; but we esteemed it not and turned away. Let us confess our unfaithfulness and the limits of our trust.
   (from *The New Century Hymnal*)

The Prayer of Confession
   Almighty and Everlasting God, always more ready to hear than we are to pray, always willing to give more than we either desire or deserve: pour upon us the abundance of your mercy; forgiving those things of which our conscience is afraid, and giving us those good things that we are not worthy to ask, except through the merits and mediation of Jesus Christ, your Begotten One, our Sovereign. Amen.
   (from *The New Century Hymnal*)

The Meditation   I WANT TO BE A CHRISTIAN
   Lord, I Want to Be a Christian

The Assurance of Forgiveness
   Listen to the words of the scriptures: the mercy and the love of God are endless; God's wrath is slow, and God's love is eternal.
   (from *The New Century Hymnal*)

The Response   AMAZING GRACE
   Amazing Grace, How Sweet the Sound

The Distribution of the Elements
   Let Us Break Bread Together   LET US BREAK BREAD
   As We Gather at Your Table   BEACH SPRING
   Draw Us in the Spirit's Tether   UNION SEMINARY
   O Bread of Life   SHENG EN
   O Love That Will Not Let Me Go   ST. MARGARET
   More Love to You, O Christ   MORE LOVE TO YOU

The Invitation   BALM IN GILEAD
   There Is a Balm in Gilead

The Commission
Come, Holy Spirit, renew the whole creation. Send the wind and flame of your transforming life to lift up the church in this day. Give wisdom and faith that we may know the great hope to which we are called. Come, Holy Spirit, renew the whole creation. Amen.

(from *The New Century Hymnal*)

The Response ALL IS WELL
Renew Your Church

The Silent Commitment

The Response of Dedication
This Little Light of Mine LATTIMER
I Love to Tell the Story HANKEY
On River Jordan's Banks I Stand PROMISED LAND
We Shall Not Give Up the Fight ONLY STARTED
Some Glad Morning I'LL FLY AWAY

The Benediction KEEP YOUR LAMPS
Keep Your Lights Trimmed and Burning

The Postlude P. Manz
On CWM RHONDDA

THE WORSHIP OF GOD
Family Sunday

Many churches incorporate into their annual worship plans a special time of emphasis on the family. The following service contributes to such an emphasis, although it also shapes a worship experience that can be meaningful on its own. Here is an affirmation of the family as an institution willed by God and of a ministry to persons for whom that institution has failed or is failing.

The Prelude   Buxtehude
    Ciaconna

The Opening Voluntary   Thiman
    Reverie on ST. PETER

The Prologue   John Ness Beck
    Festival Introit on Psalm 46

The Call to Worship
    Leader: We who have moved through another week gather for worship.
    People: **Well-worn by our familiar steps, our ways are not your ways, Holy One.**
    Leader: Our gait changes with the winds of public opinion; our sights are set on mirage-like destinations that are disappointing substitutes for commitment to your purposes.
    People: **Often we are like inexperienced young travelers, asking again and again, "How much longer?"**
    Leader: Gracious God, forgive our impatience and stumblings as we learn to follow you.
    People: **Be our companion on this journey, Friend, and remind us today of your presence with us.**
    Leader: O Mortal, what does Yahweh require of you but to do justice, love kindness, and walk humbly with your God?

People: **May we place our living on your favorite path, O Christ, and move as your faithful people at the call divine.**
All: **Amen.**

(DWN)

The Processional Hymn ST. DENIO
God Made from One Blood

The Old Testament Lesson Psalm 91
Leader: This is the Word of the Lord.
People: Thanks be to God.

The Meditation Mendelssohn
Cast Thy Burden upon the Lord
from *Elijah*

The Prayer of the People
O God, when through the word of the Bible or the music of Mendelssohn we hear that invitation to cast our burdens on you, we stop short, listen for a trailing comment, and wonder if you mean it. We're not accustomed to people asking us to share our burdens. Most folks don't even want to hear about the loads we carry, much less help us carry them.

Thank you, God, for asking us to allow you to help us and thus increasing the prospect that we can stand up straight again unbent by heavy burdens. Take our cynicism—it is eating away our joy. Lift our sorrow—we are weary of weeping.

We toss to you our anger—it coils like a rattlesnake in our souls. We give you our judgment—we're not good at playing God. Here, too, is our duplicity—living dishonestly is destroying us. We hand you our bitterness—it's a blight on our faith. Here is our guilt—we finally prefer mercy over misery.

Take our worry—it's futile to fret over that which we have no control. Accept our envy—it's driving us mad. Carry off our competitiveness—it's turning everything into a game of winning and losing. Have at our resentment—it's about done us in. Save us from our overblown sense of self-importance—we're tired of trying to be perfect.

God, we hope this is not too much to lay on you. But you did ask. Honestly, there is more. Once we can allow ourselves to admit our burdens, it is so lightening, so freeing, for us to give them away.

Praise be to you, O burden-accepting God. Please don't carry them for us. We carried them too long. Just throw them away. Yes, just get rid of them, God. Amen.

(CWG)

The Response J. Ness Beck
I Need Thee Every Hour

The New Testament Lesson Galatians 5:13-16, 25; 6:1-2
Leader: This is the Word of the Lord.
People: Thanks be to God.

The Hymn THE GIFT OF LOVE
Though I May Speak

The Litany
Leader: God, I retreat to the safety of hiddenness.
People: And, as David hid himself from Saul in the cave, I hide my tears in smiles, veil my grief in busyness, mask my pain in,
Leader: "Oh, I'm fine—just a little tired."
People: In the aloneness of my hiding, I seek to be found by you, crying out to you, O God, demanding, hoping, praying: You see through my veils, behind my masks.
Leader: I want to be known. I want to be known. In my times of need, I want the darkness I remember when as a child I buried my face in the loving embrace of Mom and Dad.
People: In my times of need I want the blinding light emerging from my cave to illuminate the protective arms that continue to surround me—all the days of my life.

(JB)

The Anthem   Joseph Martin
    My Friend, Do Not Forget

The Sermon
    "When Families Hurt"

The Offerings of Our Lives and Labors unto God

The Meditation   J. Brel
    If We Only Have Love

The Invitation

The Commission
    Go now with your eyes open to the hurts and needs of families around you; with your ears open to both shouted and whispered pleas for help; with your hearts open to the reality of God's mercy experienced in every form of family; and with your hands open to the possibility of touching needs with help and hurts with healing. Go as members of the family of God to encounter every family with the love of God. Amen.
                                                                                    (CWG)

The Recessional Hymn   BEACH SPRING
    The Servant Song

The Benediction
    Mother and Father of the whole family of humankind, Loving God of every family on the face of this earth: As we go from this place, continue to call us into loving relationships. Strengthen us for the keeping of promises. Give us wisdom for resolving conflicts. And, please God, when we fail, do not give up on us or allow us to give up on one another. Walk with us, God. Stay with us, God. Help us, God. Heal us, God. And, God, make us healers. Amen.
                                                                                     (CWG)

The Closing Voluntary   J. S. Bach
    Come, O Creator, Spirit Blest

The Pealing

THE WORSHIP OF GOD
Mother's Day

Mother's Day observances were begun by Julia Ward Howe as a means of promoting peace. Since the inception of this special day, its meaning has involved more than honoring mothers. Mother's Day invites a focus on the kind of lives that make for peace—an invitation welcomed by all who desire to explore the spiritual potential in recognizing this day. The following service acknowledges the extreme importance of motherhood and focuses on enduring truths that make a difference in the quality of life for both men and women, adults, young people, and children.

(Prior to the service, distribute flowers to the congregants as they enter the worship center. Place books of various sizes at random heights across the altar. Lay a garland of greenery across the full length of the communion table. This garland should include runs from the sides and frontal drops, creating a liturgical parament of fresh greenery that will receive the congregants' flowers of remembrance later in the service.)

The Silent Meditation   Psalm 91
    "And He shall give his angels charge over thee,
        to keep thee in all thy ways."

The Prelude   H. Ley
    Prelude on "Down Amprey"

The Gathering
    Leader: "Mother is the name for God on the lips and hearts
                 of children."
                              (William Makepeace Thackeray)

The Prologue   M. Durufle
    Ubi Caritas

The Call to Worship
    Leader: The universal law of life is love. Let us gather in this
                 place to learn again the lesson of the Divine.

People: **We come to reflect upon the cherished human experiences of acceptance, to study spiritual discovery through the gifts of goodness, to change and become enlightened by grace for the sake of others.**

Leader: The eternal presence of a mothering God offers blessing and companionship as we gather for nourishment and growth. Come, learn once again the qualities and delights that shape our natures as children of God.

People: **We want to know more of our Parent-God. We are here to be "raised" in the compassion and consciousness of eternal love.**

Leader: Let us celebrate the goodness of a Mother-God. Let us sound praises for the lessons of truth in this hour. Let us rediscover the reality of love and dance again for the joys of life.

(DWN)

The Invocation

Holy God, we speak to you as people of many voices whose words are shaped by different situations. Even on this day to honor our mothers, each of us is filled with unique sentiments. To some, the word "mother" evokes warm feelings of love and expressions of gratitude. To others, however, the word brings to mind thoughts of abuse, manipulation, control, and guilt and spawns reactions that are negative. For some of us, the word "faith" represents an invitation to pilgrimage and fulfillment. For others, though, "faith" is associated with closed minds, narrow orthodoxy, and creedal rigidity.

God, we cannot escape words and the baggage each word carries. We do pray, however, that you will take us beyond words. Fill us with visions of new possibilities, gratitude for loving relationships, and resolve to move away from associations that depersonalize and to grasp experiences that make us whole persons.

In this time of worship, turn us to the One we know as "the word made flesh." In his presence teach us of parenting, faithing, loving, and growing. Deliver us from allowing status or role to define self-worth and fill us with the assurance that all of us are, each of us is, greatly loved.

O God, we speak to you and seek life in relationship to you with praise and gratitude.

(CWG)

The Hebrew Lesson — Proverbs 1:7-8

The Meditation — Kasia Livingston
My Mother's Faith
From the CD *Broken* by Cynthia Clawson[9]
(Either play this piece of music or have a soloist sing the lyrics.)

The Gospel Lesson — Mark 9:35-37

The Meditation — N. Sleeth
God of Great and God of Small
Children's Choir

The Morning Prayer
God our Mother, God our Father,
thank you for children,
signs of the kingdom
growing by leaps and bounds among us.

With unconditional love,
may we gather them into our circle.
Let us tell them your story
again and again and again
until they imagine it, paint it, sing it,
act it, dance it, write it—
until it sinks deep into
their bodies and spirits and voices,
until they express their joy and sadness
from head to toe.
Remind us that children come
"trailing clouds of glory,"
not so far from the wonder of your face.

Forgive us for watering down the gospel
until you are just another grown-up
who "went about doing good" long before they were born.
Forgive us for telling them to be kind and loving
without offering them the faith and hope they need
to live authentically in the world.

Even as we try to shelter them from storms,
help us model compassion that enters the pain of others.
Let us nurture all that makes them precious gifts,
daughters and sons made in the image of God.

Above all, as we grow alongside our children,
may our dependability and faithfulness
show them they can trust your tender love
now and forever.

(Sharlande Sledge[10])

The Hymn   RHOSYMEDRE
O God, Whose Steadfast Love

The Lesson   Robert Munsch[11]
I'll Love You Forever
(A worship leader reads the entirety of this children's book.)

The Silent Remembrances and Thanksgiving

The Anthem   J. Martin
My Friend, Do Not Forget

The Sermon
"Life Lessons"

The Response   Proverbs 31:10-31
(During the reading of this text, invite congregants to present flowers at the chancel as offerings of thanksgiving for the lives of women who have mothered the children of the world. A worship leader receives the flowers and weaves them into a liturgical vestment—a floral blanket that undergirds the books of lessons on the altar.)

The Recessional Hymn   Abbot's Leigh
God Is Love

The Commission
"We never know how high we are till we are called to rise; and then, if we are true to plan, our statures touch the skies." Let us go into the world to live out the lesson of life. Let us leave this place with the reassuring peace that love will never let us go. Amen.

      (Based on a poem by Emily Dickinson)

The Postlude   A. Fedak
 O Sons and Daughters, Let Us Sing

THE WORSHIP OF GOD
Father's Day

Father's Day presents multiple opportunities for worship-related emphases. Either honoring fathers or considering the blessing of fatherhood inspires a consideration of the importance of responsibilities related to fatherhood. Because of the Bible's numerous references to God as "Father," this day is a good occasion for examining why this term was related to God. The following service includes these emphases along with a sermon that examines one preacher's hopes and prayers for the physical offspring who call him "Father."

The Prelude   H. Starks
My Father's Beautiful World

The Prelude   P. Wohlegemuth
Of the Father's Love Begotten

The Call to Worship
  Leader: Gather children of the faith, "Our Father is coming—not tomorrow, but today; not next year, but this year; not after our misery, but in the middle of it; not in another place, but right here where we are standing."
  People: **We reach to a loving Father-God sharing our burdens, confessing our weaknesses, and seeking new visions of hope and promised strengths.**
  Leader: The "steel-velvet God" offers rest to all who search for healing, to each who long for acceptance and those who dream of liberation. Come, heirs of God's kingdom; here find a place where voices bid you welcome and sisters and brothers are open to risk and change.
  People: **We long to live as authentically as Christ lived. We seek to journey farther than fear and dream beyond imagination the intentions of our Father-**

God. May the Creator of life challenge us this day to adopt our legacy and turn towards home.
(Henri Nouwen, adapted[12])

The Introit   J. Ness Beck
Song of Exaltation

The Hymn of Praise   FOREST GREEN
I Sing the Almighty Power of God

The Silent Prayers of People's Praise

The Meditation   H. Hopson
Prayer of Thankful Praise

The Hebrew Lesson   Deuteronomy 5:1-9; 6:1-9

The Response   J. Marshall
Blessed Is the Man

The Morning Prayer

    Oh God, some of us can call you "Father" and experience an overwhelming sense of security, peace, intimacy, and joy. We associate the word "Father" with love, exemplary behavior, and provisions of both a physical and spiritual nature. Calling you "Father" is another way of saying, "We love you."

    We give thanks for the men in our lives who made the word "Father" a mode of address synonymous with something divine. But not all people share that sense of the word. For some individuals, the term "Father" conjures up visions of pain and abuse and incites feelings of anger and fear. Hearing the word "Father" causes some people to curl up into a fetal position emotionally and stirs a will to run away, rapidly. For these friends and acquaintances, you must forever be addressed as "Mother" or "Lover" or in some other manner. Of course, you understand.

    Oh God, deliver us from thinking that we can ever define who you are only by terms we know and by experiences from our past. You are Father, Mother, Shepherd, Rock, Royalty, Light, Creator, Grace, Lover, and more—so much more.

Thank you, God, for people whose lives have given us insight into your nature. Help us to live in such a way that our words and actions will cause others to know you better, to open up to you, and to experience your love.

Hear our prayer, O Transcendent Love, and fill us with the peace that accompanies your presence. We pray in the name of the one who first gave us the idea of calling you "Father." Amen.

(CWG)

The Response					A. Malotte
The Lord's Prayer

The Gospel Lesson				Luke 15:11-24

The Hymn				Tryggare Kan Ingen Vara
Children of the Heavenly Father

The Contemporary Lesson			Carl Sandburg[13]
"The People, Yes"

A father sees a son nearing manhood.
What shall he tell that son?
"Life is hard; be steel; be rock."
And this might stand for the storms
And serve him for humdrum and monotony
And guide him amid sudden betrayals
And tighten him for slack moments.
Or should he say,
"Life is soft loam; be gentle; go easy."
And this too might serve him.
Brutes have been gentled where lashes failed.
The growth of a frail flower in a path up
Has sometimes shattered and split a rock.
A tough will counts. So does desire.
So does a rich soft wanting.
Without rich wanting nothing arrives.
Tell him too much money has killed men
And left them dead years before burial:

The quest of lucre beyond a few easy needs
Has twisted good enough men sometimes into dry thwarted worms.
Tell him time as a stuff can be wasted.
Tell him to be a fool every so often
And to have no shame over having been a fool
Yet learning something out of every folly
Hoping to repeat none of the cheap follies
Thus arriving at intimate understanding
Of a world numbering many fools.
Tell him to be alone often and get at himself
And above all tell him no lies about himself
Whatever the white lies and protective fronts
He may use amongst other people.
Tell him solitude is creative if he is strong
And the final decisions are made in silent rooms.
Tell him to be different from other people
if it is natural and easy being different.
Let him have lazy days seeking his deeper motives.
Let him seek deep for where he is a born natural.
Then he may understand free imaginations
Bringing changes into a world resenting change.
He will be lonely enough
To have a time for the work
He knows as his own.

The Response   S. Wesley
    Thou Wilt Keep Him in Perfect Peace

The Sermon
    "A Father's Prayers"

The People's Silent Prayers of Dedication

The Meditation   J. Bert Carlson
    He Comes to Us as One Unknown

The Commission
> Do not pray for easy lives; pray to be stronger women and men. Do not pray for tasks equal to your powers, but for power equal to your tasks. Then, the doing of your work will be no miracle—you will be the miracle. Every day you will wonder at yourself and the richness of life which has come to you by the grace of God.
>
> (*New Century Hymnal,* Prayers of Benediction)

The Recessional Hymn   HYFRYDOL
> *God of Justice, God of Mercy*

The Postlude   M. Hayes
> *Children Medley*

THE WORSHIP OF GOD
Heritage Sunday

Though becoming a Christian means beginning a new life individually, each personal pilgrimage of faith takes place within a historical context rich with experiences of innumerable pilgrims on the same journey. God has not left us bereft of the benefit of wise counsel and courageous models from those who have gone before as the people of God. The following service sensitizes worshipers to the significance of our Judeo-Christian heritage and encourages an identification with that heritage that results in appreciation and rejoicing.

(Create a succor, or canopy of thanksgiving, over the communion table. Set the communion table with a collection of symbols from the Jewish and Christian traditions of faith—both symbols held in common and symbols distinct to each tradition—e.g., a menorah, a cross, a scroll of the Torah, a loaf of bread, a cup of wine, a cellar of salt, a candle, and a bowl of water.)

The Preludes .... Louis Vierne
Pieces in Free Style

The Welcome

The Opening Voluntary .... Mary J. von Appledorn
Shabbat Shalom

The Prologue .... Deuteronomy 6:4-9
The Shofar Call
The Shema
(Traditional Shabbat)

The Voice of a Pilgrim
 To set out in such a frail craft seems lunacy. Whose idea was it anyway? From this perspective the water is dark, deep, and definitely cold. How can I possibly hope to traverse that wet expanse? I cannot walk on water like Jesus did. I cannot part it like Moses did. There is no spector in a Grecian death mask to ferry me across the Styx.

I feel no fear, only perplexing amazement that it should be ordained that I must travel this course, that the departure would be so imminent. Why am I here at this timeless shore looking at such a still sea with no discernible shore that could be a destination? . . . From this vantage point, only a misty distance.

Could that mist hide a cloud of witnesses? Could the hint of parents around my bed days ago be a foreshadowing of traveling companions? Are there only questions? Does there have to be ignorance for faith to come into play? I am not particularly frightened on this ceaseless seashore, only lonely and a bit sad. I keep looking into the black water and the gray mist, waiting for the fog to part like a heavy, moist curtain and to reveal him walking across the waters smiling, arms outstretched to embrace me, with them following. . . .The conviction of things not seen.

(RC)

The Call to Worship
> Leader: Our story stretches back to the first breath of creation, moves forward through the life-blood of the saints of our faith, and pulses in the lives of ordinary folks like ourselves.
> **People: God placed Abraham and Sarah in the middle of a story and journeyed with them toward a land of hope and promise.**
> Leader: From them descendants were born, as numerous as the stars of the sky and the grains of sand on the seashore.
> **People: We are in the company of "great clouds of witnesses" who write the story with us.**
> Leader: The story is still unfolding, and in faith we make it our own. It forms our memory and our hope. God is at work beyond our story and our imagining throughout all time and space.
> **People: Tell the story! Sing "Alleluia" to our God!**

(SS)

The Meditation J. Leavitt
How Lovely Is Your Dwelling Place

The Prayer of Praise and Adoration
For stories, encouragement, hope, affection, grace, memories, and love that the generations before us have passed down to us; for stories, encouragement, hope, affection, grace, memories, and love that we pass to our friends and neighbors; for stories, encouragement, hope, affection, grace, memories, and love that we pass to the generations to follow—we give thanks to you, O God, who surrounds us with love, now and forever and ever. Amen.

(SS)

The Introit K. Nystedt
Cry Out and Shout

The Processional Hymn LEONI
Yigdal Elohim Chai
("The God of Abraham Praise")

The Litany of the Great Cloud of Witnesses
Leader: Sisters and brothers in Christ, let us call to mind those who have lived, worked, spoken, and witnessed to our faith in this and other ages.
People: We remember those through whom you have acted in the world, in the church, and in our own experience. We invoke their names that they might stand with us and offer the encouragement of their prayers.
Leader: Abraham and Sarah, believers in your promise to create a holy nation,
People: Stand with us.
Leader: Moses, who led the exodus under the cloud of your presence, and Ruth, whose loyalty to Naomi became a model of faithful love,
People: Stand with us.
Leader: Isaiah, who in a time marked by terror proclaimed that the lion would lie down with the lamb,

People: **Stand with us.**
Leader: Mary, who mothered Jesus on earth, and John, beloved disciple,
People: **Stand with us.**
Leader: Paul, Barnabas, Lydia, and Timothy, who nurtured the birth of the church,
People: **Stand with us.**
Leader: Augustine, whose restlessness found rest in God,
People: **Stand with us.**
Leader: Francis of Assisi, who pursued poverty because Jesus was poor and saw God in the light and life of creation,
People: **Stand with us.**
Leader: Julian of Norwich, Bernard of Clairvaux, Teresa of Avila, and Hildegard de Bingen, who caught a glimpse of the mystery of God,
People: **Stand with us.**
Leader: Martin Luther, who spoke of salvation by grace through faith,
People: **Stand with us.**
Leader: Lottie Moon, who preached the gospel where the gospel had not been heard,
People: **Stand with us.**
Leader: Sojourner Truth, who dreamed of women and men, black and white, all of them free,
People: **Stand with us.**
Leader: Walter Rauscehenbusch and Clarence Jordan, voices of liberation,
People: **Stand with us.**
Leader: Dietrich Bonhoeffer, confessor in chains, and Corrie ten Boom, resister of evil to humanity,
People: **Stand with us.**
Leader: Children of the synagogue: Elie Wiesel, Oskar Schindler, Etty Hillesum, and Anne Frank,
People: **Stand with us.**

Leader:	Martin Luther King, prophet of the day when we all will be judged by the content of our character, not by the color of our skin,
People:	**Stand with us.**
Leader:	Henri Nouwen, beloved brother of the handicapped, and Thomas Merton, who met you best in solitude and prayer,
People:	**Stand with us.**
Leader:	Mother Teresa of Calcutta, who made her home among the homeless, fed the hungry, and found her joy in service for love's sake,
People:	**Stand with us.**
Leader:	Hezekiah Stewart, Amy Butler, and Jimmy Dorrell, who look into the eyes of our cities' poor and see the face of Christ,
People:	**Stand with us.**
Leader:	Jimmy Carter, Millard Fuller, and Lee Piche, who believe each person should have a decent place to live and build houses in your name,
People:	**Stand with us.**
Leader:	Ed Wilson, Jack Diddie, Lindsay Little, Bob Watts, Scott Bryson, Suzi Paynter, Sam Osborne, Annie Londos, Tom McGahan, and all those who shared their lives with this community of grace,
People:	**Stand with us.**
Leader:	Our friends in the faith, saints in our church and community today, who encourage us and walk beside us,
People:	**Stand with us.**
Leader:	Almighty God, you have surrounded us with a great cloud of witnesses. Encouraged by the good example of these, may we persevere in running the race that is set before us until at last we live in the communion of your saints and eternal joy.
People:	**Through Jesus Christ, who lives and reigns with you, and the Holy Spirit forever and ever. Amen.**

(SS)

The Pastoral Prayer
>	Great God, what a history! What a fellowship! What a community! We know you better as a result of becoming more familiar with your people in the days that have preceded this hour.
>
>	Among your followers in earlier ages we recognize our spiritual kin—persons of faith who struggled with doubts, people whose songs of praise arose from sighs accompanied by tears prompted by problems, individual believers who made sacrifices while preferring an easier way, prophets who, within their souls, hosted a wrestling match between mercy and judgment, disciples with good intentions who needed encouragement, and messengers of good news who longed for acceptance and rest. On and on the identification goes.
>
>	It is good for us to look back. We see sources of assistance for doing your work today and find inspiration for staying at tasks that we have considered quitting.
>
>	But, guiding God, please do not allow us to spend so long looking over our shoulders that we trip into the future. Enable us to find in the past the roots of faith and hope that will come to full flower in our lives as we engage the present and prepare for the next day.
>
>	We pray in the name of the Ultimate Pilgrim. Amen.
>
>	(CWG)

The Hymn									BEACH SPRING
>	*God of Abraham and Sarah*

The New Testament Lesson		Hebrews 11:1-3, 7-32, 39-40; 12:1-2
>	Leader:	This is the Word of God.
>	**People:	Thanks be to God.**

The Anthem									Shaw/Parker
>	*Saints Bound for Heaven*

The Sermon
>	"Looking Toward Judah"

The Offering of Our Lives and Labors unto God

The Meditation
> Leader: We are reminded, our God, of our rich heritage, and it is with thanksgiving that we hear the stories that have brought us to where and who we are.
>
> **People: It is with gratitude that we acknowledge our part in a larger whole: our debt to those who have gone before—our responsibility to those yet to come.**
>
> Leader: We are the people of God in this time and this place,
>
> **People: And it is in the interaction of one with others that we learn more of who we are—more of who we can be and more of who you are, our God.**
>
> Leader: We celebrate these words of God made flesh—in our midst and in our experience.
>
> **People: Thanks be to God.**
>
> (JB)

The Invitation

The Recessional Hymn   ST. PETER
> *In Christ There Is No East or West*

The Scriptural Benediction   Numbers 6:24-26

The Choral Benediction   John Rutter
> *The Lord Bless You and Keep You*

The Closing Voluntary   L. N. Clerambault
> *Basse de Cromorne*

THE WORSHIP OF GOD
Baptismal Service

Whether in a body of water in the great outdoors, in a baptismal pool inside a church, or beside a baptismal font in a grand cathedral, the act of Christian baptism is an act of worship of great significance for all believers. The following service both reverences the importance of the baptism of an individual and draws all worshipers into the celebration of a person's publicly-declared, dramatically-enacted faith.

(Insert in each printed order of worship wet paper towels folded and sealed in clear plastic bags.)

The Prelude   Paul Manz
  If You But Trust in God to Guide You

The Opening Sentences
  Surrounded by miracles, I pray to be released from all that blinds my eyes and binds my heart. Free me of my illusions, assumptions, and expectations, that I might participate more fully in the life and love of my God.
                                                  (JB)

The Call to Worship   Joseph Martin
  The Canticle of Hope

The Prayer of Approach
  Holy God, we are here because we believe that you can change us. We are terrified by that thought, for we love the certainty of our imperfections. By your presence and power, make us willing to accept what you can do with us. Turn us from water into wine, not for our own glory, but as witness to your dominion. Give us grace to trust your working in and through us.
  We pray in the name of Jesus, the baptized one who revealed your strong and tender love for the world. Amen.
                                                  (PR)

The Introit   Schutz/Hopson
  Festive Introit

Special Services

The Processional Hymn LYONS
We Worship You, God

The Scripture Lesson 1 Corinthians 1:26-31
    Leader: This is the Word of God.
    People: Thanks be to God.

The Meditation Joseph Clokey
    O Make Our Hearts to Blossom

The Prayer of the People
    Dear God, we all gather around the waters of baptism this day to be immersed in your loving, powerful presence. We come to be bathed. Sometimes you bathe us like new parents bathing a newborn, gently and soothingly. Sometimes we're like toddlers in the bath, kicking and screaming all the way, voicing our defiant "no's" to you. Other times, like children, we take great delight in playing in the bath, knowing you take great delight in us. However it's done, you do bathe us, scrubbing us of our sin, then wrapping us in your peace like big warm towels fresh from the dryer. Then you dress us in new clothes and send us out shining like the sun to all the world about the new day of your kingdom, that they too may be bathed in your loving, transforming, powerful presence. Let us live as baptized people, through Jesus Christ our Lord, Amen.

                                                                          (JWC)

The Response B. Hunter
    In the River of Jordan

The Scripture Lesson Romans 6:3-4
    Leader: This is the Word of God.
    People: Thanks be to God.

The Hymn BEACH SPRING
    Wash, O God, Our Sons and Daughters

The Meditation on Christian Baptism
    Baptism is an act that looks back with gratitude on what God's grace has already accomplished; it is here and now an act of

God's grace, and it looks forward to what God's grace will effect in the future. Baptism signifies the washing away of sin, the pouring out of the Holy Spirit upon us, our burial and resurrection with Christ, and our experience of being born of water and the Spirit. These grace-filled events happen to us over the course of a lifetime, because baptism happens not only while we are in the water; but our baptism also anticipates a lifetime of further and deeper experiences with God. When someone is baptized, it is a significant and life-changing event in the life of both that person and the church. What happens to the one being baptized will make a difference to every member of the community of faith. The rest of the church can never again be the same.

(KMF)

The Response   LANDAS
    My Faith Has Found a Resting Place

The Act of Christian Baptism

The Response to Christian Baptism   D. Schwoebel
    Not What My Hands Have Done

The Sermon
    "A Matter of Identity"

The Responsive Meditation   A. Hill
    Fix Me, Jesus
(During the singing of the meditation, each worshiper is requested to remember his or her own own baptismal experience by using the wet paper towel in the plastic bag to wash and simultaneously to recommit to an identity as a follower of Christ.)

The Invitation

The Offering of our Lives and Labors unto God
(During the offertory the persons baptized earlier in the service will stand at the front of the worship center to be greeted, blessed, and encouraged.)

Special Services

The Commission
    To be baptized in the name of Jesus is to be commissioned by God for service. Go now, all of you, as people immersed in the love of God, ready to share that love with those who need it—those who need love as badly as a thirsty person needs water.
    (CWG)

The Recessional Hymn   HYFRYDOL
    Like a Tree Beside the Waters

The Benediction
    As you go, be assured of the love of God who wants to say to us, even as to Jesus, "You are my beloved in whom I am well pleased." Amen.
    (CWG)

The Response   Shaw/Parker
    Saints Bound for Heaven

The Closing Voluntary   Paul Bunjes
    Aurelia

THE WORSHIP OF GOD
Funeral Service

The following service was created as a response to the life and death of a charter member of our church, Dr. Thomas G. Stricklin, who enjoyed a distinguished career as a professor of history at a state university. Very personal in nature, this service takes seriously the uniqueness and worth of this child of God. The service centers on the sufficiency of faith and thus resounds with expressions of assurance and comfort.

(A funeral in the context of worship within a church differs from a funeral in other settings. For example, we keep in place the flowers that typically enhance the altar—two large urns filled with white flowers. Other floral contributions related to the death are taken to the place of burial rather than into the sanctuary. The pall-covered casket remains in the narthex until the time for the service to begin or until the singing of the processional hymn. The pall provided by the church symbolizes the truth that we are all equal in the sight of God. Family members of the deceased person enter the worship center behind the casket during the processional hymn.)

The Prelude   Hovaness
> *Prayer of St. Gregory*
> (with trumpet)

The Tolling of the Hour

The Prologue   J. Weaver
> *Psalm 46*

The Opening Sentences
> Worship both brackets and pervades the life of a Christian. We worship God at birth, at death, and at all points in between. In these moments, we have gathered to honor the life of Tom Stricklin, to grieve his death, to give thanks for his time among us, and to worship God. May this be a time of reflecting, grieving, finding comfort, hoping, and taking the first step beyond this moment.
>
> (CWG)

The Prayer of the People
> God, we know that for some reason you put each of us in this world, a world where sometimes bad things happen and people whom we love sometimes die, and we ourselves live in grief. We cry to you out of the darkness and confusion that so often surround us. We ask that you would open our eyes to the light, to your presence that is with us in our grief. We ask for your healing. We ask for your wholeness. We ask the same for others in our community who cry out at this time. We know that you can turn the sadness into joy; we've seen you do it. Today we offer our broken lives and hearts and bodies along with our grief to you for healing. In the name of the Christ, whose body was broken that we might be whole, Amen.
>
> (LKC)

The Assurance of the Scriptures   Romans 8:38-39

The Processional Hymn   ST. ANNE
> *O God, Our Help in Ages Past*

The Words of Comfort   Psalm 23 from *Psalms Now*
> Leader: The Word of God.
> **People: Thanks be to God.**

The Hymn   NEWMARK
> *If You But Trust in God to Guide You*

The New Testament Lesson   Romans 5:1-2
> Leader: This is the Word of Truth.
> **People: Thanks be to God.**

The Anthem   S. Adler
> *How Sweet the Sound*

The Homily
> "A History Lesson"

The Response   J. Rutter
> *I Am the Resurrection and the Life*
> from *Requiem*

The Prayer of Thanksgiving

O God, through your inspired word you have instructed us to give thanks in all things and to rejoice in all situations. That is not always easy, despite our good intentions regarding obedience to your word. At this very moment, grieved by the death of a beloved family member, a good friend, a faithful church member, and a dedicated educator, thanksgiving is not immediately forthcoming. However, reflection on this occasion and meditation on your provisions in it generate gratitude.

Thank you for the gift of Tom Stricklin's life. He was always a gift to us, not a possession on which we staked claims of ownership. Thank you for the overwhelming comfort that reaches deep into our beings to touch the grief that grinds in our souls. Thank you for the amazing strength available in a dedicated family of faith. Thank you for the assurance of a faith that can sustain us as we carry on the work that was so important to this man and so crucial to your reign.

We hurt, God, but we also hope. We grieve, but we also sense your grace. Even if right now we are weeping, our thoughts and words are scrambling to address you with genuine thanksgiving. Amen.

(CWG)

The Litany

Leader: How precious is human life!
People: How precious, human love!
Leader: With life comes death, the sweet release.
People: With love comes pain, the sweet remembrance.
Leader: There is no life that has no death coursing through its veins.
People: There is no love that has no pain running through its heart,
Leader: So let us press our common pulse, quickening enemy and friend—
People: For that pulse is our lifeline and the heartbeat of God.

Leader: Let us join hands with joy, made bright by the shadow of death;
People: And let us embrace our grief, made dark by the glory of life.
Leader: Let us reach toward our ecstasy, made high by the depth of pain;
People: And let us bend toward our despair, made deep by the height of love.
Leader: For we know that where there is joy and grief, God shall be the sweet release;
People: And where there is ecstasy and despair, Christ shall be the remembrance sweet.

(Everett Tilson and Phyllis Cole[14])

The Meditation   A. Copland
At the River
solo

The Commendation
Leader: The Lord bless him and keep him, the Lord make his face to shine upon him and be gracious unto him. The Lord lift up his countenance upon him and give him eternal peace.
    And now may the God of peace make each of us perfect in every good work to do the will of God, working in each one that which is well pleasing in his sight. Through Jesus Christ, to whom be glory forevermore. Amen.

(DWN)

The Benediction   J. Rutter
God Be in My Head

THE WORSHIP OF GOD
The Service of Christian Marriage

A wedding ceremony in a church is an occasion for the public worship of God. The following service provides an opportunity for the bride and the groom and for all present to reflect on the meaning of the covenant of marriage and to express praise to the God who makes marriage possible.

(All floral offerings displayed in the sanctuary should enhance the architectural beauty of the room and direct worshipers' attention to the exchange of promises and the commitment of lives to each other and to God.)

The Preludes
(Because a decision was made to conduct this ceremony in a place of worship, all music selected for inclusion in this service must be appropriate for the worship of God. Aware of both the variety of instrumentations and ensembles available for musical offerings and the central roles of choirs and organs in most churches, here are possible selections for a wedding in a church setting.)

"Nimrod" (from Enigma Variations)	Edward Elgar
Concerto in E	Charles Avison
Air, Minuet, and Rondo	Henry Purcell
Brandenburg Concerto # 3	J. S. Bach
The Four Seasons	A. Vivaldi
Andante and Allegro	W. A. Mozart
Sheep May Safely Graze	J. S. Bach
Rondeau	Mouret
Alleluia	Mozart
Canon in D	J. Pachelbel

The Wedding Processionals
Trumpet Tune in D	John Stanley
Hornpipe (from *Water Music*)	G. F. Handel
Trumpet Tune	Henry Purcell
Fanfare	Sand Lawn
Trumpet Voluntary	J. Clarke

The Call to Worship
> Minister: We gather this evening to worship God as we share in the celebration of marriage.
>
> **People: We rejoice in the love of God as in the love James and Amanda share with each other and happily encourage their marriage.**
>
> All: We affirm the faith, hope, and love with which Amanda and James come to this moment and pray God's blessings on them as they enter the marriage covenant.
>
> (DWN)

The Recognition of Marriage

Christian marriage is a divinely-blessed institution growing out of the wisdom and kindness of Almighty God. The origin of the marital relationship resides within God's intention in creation. According to the author of Genesis, God brought together the first man and the first woman, made them husband and wife, and declared it to be "good." Jesus affirmed the significance of marriage through his presence at a wedding in Cana of Galilee and by his words, "For this reason (for the reason of marriage) a man will leave his father and mother and unite with his wife, and the two will become one."

Marriage is both a social institution and a sacred covenant. Marital partners are to enjoy the blessings of this relationship and to accept the responsibilities inherent in it. So, both the best of personal efforts and the constant presence of God are needed as two people unite their lives.

The revelation of God in Holy Scripture provides both instruction and inspiration for living in a covenant relationship. Since each of you knows the Bible, I would encourage you together to turn to the Bible for guidance related to your love, your beliefs, and your practices. As the two of you build a home, if you will permit the Word of God to give you direction, you not only will find happiness in one another, but also you will be a source of strength to one another as long as you live.

Both the truth of the biblical revelation and the nature of your own personal experiences also sensitize you to the important role a family of faith plays in the building of your life together. Northminster Church happily embraces you as members of this family of faith and accepts your embrace of us. We promise to be available to you as a community of fellowship, support, refuge, and grace.

Looking ahead benefits from looking back. The gifts of scripture, faith, and church in your past point the way to your best future and inspire praise. Now, as a congregation supportive of your union, we stand to lift our voices in a hymn of praise to God.

(CWG)

The Hymn of Praise   NORTHMINSTER TE DEUM
Alleluia! Sing Te Deum
p. 305

The Prayer of Illumination
Let us ask for God's blessing on this particular covenant-making service of worship and for God's guidance as you unite your lives.

Thanks be to you, O God, for the gifts of life and love. As Amanda and James nurture the union of their lives, bless them with a sense of your presence and an awareness both of the joys and responsibilities of a life shared together in love. As they repeat their promises to each other, enable them to commit themselves to you—the One without whom neither life nor love is complete. Amen.

(CWG)

The Declaration of Intention
James, do you accept Amanda as your wife and the consequent responsibilities to live with her according to God's purpose for marriage and under the guidance of God's word, to love her, comfort her, honor her, keep her, and provide for her needs as you stand faithfully with her throughout your lives? (I do)

Amanda, do you accept James as your husband and the consequent responsibilities to live with him according to God's

purpose for marriage and under the guidance of God's word, to love him, comfort him, honor him, keep him, and provide for his needs as you stand faithfully with him throughout your lives? (I do)
(CWG)

The Families' Blessing of Union
Each of you comes to this moment out of a family in which you have been loved, nurtured, and encouraged. Who represents the families from which you come, the families that now bless the union of your lives? (I do)
(CWG)

(After the representative of the families responds with "I do," the minister turns and moves up the steps to the chancel. Once the minister is in place, the bride and groom ascend the steps and position themselves in front of the minister. If a flower girl and a ringbearer are involved in the ceremony, they move to the chancel area and stand beside the bride and groom respectively. The best man and the maid or matron of honor then move to the chancel and position themselves beside the groom and bride respectively.)

The Christian Scriptures   1 Corinthians 13
The marriage covenant is essentially a covenant of love. Love has its source in God and finds its clearest expression in Jesus Christ. Within a marriage, love is the means of communication and that which is communicated, the source of individual freedom and the bond of a shared life, the inspiration for promise-making and the strength for promise-keeping. Amanda and James, you will need to nurture the love that brings you together now and from time to time reaffirm your commitment to the responsibilities of this love in relation to your marriage.

The apostle Paul provides a beautiful description of the promise-making, covenant-keeping love that is essential to marriage. Let us hear these words and be instructed by them.
(CWG)

(The minister or a lay worship leader reads 1 Corinthians 13.)

Leader: This is the Word of God.
People: Thanks be to God.

The Hebrew Scriptures *from Song of Songs*
A Wedding Song for Jennifer

"Prologue"
p. 307

If I speak as a mortal or angel and have not love, I only make noise, as a clanging gong. If I have not love, I am nothing. (1 Cor 13:1)

"Blessing of Friends"

We rejoice and delight in you . . . in your love. We will praise your love more than finest wine. (Sg 1:4)

"The Lovers' Song"

Come away, my love, and be like a gazelle, or like a stag on a spice-laden mountain. (Sg 8:14)

Lo! The winter is past, the rains are all over and gone. Flowers appear on the earth. The time of singing has come. The cooing of doves is heard in the land. (Sg 2:11-12)

Awake, north wind, and come, south wind. Blow on my garden. Spread its fragrance abroad. Let my lover come into this fine garden and taste its choice fruits. (Sg 4:16)

Set me as a seal upon your heart, as a seal upon your arm, for love is strong as death, unyielding as the grave. Many waters cannot quench love, neither rivers can wash it away. (Sg 8:6-7)

Come away.

(D. H. Clark)

The Homily
"A Profound Mystery"

The Covenant of Marriage
James and Amanda, please hold hands, face each other, and repeat after me your marriage vows.

I James, take you Amanda / to be my lawful, wedded wife / to live together according to God's purposes / in sickness and in health / in poverty or in wealth / in the good times and the bad times / and I do promise to love you always / and will faithfully perform unto you / all the duties / that a husband owes to a wife / as long as we both live.

I Amanda, take you James / to be my lawful, wedded husband / to live together / according to God's purposes / in sickness and in health / in poverty or in wealth / in the good times and the bad times / and I do promise to love you always / and will faithfully perform unto you / all the duties / that a wife owes to a husband / as long as we both live.

(CWG)

The Blessing and Exchange of Rings
The two of you have provided rings for each other. These rings symbolize the love that has brought you to this hour and the commitments you have just made. Both the form and the beauty of each ring bring to mind the completeness of love and the never-ending nature of love.

James, as you place this ring on Amanda's finger, please repeat after me: Amanda, with this ring I accept you as my wife/ and pledge to live as your husband.

Amanda, as you place this ring on James' finger, please repeat after me: James, with this ring I accept you as my husband/ and pledge to live as your wife.

(CWG)

The Pronouncement of Union
Amanda Alice Reynolds and James Welton Gaddy, by virtue of the authority vested in me as a minister of the gospel of Christ, I pronounce you husband and wife and pray that God will seal your promises to one another and make you a blessing to each other as long as you both live.

(CWG)

The Prayer of Intercession
> Leader: Eternal God, look with favor upon Amanda and James whom you have made one in holy matrimony.
>
> **People: Give them wisdom and devotion in the ordering of their common life, that each may be to the other a strength in need, a counselor in perplexity, a comfort in sorrow, and a companion in joy.**
>
> Leader: Grant that their wills may be so knit together in your will, and their spirits in your spirit, that they may grow in peace with you and each other all the days of their lives.
>
> **People: Give them grace when they hurt each other to recognize their fault and to seek each other's forgiveness as well as yours.**
>
> Leader: Make their life together a sign of Christ's love to this sinful and broken world that unity may overcome estrangement, forgiveness may heal guilt, and joy may conquer despair.
>
> **People: Give them such fulfillment of their mutual affection that they may reach out in love and concern for others.**
>
> **All: Grant that your will may be done on earth as it is in heaven, where you, O Father, with your Son and the Holy Spirit live and reign together, both now and forever more. Amen.**
>
> (DWN)

The Prayer of Jesus

The Offering of Praise   G. F. Handel
> *Let the Bright Seraphim*
> from *Samson*

Let the bright seraphim in burning row, their loud, uplifted angel trumpets blow. List the cherubic hosts, in tuneful choirs, touch their immortal harps with golden wires.

(John Milton)[15]

The Blessing and the Commission
> Now as you go, James and Amanda Gaddy, remember that God is the One who provided the love that brought you to this hour. God is the One who has joined you together. Let nothing take precedence over that love and let no one pull you apart. Live together in love with God's blessings and with ours.
>
> (CWG)

The Recessional   Widor
> *Toccata from Symphonie V*

THE WORSHIP OF GOD
The Dedication of a Baby

The birth of a child inspires gratitude and evokes joy. The gift of new life also sensitizes us to the responsibility of providing an environment in which this child can be loved and nurtured toward Christian maturity. The following service celebrates new life, affirms and challenges the parents of the recently born baby, and draws an entire community of faith into a commitment to raising this child in a manner that will enable the child-become-adult to live as a dedicated person of faith.

(Prior to the service, place a garland of flowers across the pulpit to symbolize the new life being offered back to God in today's service. Create another garland of flowers, using as a base concrete cherubs positioned on the communion table.)

The Carillon Prelude — Paraphrase on an Easter Hymn

The Prologue — Carl Sandburg
"God's Opinion of Life"
from *Remembrance Rock*

The Opening Voluntary — Purcell-Rabinoff
Chaconne on "Dido's Lament"
from *Dido and Anaeus*

The Call to Worship
Leader: Buried deep within us is the sense that we were created for more than that for which we settle.
People: Resurrect in us the dream of life more than existence—the richness of living the way God envisioned: loving God and each other as we grow in freedom toward incarnate love.
Leader: You see, all too often our blind eyes throw out the gift of the present, staring at what we expect to see—or want to see—or think we should see.
People: Surprise us, God, with what is: your grace calling us into abundant living.

(JB)

The Introit	Yannerella
Sing unto the Lord	
The Response	Psalm 100
The Processional Hymn	DIX
For the Beauty of the Earth	
The Old Testament Lesson	Deuteronomy 6:4-7

The Presentation

> Leader: Today we celebrate miracles, for life is God's most precious gift.
>
> Parents: We hold in our arms the present of God—lovingly shaped in the image of God—named out of our most sacred faith in what God continues to do—our deepest hopes for the future and our abiding love for each other and this community, even unto the ends of the earth.
>
> Leader: You hold in your arms a marvelous incarnation—of love made flesh in relationship—of potential being realized in the wonder of individual growth.
>
> Parents: We are in awe of our responsibility and our privilege. Our joy is being made far more complete in this lifelong investment—this lifelong commitment.
>
> Leader: From the heart of God into the heart and arms of this community:
>
> **People: We are those to whom these children are entrusted. We are those who commit ourselves to being a part of the process of their living. May we model for them the joy, the discipline, the excitement, the pain, and the work of the abundant life. May our living with them reveal the depths of God's dreams for us and our world—as our concept of who we are is expanded—as we affirm the intimacy that is enhanced by the inclusion of others into it.**

(JB)

(At the conclusion of the litany of presentation, the minister invites the parents and/or the godparents of the child to be dedicated to come forward during the singing of the hymn and to stand at the chancel for the charge and the prayer of dedication.)

The Hymn   STUTTGART
Child of Blessing, Child of Promise

The Charge
Leader: Our Lord has expressly given little children a place among the people of God. Remember the words of Jesus Christ, spoken in love and acceptance, when he said, "Let the children come to me, do not hinder them; for to such belongs the Kingdom of God." Would you bring your daughter now to be dedicated to God? In bringing her, do you confess your faith in our Lord and Savior Jesus Christ? Do you accept your privilege to live before Jordan a life that becomes the Gospel? Will you endeavor to keep Jordan under the guidance of God's Church until she accepts for herself the gift of God's grace and salvation? Jordan, you are God's gift of life to your parents, to your grandparents, and to all of us. You are wonderfully made by God, who knows and loves you. We are grateful that God has chosen us to be a small part in caring for you and nurturing your faith.

Parents: Jordan, you are our beloved daughter. Being your parents is a profound blessing for us. We know that you belong to God, and we pray that we will always teach you the way of faith in Christ by our example. We love you and want you to experience our love, and also to know the love of God and grow up to become all that God has created you to be. From this congregation we ask for support and encouragement as we raise our daughter. We entrust our child to your loving care in the days that she will worship among this congregation, and ask you to help us teach her about God's love and grace.

Leader: People of God in this congregation, Don and Cathe have asked for our encouragement and support in the Christian nurture of their daughter. I charge you to accept this privilege of being a part of Jordan's family of faith.

Church: **You have asked us to participate in the nurture of your daughter. We are honored and humbly accept our partnering responsibility for encouraging Jordan's spiritual, emotional, and physical well-being. We offer the gift of ourselves, as representatives of God's large family, to you and to Jordan. By our example and our words we will support your calling as parents. Jordan, we promise always to include you as a cherished member of our family of faith, to affirm you as you grow in grace, to call forth the gifts God has placed within you, to encourage you to seek God's path for your journey, to nurture you and help you to hear God's call, and to affirm God's call on your life and bestow our blessings upon you with joy.**

(KMF)

The Prayer of Dedication

God of Grace, Perfect Parent of us all: Thank you for the gift of children, their minds bright with wonder, their eyes open with amazement, their hearts tender and overflowing with love. You have set them in the center of us and challenged us to be like them. You have shown us how to love them unconditionally and set them free to become all that they can be. So we pray your presence alongside them, and us, as we grow up together.

Teach us to laugh with your joy, and remember that what really matters is loving each other and living in peace. Teach us to dream with our children and to discover that nothing is impossible when hearts and minds work together. Teach us to open our arms as wide as a child's to take everyone in and believe life is good, because we do not want to learn to hate and to discourage.

Shepherd of tender sheep, guard your children, big and small from all that would harm or frighten. When the hurts of life come—as they surely will—send arms of comfort, protection, and healing to make us well again. Send us gifted teachers, attentive caregivers, and enthusiastic encouragers so that we will be strong and caring and sure of whom we are. Nurture us, O God, so that we may grow into the children of your kingdom you have created us to be.

Through Jesus Christ your own Son. Amen.

(SE)

The Anthem   J. Rutter
All Things Bright and Beautiful

The Sermon
"Will Our Children Have Faith?"

The Offering of Our Lives and Labors unto God

The Meditation   R. Thompson
The Lord Is My Shepherd

The Invitation

The Recessional Hymn   ELLACOMBE
We Sing the Mighty Power of God

The Benediction
O God, your benediction is upon us in the gift of your grace that brings us into the world, draws us toward you during all the days of our lives, and offers us meaning even in the presence of death. Thanks be to you, good God. In the name of the One who pleaded, "Let the children come to me," we depart with your benediction. Amen.

(CWG)

The Closing Voluntary   Gigout
Grand Choeur Dialogue

The Carillon Postlude   Easter Alleluias

NOTES

[1] C. Welton Gaddy, *Coming Home: For All Who Dream of a New Church* (Macon GA: Smyth & Helwys, 1995) 5.

[2] See the text and the music for this hymn by D. H. Clark on pp. 305-306.

[3] *Psalms Now*, Leslie Brandt (Concordia Publishing House, 1973).

[4] Taken from *The Gates of Heaven*, the basic book of liturgy in synagogues in the tradition of Reformed Judaism.

[5] Based on excerpts from Jewish liturgical materials, primarily taken from *The Gates of Heaven*.

[6] From *Yes, We Sang! Songs from the Ghettos and Concentration Camps*, Shoshana Kalisch with Barbara Meister (New York: Harper and Row, 1985) 38, 44, 109.

[7] Based on selections from Psalm 51 and *Gates of Prayer: The New Union Prayerbook* (New York: Central Conference of American Rabbis, 1975).

[8] *The New Century Hymnal* (Cleveland OH: The Pilgrim Press, 1995).

[9] Cynthia Clawson, "My Mother's Faith," on compact disc *Broken: Healing the Heart* (Topongo CA: Civic Record Group).

[10] Sharlande Sledge, *Prayers and Litanies for the Christian Seasons* (Macon GA: Smyth & Helwys Publishing, 1999) 95.

[11] Robert Munsch, *I'll Love You Forever* (Ontario: Firefly Books Limited, 1986).

[12] Henri Nouwen, *The Wounded Healer*, (New York: Image Books, Doubleday, 1972).

[13] Carl Sandburg, *The Complete Poems of Carl Sandburg, Revised and Expanded Edition* (New York: Harcourt, Brace, and Jovanovich, 1970) 449.

[14] Everett Tilson and Phyllis Cole, *Litanies and Other Prayers, Year B* (Nashville TN: Abingdon Press, 1990) 114.

[15] From *The New Oxford Book of English Verse 1250—1950*, ed. Helen Gardner (Oxford: Oxford Press, 1972).

Outcast of Beauty

"Fanfare for a Common Man"

A Festive Call to Praise

Special Services 301

"Honoring the memory of a saint"

Child of Blessing, Child of Praise

APPENDIX
Visual Enhancements

The celebration of Advent is impacted by nature and its surroundings as well as by events specific to this time of the year. The theme unfolds in a natural progression with a new dimension of the season emerging each week. Worshipers need to witness this progression visually and to feel it emotionally.

The universal themes associated with the four Sundays of Advent—Hope, Peace, Joy, and Love—can be experienced visually in a manner that reveals the natural progression of the season. Begin Advent—the coming—with the presence of a simple bare branch. If more than one area for floral arrangements is available, each can display a bare branch. As Advent unfolds, the progression of the season will be seen in what happens to these bare branches.

An alternative manner of display uses the altar as the focal point of worshipers. Begin the season with four bare trees positioned around the altar.

For the first week of Advent, display the first branch at the far left of the altar. This branch stands symbolically as the root of Jesse. Though at first glance it appears hopeless, closer observation detects new life springing forth from the root. Asparagus shoots placed around the base of the branch and covered in sheet moss will convey the truth of emerging hope.

During the second week of Advent, add a second branch displaying noticeable growth and a more mature form. Full foliage and flowering buds should appear on this branch. Cut pieces of salal wired to the bare branch convey this developing maturity. Ligustrum or camellia branches can provide a similar effect. Choose greenery that can be wired to the branch and still remain fresh outside of water.

During week three of Advent, worshipers should be able to see full blossoms. The branch has burst forth in a prolific and glorious array of blooms. Open roses, camellias, full-blown carnations, or massed freesia will provide the best display of joy. These blossoms should be placed in floral water tubes and wired to the branch. The mechanics can be disguised with sphagnum or sheet moss.

On the fourth Sunday of Advent, add the final branch which also is in full bloom. As worshipers meditate during a choral selection following the morning prayer, members of the altar guild remove the blossoms from the branches and gather them into garden baskets. The blossoms then can be used to create a large garland extending across the communion table or carried to the vestry where flowers are prepared for those who are ill or those who have experienced recent deaths in their families. Yet another idea is to distribute the blossoms to the congregants who in turn share them with people they cherish.

A second visual approach to Advent focuses on the season's central theme of the gift. Develop the progression of this concept as follows:

During week one, focus on the numerous places from which gifts are gathered. Overload a space with catalogs, store fliers, pictures of gift ideas, and magazines that portray the innumerable ways in which gifts can be acquired.

During week two of Advent, center on the purchase of a gift. Worshipers are well aware that Christmas Day is drawing near and that purchases of gift selections must be made. Display unwrapped boxes, shopping bags, tags, and other symbols of shopping purchases.

Week three conveys the joy achieved when people filled with hope find rest in the assurance that their special gift to someone is wrapped and on display. Anticipation mounts as the realization grows that this gift meets the specification of dreams.

Week four of Advent reveals the truth. Love is made known. As in any gift-giving exchange, it is the expression of love given from the heart that is important. The actual gift is only the vehicle for revealing the truth that love is the reason for giving. On the fourth Sunday of Advent, worshipers should see all of the packages laying open except for one large wrapped box left for the Christmas Eve service. Box tops and tissue paper create a display of the indescribable moment shared when gifts are exchanged.

Finally, on Christmas Eve, the remaining box to be unwrapped has become larger than life. Each outer wall of the package is 4'x8', created by sheets of foam core. The box is totally wrapped and tied with a massive bow. Not until the homily for Christmas Eve is the content of this gift box revealed. The minister cuts the ribbon and allows the walls to collapse. Inside the box a mother and child wait to remind us of the greatest gift ever given. The culmination of all hope, peace, joy, and love is contained within the gift of the season.

(DWN)

Appendix

Appendix

310 Volume 2, Annotated Orders of Worship

Appendix

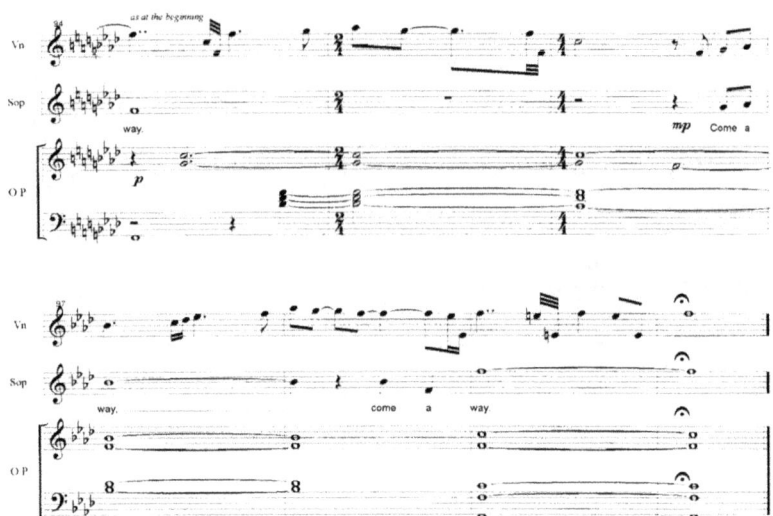

www.ingramcontent.com/pod-product-compliance
Lightning Source LLC
Chambersburg PA
CBHW071653160426
43195CB00012B/1453